IMPOSSIBLE STORIES

NEW SUNS:

RACE, GENDER, AND SEXUALITY IN THE

SPECULATIVE

Susana M. Morris and Kinitra D. Brooks, Series Editors

Impossible Stories
On the Space and Time of
Black Destructive Creation

John Murillo III

THE OHIO STATE UNIVERSITY PRESS
COLUMBUS

Copyright © 2021 by The Ohio State University.
All rights reserved.

Library of Congress Cataloging-in-Publication Data
Names: Murillo, John, III, author.
Title: Impossible stories : on the space and time of Black destructive creation / John Murillo III.
Other titles: New suns: race, gender, and sexuality in the speculative.
Description: Columbus : The Ohio State University Press, [2021] | Series: New suns: race, gender, and sexuality in the speculative | Includes bibliographical references and index. | Summary: "Merging theory and praxis, Murillo engages with Gayl Jones's *Corregidora,* Octavia Butler's *Kindred,* Toni Morrison's *Beloved,* Kiese Laymon's *Long Division,* Dionne Brand's *A Map to the Door of No Return,* and Paul Beatty's *The Sellout* to show how Afro-pessimism offers new ways to think about anti-Black racism and practice Black creativity"—Provided by publisher.
Identifiers: LCCN 2020029421 | ISBN 9780814214596 (cloth) | ISBN 0814214592 (cloth) | ISBN 9780814280874 (ebook) | ISBN 0814280870 (ebook)
Subjects: LCSH: American literature—African American authors—History and criticism. | Racism. | African Americans—Race identity. | African Americans—Intellectual life. | Race relations in literature. | Space and time in literature.
Classification: LCC PS153.N5 M86 2021 | DDC 813/.5409896073—dc23

LC record available at https://lccn.loc.gov/2020029421

Cover design by Black Kirby
Text design by Juliet Williams
Type set in Adobe Palatino

CONTENTS

Acknowledgments	vii

Introduction: The Black (W)hole of It All	1

FIRST ARRANGEMENT • BLACK (IN) TIME: UNTIMELY BLACKNESS

I Prelude: Untimely Fragments and the Beginnings of a Reflection	23
II Black Holes and Generations	33
III Untime	53

SECOND ARRANGEMENT • THE UNTIMELY WORKS AND WORLDS OF IMPOSSIBLE STORIES

IV Prelude: Trauma Work	77
V Of Shadows and Diamonds	95
VI Elliptical in Love Dot Dot Dot	121

THIRD ARRANGEMENT • TRANSMISSIONS FROM OUT OF NOWHERE

VII Prelude: No Place, Not Any Place, Out of Place	137
VIII Nowheresville	147
IX Stanky Shrines and Hollow Bastions	163

Outro: Out of Time in the Middle of Nowhere	185

Bibliography	195
Index	201

ACKNOWLEDGMENTS

I, We

THE ONES I LOVE deserve the first, last, and most gratitude.

To my mother and father, D'Juana and John, who cared for and carried and continue to care for and carry me on the wings of their continued and boundless wisdom and experience, and their insatiable desire for a dreaming they do not name, but no doubt perform.

To my brothers, Joshua and Jeremiah, who provide me the opportunity to judge my capacity to teach and to be taught; they, in their love and peculiarity—a peculiarity that drives us all to create—drove and drives me to aspire to blur the lines between student and teacher so that I might more carefully and imaginatively consider the words and worlds I sought to put down on paper.

To my aunt, Veritta, who, like my grandmother, Brenda, stands stalwart through sickness, faithful through trial, and not only embodies a relentless aspiration to heal and be healed but also puts this aspiration into practice; healing becomes devotional, spiritual, and mobile through her.

And to all of my family: Their very being nurtures me, drives me, compels me to make and keep making time and space for my own thoughts, and so for them and all they have been and might be.

To the love of my life, Chinyere Amobi, I express gratitude that cannot be made legible in the grammar and language available to me; this is ultimately a failure. But for being refuge and rock, advisor and caregiver, for being my partner, closely journeying with me through all the trauma and work, for holding me, my hand, and my head, in the hold of this ship—for being all and more than I could ever need or dream of, I thank her.

To Frank Wilderson, Jared Sexton, and Christina Sharpe, who, from afar, offered valuable conceptual and philosophical insight into my work, into navigating the academy, into diving deeper and deeper into this oblivion of thought I've leapt into, and to never stop moving, writing, thinking, and caring, I offer my sincerest appreciation and thanks.

To past mentors Ellen Rooney, Philip Gould, Deak Nabers, Daniel Kim, Rolland Murray, and Stuart Burrows, I offer my thanks for the various iterations of practical insight and advice into my writing and into my career you provided at different points along this journey.

To everyone and anyone who might have expressed, in any way, doubt or disbelief in my capacity to find something creative, imaginative, caring, brilliant, beautiful, and Black beyond the event horizon; to everyone who, in that same breath, revealed their unwillingness to take the imaginative and conceptual leap, let alone wish me well as I did so, I thank you for what became fuel to the flame of my drive and my expression, here, in this project, and beyond.

And to God, in whom I have been faithful, flawed as my expression of that faith might have been at times; that faith has guided me beyond myself, beyond this work, beyond the imaginable, and into a ceaseless, difficult, promising, unsettling, and loving project that, as I envision it, "can never really be done."

INTRODUCTION

The Black (W)hole of It All

"I am shattered," I start to think before
sinking into the paper, like I am ink.¹

Shambles.²

IN THE CUT and clatter of the shatter, I struggle to find my bearings. The words are jagged, sharp, and ubiquitous, so much so that all thought feels imperiled by the threat of being flayed. Like a nebula, the cluster is awesome in both its violence and its resplendence; it is at once the dangerous cosmic effluvia of death and decay, and the brilliant potential for otherworldly creation. Either way, the system through which my mind drifts is a living celestial body composed of fragments. And while I fail to orient myself to the glimmering chaos, I can discern that these shards of the scenes of life, joy, laughter, depression, anxiety, death, and mourning that constitute the gray matter behind my eyes pass, clash, crash, and clamor for attention—amid the chaos, I can only make out that they want to be held and beheld.

The fragments are everywhere, and they demand that they be handled with care.

---

1. Listen to Mos Def's "Love" from *Black on Both Sides* (1999) for the specific reference (though I know the lines originate from "I Know You Got Soul" by Eric B. & Rakim). This album (and this song specifically) is my absolute favorite hip hop album and is very formative for me as a writer.

2. Perhaps a strange reference, but I am deliberately evoking the use of the word as used by Trafalgar Law of the manga and anime *One Piece*, who proclaims "Shambles" to invoke his terrifying spatial manipulation abilities.

I am being called to work with them, to cradle them and see what they show, heed what they sing. The work of curating those that resonate with the greatest prominence has been, is, and will be disorienting; trying to create with and through destruction is a dizzying endeavor. Failure to triumph over this violent vertigo with the aim (and responsibility) of generating new knowledge and novel stories from bits and pieces feels inevitable. Work under these conditions feels impossible.

This cannot be reassembly or redress. Reparation, if wholeness is the telos, will fail before the thought fully forms. These are not the pieces put together by the revenant remnant of this or another self. Instead, tumbling in the cut, I can only try to look and listen carefully for the fragments that shine and sing at the most resonant frequency, hold and behold the ones I can gather with determination, and try to make the arrangements that form something like analysis, something like storytelling, something like creation.

Making the arrangements—working with the derangement of fragments—requires a set of organizing principles and questions. I must establish at the outset what influences, if not wholly governs, this process of making a way with disarray. I must distill what will help tune the ear, prime the eye, and guide the hand because this will aim and narrow the practice, prevent it from becoming overwhelming; or, by reckoning with the unbearableness of the task at hand, this will clarify the limitations, scope, and scale of this perilous creative enterprise.

We must map our premises. Black "life" and "death" do not matter in this world. This is the structural truth of the anti-Black world in which the terms "life" and "death" do not adhere to Black folk the way they do for others because this world violently warps the way Black folk, as socially dead beings, relate to the conditions of being alive or dead. This truth (or "fact"[3]) telegraphs an unethical, gratuitously violent antagonism between Black folk who "live" and "die," and the anti-Black world that sanctions, desires, and demands the meaninglessness of even those quotation marks.[4] The most

---

3. Pace Frantz Fanon, this is an explicit reference to the fifth chapter of *Black Skin, White Masks* (1967), "The Fact of Blackness." Let me also point out that I'm citing an edition of the Markmann translation of *Black Skin, White Masks*. This is a conscious decision: Peculiar omissions and translation choices in the more widely accepted Philcox translation appear to elide the depth and scope of Fanon's choices in this chapter, producing misreadings and misuses of the chapter.

4. Pace Hortense Spillers, this is a reference to "Mama's Baby, Papa's Maybe," in which Spillers writes of the dereliction of the idea of "freedom" or "liberation" for Black flesh: "Even though the captive body/flesh has been 'liberated,' and no one need pretend that even the quotation marks do not *matter*, dominant symbolic activity, the ruling episteme that releases the dynamics of naming and valuation, remains grounded

attentive Black thought and action works to examine the forces that drive the anti-Black world, and contend the destructive, terrorizing manifestations and effects of those forces as they position Blacks in space and time. This project attempts to map these forces from a Black position through a careful examination of twentieth- and twenty-first-century Black literature. I am guided by this set of questions: How do the violent forces that position Blacks in space and time affect the literary creation we might produce? How might we engage Black literary creation? And what is at stake in both Black literary creation and our engagements with it?

"Living," "dying," and creating in the "afterlife of slavery," the haunting and structural subjection that seals Black folk into "crushing objecthood,"[5] is to "live," "die," and create in relation to an antagonism that is temporal, spatial, and political-ontological in nature.[6] As Dionne Brand writes in *A Map to the Door of No Return*, slavery violently disfigures time and space, creating a "tear in the world . . . a rupture in history, a rupture in the quality of being [and] a physical rupture, a rupture of geography."[7] Time and space shatter in slavery's unending wake such that slavery persists as an afterlife, framing and disfiguring the scenes of subjection[8] we endure and bear witness to across time and space. Tear. Rupture. Shatter. In this writing, we will investigate Black creative work while inhabiting the totality of this spatiotemporal fragmentation. We read time and space in and through Black literature, and draw from physics to help develop a nuanced, unique approach that both merges my interests in Black studies and theoretical physics and also illuminates what I understand to be two, underthought—or uncritically thought of—fundamental features of being: time and space. By holding and behold-

---

in the originating metaphors of captivity and mutilation so that it is as if neither time nor history, nor historiography and its topics, show movement, as the human subject is 'murdered' over and over again by the passions of a bloodless and anonymous archaism, showing itself in endless disguise" (68). I carefully dissect this passage among other key passages from her groundbreaking text in the First Arrangement, but her work is integral to my thinking throughout and beyond this writing.

5. Frantz Fanon, *Black Skin, White Masks* (London: Pluto Press, 2008), 82.

6. Writing these lines, I am evoking and conjuring the words of Fanon and Hartman, who in *Black Skin, White Masks* and *Lose Your Mother: A Journey along the Atlantic Slave Route*, respectively, wield some of the clearest, most compelling, and most precise language to describe the conditions that I'm laying out as I begin making my claims. Hartman's words in particular resonate very prominently: "This is the afterlife of slavery—skewed life chances, limited access to health and education, premature death, incarceration, and impoverishment. I, too, am the afterlife of slavery" (6).

7. Dionne Brand, *A Map to the Door of No Return: Notes to Belonging* (Toronto: Doubleday Canada, 2001), 4–5.

8. See Saidiya Hartman, *Scenes of Subjection: Terror, Slavery, and Self-Making in Nineteenth-Century America* (Oxford: Oxford University Press, 1997).

ing the fragments of lived and literary Black stories that speak to the fractured relationship between Blackness, time, space, and creation, we aim to establish a more precise understanding of Black temporality and spatiality. Our claim and aim and hope are that a better grasp of how Black folk relate to space and time clarifies the stakes and mechanics of Black creative work, and that thinking about Black creative work as being made from out of time and out of nowhere opens us into the impossible forms of Black creation that just might transform the cosmos as we know it.

On the one hand, it is as if time "shows no movement"; slavery's persistence as "afterlife" throws the idea of linear progress (read: the movement of time "forward" and away from slavery) into violent disarray. On the other, it is as if all possible temporal movement and "all moments" in the anti-Black world "somehow gesture back"[9] to this inaugural rupture, creating a series of endless, overlapping loops entangling all of time with the time of enslavement. This untimely problem is what girds the *longue durée* of social death: Slavery creates a problem that halts and loops time, dispersing the political-ontological[10] position of the socially dead across all temporal moments and movements in its wake. Blackness and Slaveness collapse into the same political-ontological position, in part *because* of a distortion, or warping, of time as we know it.[11]

In the **First Arrangement** of *Impossible Stories* entitled "Black (in) Time: Untimely Blackness," I move through Black "stories about time" that offer insight into this untimely force. In chapter 1 of this section, "Prelude: Untimely Fragments and the Beginnings of a Reflection," I begin by creatively moving through an arrangement of narrative fragments, a collection of bits of stories of anti-Black violence. Each narrative fragment draws our attention to a particular temporal problem that characterizes the larger problem of Black time. "Fragment 0: Loops" deals with the "looped" or repetitious experience of familiar scenes of anti-Black violence against Black women, "Fragment 35: Lapse" considers Sandra Bland and compels us to think about the lapses or gaps in the continuity of Black time, and "Fragment 24: Loss" struggles with the tragedy of Kalief Browder in order to think about the "lostness" of Black time. Taken together, this arrangement

---

9. Brand, *A Map*, 24–25.

10. I say political-ontological in the vein of Afropessimistic scholarship, which contends that the racial calculus begotten by enslavement (the political) had metaphysical consequences for the way we understand being itself (the ontological) that persist in ways that govern Black and non-Black being in the anti-Black world. The term "political-ontological" captures the entanglement between political and metaphysical conditions.

11. So when Fanon writes, "the problem to be considered here is one of time" (*Black Skin*, 176), I take his words very seriously.

of narrative fragments provides the foundation for how we will think about the Black problem, with time discussed more thoroughly in the next two chapters.

In chapter 2, "Black Holes and Generations," we engage recent work by Michelle M. Wright who, in *Physics of Blackness*, examines the prevailing assumptions about time's relation to Blackness in and outside the academy, suggesting that a novel understanding of this relation might produce deeper, more inclusive investigations into what it means to be Black in the anti-Black world. I contend with her theory of "epiphenomenal time" on the grounds that although it is founded on a proper critique of the way Black thought (and all thought)[12] takes its understanding of time for granted by uncritically clinging to an outdated, "Newtonian" theory of time,[13] it is too carelessly recuperative. Specifically, she sets aside the violence at the heart of the relation between Blackness and time in order to present "epiphenomenal time" as a corrective to how we generally think about Black temporality. In order to redirect us toward a more expansive, if more devastating, corrective to the assumptions Wright aims to dispel through her concept, I turn to Black literature.

Taking a lesson from our encounters with Black narrative fragments, we turn again to Black narrative as we continue our search for this more expansive and precise theory of Black temporality. We first turn to Gayl Jones's 1975 novel, *Corregidora*, as it provides useful insight into the persistence of slavery's violence across generations. The novel follows Ursa Corregidora, a descendant of a Portuguese slaver and seaman named Corregidora, who sings the blues in Kentucky from the mid-1940s to the late 1960s. The fourth generation in a line of women committed to bearing witness to the sexual violence Corregidora inflicted upon their lives and stitched into their existences, to living *as* the evidence, and to "making generations" to continue their commitment, Ursa must suddenly confront her own relationship to sexual violence, temporality, and creativity when her drunk husband, Mutt Thomas, pushes her down the stairs, which results in her needing a hysterectomy. Through Ursa's narrative, Jones mobilizes the violence of time to produce questions about relationality and generation—both procreative and creative—that meditate on how untimely Blackness creates problems for the relations between and among Black folk, and between Blackness and

---

12. See Jared Sexton, "Ante-Anti-Blackness: Afterthoughts," *Lateral* 1 (2012), particularly the opening lines, which include "1) all thought, insofar as it is genuine thinking, might best be conceived of as black thought . . . Blackness is theory itself."

13. We will think more about Newtonian's theory of absolute time, which theorizes time as purely, uniformly linear in this second chapter.

the possibility of (pro)creation. Jones's recognition of the importance of violence to thinking about Black temporality exposes some of the limitations of Wright's concept of epiphenomenal time, and it also introduces important linkages between Black making/generating, Black "untimeliness," and Black relationality that transform the stakes of examining Black temporality. Thinking about and better theorizing Black temporality leads us into new considerations of Black being that alter how we understand Black creative and relational possibilities; Jones confirms that Black time presents a temporal and philosophical problem for thought with profound consequences for *how* we make, *what* we make, and how we *relate to* one another. Of particular interest to us is Ursa Corregidora's own brand of Black creation in the wake of her own physical, psychological, and existential trauma. A comparison between how Ursa sings the blues prior to and then after her traumatic fall and hysterectomy allows us to begin building a theory of Black destructive creation under untimely conditions. From physics, we look at the blueshift phenomenon (both the Doppler and gravitational kinds), a phenomenon involving both the structural and phenomenological nature of wavelengths and how they are perceived, in order to think about the structural and phenomenological nature of Black creation as embodied by Ursa's blues. And from Black feminism, we read Hortense Spillers's "Mama's Baby, Papa's Maybe: An American Grammar Book" to think about how Ursa's "blueshifted blues" offer insight into the "praxis and . . . theory" of, and "method for reading" and hearing, Black creation. My aim is to heed Ursa's call to "leap in to the black hole" toward what will be a new vocabulary to describe Black temporality, one developed in the same spirit as "epiphenomenal time," but with a radically different foundation and direction.

Chapter 3, "Untime," the final chapter of the First Arrangement, continues this exploration, "boldly going" through with an attempt at (re)naming a "corrective" to the problems of Black temporality. Through David Marriott and Frantz Fanon, we extend our engagement with these problems into a theorization of the "deathliness"[14] that characterizes what I call "untime" to name the force behind the violent relation that Jones traces. To flesh out the psychic and imaginative implications—the implications for how one imagines selfhood and relationality, and for how/what one is able to imagine in general—we end with a close reading of Octavia Butler's *Kindred*, which takes untime's force very seriously, mobilizing it as a significant problem in the novel. Incorporating some of the fundamental, physical characteristics of

---

14. David Marriott, *Haunted Life: Visual Culture and Modernity* (New Brunswick: Rutgers University Press), 231.

black holes to help amplify the reading, we conclude with deepening questions about the possibilities of destructive, violent, radical Black creation.

Untimeliness has real and mixed consequences for the possibilities of Black creation. The **Second Arrangement** of *Impossible Stories*, "The Untimely Works and Worlds of Impossible Stories," examines the literary creation this "untime" makes available to Black folk. Throughout this section, we incorporate narrative fragments from my teaching experience that tonally and creatively contextualize and magnify our concerns. Animated by Christina Sharpe's essay "Black Studies: In the Wake" and the book that followed it, *In the Wake: On Blackness and Being*, we continue our work with chapter 4, "Prelude: Trauma Work." We read untimely Black creation as a form of "wake work," work in the ceaseless wake of slavery that seeks to "care for, comfort, and defend the dead, the dying, and those lives consigned, in the aftermath of legal chattel slavery, to death that is always-imminent and immanent."[15] We unpack Sharpe's conceptualization in order to examine how Black literary work acts as a conduit for the untimeliness of the "wake." By building from and interrogating the "work" element of "wake work," we develop an ensemble of questions about the work of Black creation, how that work works, and to what ends we even attempt to perform that work. And reinvigorated by these questions about the nature of "work" performed under untimely conditions, we sharpen the vector of our exploration of the stakes and possibilities of Black creation.

In chapter 5, "Of Shadows and Diamonds," we turn to Toni Morrison's *Beloved*, which offers an interesting set of questions about "narrative" and the way these stories never "pass on"[16] (never die, become ghastly and ghostly); are, or must not be, "passed on" (either avoided or dismissed); and must be "passed on" (shared, distributed, dispersed). We do this because after spending so much time diagnosing the problem of Black time as untime and arriving at questions about "what to do" with all of that, we begin to wonder about how to do the "wake work" of Black creation under the conditions we have mapped out. Specifically, *Beloved*'s concept of "rememory" introduces a mechanism by which we might perform "wake work" in Black creative/destructive ways. Reading the catalytic phrase that initiates the first performance of rememory in the novel "Tell me your diamonds,"[17] we analyze the physical properties of diamonds as a way of thinking as meticulously as possible about how rememory works and what it reveals

---

15. Christina Sharpe, "Black Studies: In the Wake," *The Black Scholar* 44, no. 2 (2014): 59–60.

16. Toni Morrison, *Beloved* (New York: Vintage International, 2004), 323.

17. Ibid., 69.

about our relationships to the untimely anti-Black trauma with which we try to work. Then, by taking seriously the honest meditations presented in Saidiya Hartman's "Venus in Two Acts," we cobble together an outline for a praxis for Black imaginative invention that might help us tell "impossible stories." Of particular import to this section is our departure from more canonical readings of Morrison's novel.[18] I find that a general tendency in readings of *Beloved* is to couch analyses of key elements of the novel, including those that interest us—rememory, the diamonds moment, and the "pass on" refrain at the novel's end—in assumptions about temporal coherence or "seamlessness,"[19] the redemptive and recuperative potential for Black folk engaging with trauma,[20] and the applicability of particular theoretical frames to Morrison's writing.[21] While we will make reference to particular essays

---

18. This gesture of analytically distancing this writing from the large and rich collection of writings about *Beloved* is in part inspired by Petar Ramadanovic's similar analytical gesture, performed at the beginning of chapter 6, "In the Future: Reading for Trauma in Toni Morrison's *Beloved*," in his illuminating book *Forgetting Futures: On Memory, Trauma, and Identity* (Lanham: Lexington Books, 2001).

19. For this language exactly, see Marilyn Sanders Mobley, "A Different Remembering: Memory, History, and Meaning in Toni Morrison's *Beloved*," in *Modern Critical Interpretations: Beloved*, edited by Harold Bloom (Philadelphia: Chelsea House, 1999), 17–26. For other writing that explicitly assumes temporal cohesion in Morrison's novel and for Black folk in general, see Lynne Pearce, "Gendering the Chronotope: *Beloved*," in *A Practical Reader in Contemporary Literary Theory*, edited by Peter Brooker and Peter Widdowson (Hertfordshire: Prentice Hall, 1996), 430–40.

20. This list is not exhaustive, but for works that in some way read *Beloved* as being a redemptive or recuperative text, one in which the characters must confront trauma in order to heal themselves or their community, or to recover or reclaim a sense of self, history, or psychic cohesion, see Linda Krumholtz, "The Ghosts of Slavery: Historical Recovery in Toni Morrison's *Beloved*," in *Modern Critical Interpretations: Beloved*, edited by Harold Bloom (Philadelphia: Chelsea House, 1999), 79–97; Ashraf H. A. Rushdy, "Daughters Signifyin(g) History: The Example of Toni Morrison's *Beloved*," in *Modern Critical Interpretations: Beloved*, edited by Harold Bloom (Philadelphia: Chelsea House, 1999), 115–39; Caroline Rody, "History, 'Rememory,' and a 'Clamor for a Kiss,'" in *Modern Critical Interpretations: Beloved*, edited by Harold Bloom (Philadelphia: Chelsea House, 1999), 155–175; Kathleen Marks, *Toni Morrison's* Beloved *and the Apotropaic Imagination* (Columbia: University of Missouri, 2002); Claudine Raynaud, "*Beloved* or the Shifting Shapes of Memory," in *The Cambridge Companion to Toni Morrison*, edited by Justine Tally (Cambridge: Cambridge University Press, 2007), 43–58; Evelyn Jaffe Shreiber, *Race, Trauma, and Home in the Novels of Toni Morrison* (Baton Rouge: LSU Press, 2010); Mae G. Henderson, "Toni Morrison's *Beloved*: Re-Membering the Body as Historical Text," in *Speaking in Tongues and Dancing Diaspora: Black Women Writing and Performing* (New York: Oxford, 2014).

21. I'm thinking here about Homi K. Bhabha's postcolonialist account of *Beloved* in relation to the concept of "worlding" in his 1994 essay, "The Location of Culture"; Claudine Reynaud's heavily psychoanalytic reading of *Beloved* in "In Pursuit of Memory" (2001 and Justine Tally's reading of the novel in "Memory Work," from her 2009 book,

from this substantial body of scholarship, we prioritize our focus on Hartman, the physics of diamond refraction, and untimeliness because I believe this alternative approach leads us to thinking about the impossibility at the heart of our analysis much more effectively.

But it is not merely about performing this "impossible" work. It is about working to "sound an ordinary note of care"[22] for Black folk under extraordinarily disastrous conditions. Recalling the reason we made the attempt to gather, arrange, hold, behold, and be beholden to the narrative fragments of Black lives imperiled by "untime" in the first place—that is, recalling that we are fundamentally animated by the fact that "each and every Black fragment matters" and that we are trying to care for them by bearing witness to them—we consider the possibility and shape of care in relation to our newfound work. In chapter 6, "Elliptical in Love Dot Dot Dot," we analyze how Kiese Laymon's *Long Division* wields untime's force while also metafictionally meditating on questions about the connections between Black life and death, Black words, Black (literary) creation, and *how love factors into these connections*. I read his text as asking: How do we write careful, caring sentences while Black in the anti-Black world? How does Black writing relate to the untimely relation between Blackness and time? And how do we care for each other across every facet of whatever impossible creation we make? Paying special attention to the novel's peculiar interest in ellipses, and in conjunction with Laymon's writing about "unreasonable love" in an essay on Trayvon Martin, we pursue with him a better understanding of the entanglement between Blackness, untimeliness, writing, and care.

The book shifts its attention to a question of Blackness in relation to space in its **Third Arrangement,** "Transmissions from Out of Nowhere," as we find ourselves troubled by *Beloved*'s final refrain. In that last sense of "this is not a story to pass on," we might ask: "Pass on" to *where*? In search of some semblance of an answer, we turn back to Dionne Brand's "tear in the world" and how it speaks to a spatial problem for Blackness. Slavery's mutation of time into a violent, anti-Black force comes with a similarly violent distortion of Blackness's political-ontological, imaginative, and physical relation to space. Black being is displaced from the anti-Black world of

---

Toni Morrison's Beloved: *Origins*, in which Tally aligns Morrison's rememory with ideas from Greek philosophy, Paul Ricoeur, and Christianity. These are all interesting and compelling readings from within the frameworks they choose to situate their analyses, but they are such far cries from the reading we will be doing that extensive corrective or argumentative engagements with them would only detract from our work.

22. Christina Sharpe, *In the Wake: On Blackness and Being* (Durham: Duke University Press, 2016), 132.

the living to a veritable "underworld" of the dying, the dead, and those who "live" in inescapable proximity to death, a deathly space, a "zone of nonbeing."[23] Black nonbeings lose "all bearings," and so vertiginously[24] lose a relation to "geography" or place, which problematizes the possibility of a Black "Diaspora" that takes for granted this relation. And Black nonbeings suffer a violent loss of a sense of being, experiencing a psychic shattering (Fanon describes this as a "split" and a "dislocation") that violently disperses Black being's fragments across a derelict psychic space.[25]

The creation of textual space from this displaced position interests me because, in a similar fashion to our considerations of Black temporality, thinking about space created from, with, and against displacement, or way-making from, with, and against no-way or nowhere, presents an important quandary for how we frame Black literary space. This Third Arrangement reads Black literature and thought that exemplify and meditate upon the creation of Black space. The ways Black folk make, inhabit, and move through literary and nonliterary spaces, and the ways Blackness relates to space in general, remain subject to certain forms of limitation and prohibition, which are spatial articulations of anti-Black violence—and we can think of the displacement of Black people due to combinations of natural disasters, scarce resources, gentrification, policing, carceral punishment, immigration policy, and so on as a complex example of these spatial articulations. With my interest in theoretical physics, I read the creation of Black spaces in relation to theories about structure formation in the cosmos; with my foundation in radical Black thought and creation, I ask us to consider the more abstract forms of "labyrinthine" structural prohibitions and limitations affecting the possibilities of Black spatial creation. As with the opening of the "timey-wimey"[26] first section of *Impossible Stories*, this final section on space begins with chapter 7, "Prelude: No Place, Not Any Place, Out of Place." In this chapter, we attend to a narrative fragment that speaks to some of the more insidious characteristics of Black spatiality as they appear in real events (i.e., the murder of Nephi Arreguin) of anti-Black violence. Through this narrative fragment of Black folk not belonging any place, perilously migrating

---

23. Fanon, *Black Skin*, 2.

24. See Frank Wilderson, "The Vengeance of Vertigo: Aphasia and Abjection in the Political Trials of Black Insurgents," *InTensions* 5.0 (2011).

25. In the passage cited in footnote 23, Fanon describes it as "sterile" and "arid."

26. This conjures the BBC program *Doctor Who*. Specifically, this quote is from an episode in season 3 of the more modern portion of the series entitled "Blink." During the episode, The Doctor, played by David Tennant at the time, describes time as "wibbly-wobbly, timey-wimey . . . stuff," and this quote has humorously, but also very seriously, helped me conceptualize my own theory of time (which we are beginning to map out here). Also, I deeply enjoy this show.

through space, and being subject to a form of totalizing containment across space, we develop the nasty sense that there might be "nowhere" in this world, or in this cosmos, where we might really get to *be* (let alone imagine, let alone create).

The next chapters take seriously this idea of "being nowhere." Crucial to chapter 8, "Nowheresville," is an engagement with Lisa Randall's *Dark Matter and the Dinosaurs: The Astounding Interconnectedness of the Universe*, which, in language accessible to both professional and lay persons with scientific interests, helps explain the nature of the mysterious "dark matter," how it might function in relation to large and small structure formation—for example, of galaxies and galactic clusters—and how this relation might offer us insight into how "we" exist in relation to each other and to the universe and its structures. I am interested in what Randall writes and says about her book as well, as she utilizes metaphor to make plain some of the more complex concepts she's elaborating. In one article in particular, "Seeing Dark Matter as the Key to the Universe—and Human Empathy," she makes a usefully anti-Black analogy between Black people and dark matter, suggesting that the characteristics of dark matter in the universe parallel the treatment and positioning of Black people in the structure of the world.

Around this anti-Black-but-useful connection made by Randall, we wield dark matter and this question of universal structure formation as lenses for considering the nature of Black spaces, their formation, and their destruction. To lay the theoretical groundwork of chapter 8, we visit with Anthony Paul Farley's "Behind the Wall of Sleep," which allows us to (fail to) map the totally vexing, dark, and labyrinthine relationship between Blackness and space, which will set up our eventual reading of Paul Beatty's *The Sellout*. Farley's article responds to Maria Aristodemou's book *Law & Literature: Journeys from Her to Eternity*. What I find most useful about Farley's response is how he interrogates and reimagines Aristodemou's retelling of the story of Ariadne and Theseus. Farley's attention to Aristodemou's take on the structure of the labyrinth as a symbolic representation of the social order serves as a way of conceptualizing how Black folk relate to space in the anti-Black world in an abstract way. In conjunction with chapter 7's focus on the grounded realities of Black spatiality, the theoretical foundation we build with Farley completes the basis for our investigation of Beatty's *The Sellout*.

We broach the subject of Beatty's novel toward the end of chapter 8, but we really begin to dive into Beatty's offering in chapter 9, "Stanky Shrines and Hollow Bastions," analyzing how this strange, hilarious, absurd, and undeniably Black narrative allegorizes the problem of making Black space (for mourning, for living, for nourishment, for being together, and so on). The novel tracks an unnamed protagonist, addressed by some of his compatriots as "Bonbon" and by others as "the sellout," whose last name is Me, and whose hometown, Dickens, California, is unceremoniously "erased" from the map of Los Angeles, California. His mission becomes "reanimating Dickens," and his strategies, in relation to Dickens's agrarian society, reveal a disturbing entanglement between the way we imagine and construct "space" in an anti-Black world and deepen the import and difficulty of answering the question, "What even is a Black space?" Of deep interest is the concept of "Stank" and how "stankiness" helps us move toward something like an answer to that question.

To close the arrangement, we sit with Dionne Brand's *A Map to the Door of No Return*, posing "questions aimed at characterizing our movement through the violent space of the "tear in the world,"[27] and also aimed at the traces of that movement we bear in our flesh, imagination, and being. Essentially, now that we have established the scope and mechanics of the problem of Black spatiality, especially in terms of making or inventing Black space under untimely conditions, we begin to wonder about how we might move relative to such space. Recalling Ursa's Fanonian call to "leap into the black hole," we consider what such passage might look like and how such passage might happen "in the middle of nowhere."

And finally, we fade out and look outward with the **outro,** "Out of Time in the Middle of Nowhere." This final bit of writing traces a thread that runs through the entire project at the levels of language, concept, and method: destruction. Each arrangement—and *Impossible Stories* as a whole—works with various fragmented theories and narratives of Black life. Every literary analysis is a close reading, a meticulous dissection of small details of the texts we choose to visit. And each reading produces, or at least orbits around, the language of destruction: Fragments, obliteration, derangement, disorder, and disturbance all emerge as essential conceptual stars along the constellation of our meditation on Black creation in and against the anti-Black cosmos. This outro grasps this thread, unravels it. Marshalling our theoretical claims from the three arrangements on time, work, and space, we visit with M. NourbeSe Philip's *Zong!*—both the text and my memory of one of Philip's performances of some of *Zong!*'s entries—to think about how Black creation inheres in destruction. As we have done throughout the entirety of this project, but doing so much more explicitly here, we consider how destruction animates Black creation, and how Black creation wields destruction as tool and weapon.

At its core, our consideration in this conclusion and throughout the entirety of *Impossible Stories* depends on working with fragments. Thinking

---

27. Brand, *A Map*, 5.

about the complex, vexing problems that emerge when creation and destruction entangle so inextricably is why we work with Black fragments as our *prima materia*, our first matter. Fragments offer us an organizing principle[28] at the levels of method (discussed below) and concept, allowing us to both stage and think about what it means to work in this impossible space at the intersection between creation and destruction. Treating the fragments of Black spatiotemporal existence, experience, and creation *as* fragments without falling into making limiting and misleading assumptions about the possibilities of reclamation, recuperation, or redress opens us up into embracing the destruction that is elemental to Black being and making in the anti-Black world. In their brokenness, these shards of narrative and concept, and how we and the Black writers we analyze carefully hold them in our attention, behold them as wholes all their own, and create *with* them—double emphasis on "with"—teach us about making untimely Black words, work, and worlds from out of nowhere. Thinking about working *with* fragments and creating *with* destruction will culminate our work, providing an unclosed closure to our theorizing of Black spatiotemporality and Black creation.

Impossible Stories aims to reorient our relation to Blackness, Black life and death, and Black creation by inhabiting the problems that emerge when we recognize and really begin to work with Blackness's shattered relation to time and space. By reframing our understanding of Black spatiotemporal existence, we open ourselves up to a form of Black destructive creation that, as fully as possible, embraces and channels the impossibility of the stories we live, tell, and dare to imagine.

Madness in/and Method

There are reasons this Frankenstein homunculus of a project looks the way it does. We can discuss this by attending to the three most pressing methodological questions I routinely receive about this (and all of my) work.

WHY THE NARRATIVE/CREATIVE ELEMENTS?

I include narrative and creative elements in this project for two reasons—three, really, but only two will likely be taken seriously. First, and as I say to my students, to my family, and to anyone who asks me about my work,

---

28. I am evoking M. NourbeSe Philip's essay "Fugues, Fragments, and Fissures," which we will discuss in chapter 5.

I am driven by a need to make this work as accessible as possible to the communities that raised me. I speak what's next with my mother's ears, heart, and mind in mind, trying to balance the challenge of critical analysis with the familiarity of narrative. The "narrative fragments" I arrange ground the sometimes difficult and strange forays into physical phenomena, critical theory, and close reading by reminding us that this work is wholly animated by, bound up with, and indebted to the realities of Black temporal and spatial trauma. This leads me to the second reason: How Black folk live and die in relation to the problems that concern us throughout the text was, is, and always will be the foundation of every thought featured here. The realities of Black subjection form the grammar that organizes the perilous abstractions we wade through together. In my mind, I would be failing as a Black scholar if I did not hold these fragments of Black life and death closely as I write, and if I did not openly attend to the relationship between my analysis and those lives and deaths. These narrative fragments amplify and contextualize the project in a way that clarifies that the core motivation of all of this is to consider how I might express care for Black folk on these pages, in these theorizations, and beyond. This is a project about Black time, space, destruction, creation, and being, *and* it is a project that at the levels of structure, style, and ideas tries to perform care for Black folk under untimely conditions in the middle of nowhere.

WHAT'S WITH THE SCIENCE?

Like the answer to the previous question, there are both personal and intellectual reasons for this. My interest in science grew alongside my interest in books as a very young Black child with countless fascinations. I did not initially plan on writing and teaching as my trade. Starting from when I was in the fourth grade and going all the way until my final year as an undergraduate student at the University of California, Irvine (UCI), I had elected to become a scientific researcher. First and until just before college, I aspired to become an astrophysicist because I was fascinated by the stars, the planets, and all the strange, scary, and completely inconceivable wonders of the cosmos. When I arrived at UCI and had to declare a major, I found myself fascinated by the equally profound cosmos of the human mind, and vowed to become a neuroscientist—specifically, one who studied memory. Not until the fall semester of my senior year was I convinced (by Michael Szalay, my professor at the time) that my talents as a writer and analytical thinker were worthy of greater development in graduate school. In sum, I have yet to relinquish my lifelong interest in the cosmos. It informs how I approach my analysis and what I theorize.

Intellectually, the physics we come across in this text amplifies and (re)directs the analysis of Black creation. I make use of different phenomena and theories for their explanatory power. Basically, the physics provides an alternative lens through which we can and should examine the constituent elements of Black space and time. It offers a different vocabulary with which we can name or at least describe the experiences and phenomena of being Black under "untimely" conditions and with "nowhere" to be. It also offers a particular strain of inquiry about the cosmos in both structural and phenomenological ways that analytically overlays with the literary, political, and philosophical approaches we otherwise wield.

Structurally, physics considers the phenomena and mechanics of the cosmos as they operate independent of and beyond human knowledge and experience. This analytically tunes to the same frequency of structural analyses of Blackness that consider the phenomena and mechanics of the anti-Black world as they operate independent of and beyond individual and collective acknowledgment.

Phenomenologically, physics offers insight into the relativistic and otherwise experiential relationships we have with these structural phenomena and mechanics, especially but not exclusively in theorizations of time, which vibes well with the way structural analyses of anti-Blackness cannot disentangle themselves from the very real, nigh infinitely variable, but fundamentally shared Black experiences *of* that anti-Black world.

And finally, physics also offers a level of metaphorical or representative utility in that some of the theories (e.g., dark matter and galactic structure formation), phenomena (e.g., black holes), and concepts (e.g., refraction) resonate with Blackness, aspects of Black life, and the experiences of Black folk. These resonances are cool in their own right, but my interest is also in the clarity they lend to the theories of Black time, space, and creation that develop across these pages.

In sum, physics offers an analytical *novelty* that will allow us to identify previously unseen, or at least unrecognized—or unrecognizable?—features of being and creating while Black; an analytical *affinity* for this project's literary, political, and philosophical approaches to thinking about being and creating while Black; and a metaphorical or representative *utility* that helps clarify and name the theories of Black space, time, and creation that crystallize throughout the project.

While diamonds, blueshifts, black holes, dark matter, and gravitational waves fascinate me on their own, they also help us more fully understand

Black being in the anti-Black cosmos. Thinking about the mechanics of light refraction through diamonds in relation with the "diamonds" of *Beloved* compels us to reconsider just how Black folk and their imaginations channel the energy of trauma. In thinking about the relationship between dark matter and cosmic structure formation, we confront the stakes, possibilities, and essential problems and characteristics of Black space-making. Whatever the phenomenon, theory, or mechanic, physics becomes a tool with which we carve out an even deeper and more expansive exploration of our questions about Blackness, space, time, and creation.

I believe that physics—and the sciences writ large—offers Black studies an underutilized set of analytical tools, procedures, and connections that can help us craft more incisive queries or previously unasked questions about Black being in the cosmos, and guide us toward answers to some of these unsettling questions asked anew and from another angle. Contrary to some of my initial ideas about this project in its fledgling stages, *Impossible Stories* is not *precisely* or *just* a project that portends a physics of Black life and death in the cosmos. A more precise description would be that *Impossible Stories* rethinks Black temporality and Black spatiality as a way of formulating something like a physics of Black being. Beyond that, though, *Impossible Stories* offers a way to critically rethink Blackness by using all of the available analytical tools at my disposal, and has implications for Black studies, literary theory, and Black creative and destructive work that depend on but exceed the creation of such a physics.

WHY *THIS* ARRANGEMENT OF SCHOLARS AND TEXTS?

There are better reasons than "these are the fragments (texts; scholars) I could gather, the ones I hold the closest," but this is still an important start. Part of what compelled me to incorporate these texts and scholars is the personal and intellectual resonance I have fostered with them over the course of several years, reading and rereading and teaching these authors and thinkers in search of questions and answers about Blackness. I enjoy these pieces of scholarship and these creative works, and that enjoyment is inextricable from the intellectual fascination and academic considerations that come into play when trying to write an academic project, however experimental with tone and tactic this project might be.

In search of texts that would help us conjure "new" definitions of Black time and space, I turned my attention to this constellation of writing because it held the richest possibilities for pursuing a fuller, more complex, and more precise understanding of the spatiotemporal problems I want to unpack. For example, periodizations of Black art (e.g., Harlem Renaissance literature, literature from the Black Arts Movement, twenty-first-century literature) and avowed intellectual affiliations (e.g., the nuanced relationships between the thought of thinkers like Frank B. Wilderson III, Saidiya Hartman, and Fred Moten—who all appear throughout this text) are useful in a broad sense, but they are inessential here. They are organizational principles that animate and direct certain kinds of conversations, which would skew my writing in unwanted ways. My organizational principles are different for this project, so while I am wholly aware that *Corregidora, Beloved, The Sellout, Ghana Must Go, Mississippi Damned, Haunted Life,* "Venus in Two Acts," *The Undercommons,* and so on all operate on different avowed creative and intellectual registers, and with different affiliations of genre or field or paradigm, I am not interested in explicitly adjudicating these differences. Instead, my organizational principles—"stories about Blackness in time," "stories about Blackness and space," and "stories about Black creation"—guide my mind as I curate the works for this project, and my readings of the texts are meant to be distillations of each text's relationship to those principles.

For example, how Hartman, Wilderson, and Moten differently relate to prevailing conversations about Afropessimism, or how *Beloved* could be and has been characterized as a ghost story about Black folk reclaiming selfhood by confronting the haunting trauma of enslavement, and how *The Sellout* could be characterized as absurdist satire about Blackness, are interesting conversations to have (and certainly on my mind), but for the purposes of the project, how Hartman, Wilderson, Moten, Morrison, and Beatty all share in a large, ongoing, and perhaps much less obvious conversation about Black spatiotemporality is my core concern.[29] Thus, my investment in the former conversations is present throughout this text, and that investment acts as a theoretical thread that only subtends the larger conversation I want to have about the latter issue, Black spatiotemporality. As an example, to me my writing makes clear in this project that I align with the Afropessimist paradigm rather strongly. I recognize the paradigm as having the most rigorous and unflinching framework with which to approach any analysis of Black life, death, and creation in the anti-Black world. It is not immune to critique, but in that vein I recognize that the Afropessimist framework is only very

---

29. While the vast, insightful, and still-growing canon of scholarship in Afropessimism and writing about *Beloved* and Toni Morrison's oeuvre, or about *The Sellout* and Paul Beatty's satirical collection of novels, has informed my own work, I cannot gesture to all of it here without muddling the text, and mean to, instead, take a divergent path into what I believe is an unexplored quadrant of the intellectual cosmos.

recently being explored, deployed, challenged, augmented, and otherwise nurtured in ways that will only increase its applicability and utility for Black folk in and, more importantly, beyond the academy. In that light, take this as one of this project's secondary aims: The claims about Blackness, space, time, and creation here continue what I see as this ongoing project of exploring, deploying, challenging, augmenting, and nurturing Afropessimism; *this is an Afropessimistic project* aimed at advancing the paradigm to new frontiers.

And while we orbit the topic of intellectual affinities, *Impossible Stories* may in many ways lend itself to conversations in or about Afrofuturism. While I do not at any point openly engage in discussions of Afrofuturism as a paradigm, I recognize that some of the selection of texts, the appeal to scientific utility, and the creative elements certainly resonate with the Afrofuturist paradigm. Further, the special attention paid to Black speculative work and to considering the nature of Black creation—especially in a future-oriented manner that wonders at what we might, can, and should make "next"—also resonates with Afrofuturistic interests in similar lines of questioning with similar objects of analysis and similar creative gestures. Beyond these resonances, and given the absence of a sustained conversation, I leave it to the reader to determine whether or not this constitutes an actual affiliation with that paradigm. That said, to the oft-asked, "Are you an Afrofuturist?" or "So, you must like Afrofuturism, right?,"[30] I would characterize my relationship to the paradigm as troubled, destabilized, or unsettled at best.

AND WHY *THIS* SETUP—THE PRELUDES, THE ARRANGEMENTS, THE OUTRO? IS . . . IS THIS AN ALBUM?

No, it's a book. Also, yes, it's an album of sorts. If you read and listen closely, you might spy the intellectual and creative cadences that organize the three "arrangements." If this is an album, it is most certainly a concept album, governed by creative, intellectual, and political principles that lace every thought that tracks through it.

But I also venture to make arrangements in two other ways. First, this is a work made of and dependent upon fragments: conceptual shards of criti-

---

30. I characterize all of this a bit casually because these are the questions as I receive them in multiple settings and across multiple platforms. My work has been shared for a few years prior to its refinement in this book, and at conferences and lectures, in classrooms, and on social media, I routinely face one or both of these questions about my writing and my intellectual affiliations.

cal theory, details of literature, particular phenomena and principles from physics, and, most important, narrative fragments of Black living and dying in the anti-Black cosmos. This work inheres in arranging these fragments into a coherent text; to write this project is to try to make the necessary arrangements. Beyond putting these elements into relation with one another, part of the challenge stems from writing in a way that actually holds and beholds the fragments of scholarship, literature, lived experience, and physical phenomena that we arrange; treating each fragment with the requisite care requires a sustained, measured, and creative approach. With regard to lived experience, we arrange each narrative fragment in a way that really demonstrates care for the Black lives and deaths we choose to carry with us. With regard to physics, we effectively explicate the particular phenomena that animate and amplify our thinking throughout. With regard to literature, we wield close reading as our analytical tool, highlighting key elements or essential facets of the literary work we choose to dissect. With regard to scholarship, we highlight, pilfer, transmute, or take seriously the concepts and claims that speak most resonantly with problems of Black spatiotemporality and creation, especially when those concepts and claims are articulated with an Afropessimistic inflection. Further, we write in such a way that we often return to fragments—or rather, since we never really abandon any as we move through the text, we look again at fragments from which we shifted our attention, or conjure them anew by making explicit reference to them in the midst of new engagements. This is a way of recognizing that this field of fragments we work with is not merely a set of stories and ideas we can neatly separate from one another for convenient analysis, but an inextricably entangled knot of interconnected lives, deaths, scenes, sentiments, and thoughts that resists the sometimes too-neatness of analytical engagement.

I account for the difficulty of this venture throughout the project in order to openly reckon with what I believe is a constitutive impossibility to the completion of this enterprise: The impossibility of repair in particular is essential to the work, especially with regard to the shards of stories of Black life and death that ground every bit of analysis and theoretical musing. Redress is impossible, but I am working with the understanding that by making the proper arrangement of the irreparably broken, beholding the fragments as they are, and attempting to hold them here, in this project, as closely as possible, we will arrange the fragments into a field that might afford us the insights about Black being, time, space, and creation we seek.

Second, I try to make these arrangements out of mourning. Mourning for the dead, the dying, the lost, the untimely, the Black folk who live under such perilously untimely conditions and who know nowhere to be or belong, I try to make the necessary arrangements in this text to hold them closely, behold them intently, and carry them through every word and thought included here. If, as Claudia Rankine writes it, "the condition of Black life is one of mourning,"[31] then the same is true of the work I/we do here and beyond, now or whenever. The condition of this work, at least in part, is one of mourning the Black lives lived and lost to the untimely forces of this nowhere where we cannot be. And so, as I understand the process, arrangements must be made.

---

31. From Rankine's essay of the same name, "The Condition of Black Life Is One of Mourning," published in the *New York Times* on June 22, 2015.

FIRST ARRANGEMENT

Black (in) Time

Untimely Blackness

I

Prelude

Untimely Fragments and the Beginnings of a Reflection

I DO NOT KNOW when else to begin but with an arrangement of fractured endings. Suspended around us, the scattered shards of lost Black life, of untimely Black death, play the familiar, broken scenes again and again. The countless faces to the names we write on T-shirts, posters, websites, and our flesh peer through the fragments, expressing a want, or perhaps issuing a demand, that we who remain among the remains, we Black folk who live too intimately with the sharp shards of their shattered existences and bear the inevitable gashes and cuts over and over again, reflect upon the temporal bits of them that we (choose to) know.

I do not know how else to begin but by submitting to the wounds and perils that come with assembling even an inevitably cracked and incomplete mirror from the jagged pieces, these sharp screens on which these scenes of subjection and untimely dying repeat. I begin in reflection driven by a genuine need to heed what I read in their eyes as a call to bear witness. More than that: I reflect upon a personal and collective need to *make* time to really see and hold these scattered glimpses of life and death close, feeling, listening, and searching for what these severed timelines might teach us. By carefully arranging all this brokenness, I aim to create a medium for us to reflect upon the untimeliness of such fractured lives and deaths, and then to consider what this untimeliness teaches us about the violently shattered relationship between Blackness, life, death, and time.

Really knowing and feeling the relationship between Blackness and time has import in and of itself because a more precise diagnosis of the conditions of Black life and death in the anti-Black world is necessary if one of our aims is to develop a more precise treatment of those conditions. This is because part of my contention is that a recognition of the unethical, derelict, and deathly relationship between Blackness and time shatters our taken-for-granted ideas about our deeply, but sometimes uncritically, held definitions of past-ness, presence, and futurity. To recognize this untimely relationship would mean throwing into crisis our abilities to know or name ourselves as present beings that create and destroy in the name of a past, present, and future because they cannot cohere *as* a past, present, or future for Black folk.

I also contend that rethinking Black temporality will profoundly reshape our relationship to Black attempts at creation and destruction. Understanding what it is to be Black "in" time temporally reorients us toward Black acts and artifacts of creative destruction and destructive creation because a more accurate understanding of Black time better orients us to the possibilities, stakes, and impacts of Black creative/destructive work. Knowing *when* we are(n't) shifts our imaginative and imagined relationships to one another, ourselves, the work we do, and how and why we do it. What and who we build and break and how, who, and what we move and make reveal what we know and feel about what I call "Black untimeliness" or "untime," unsettled, unimaginable, shattered time.

These narrative shards and the forthcoming analyses of Black literature and scholarship—of stories about and theorizations of Blackness and time—unpack "untime" as Black time, creating an opportunity to reconsider why, how, and what we should create, from street to page to screen to stage to every-when/where in the name of caring for Black folk under such untimely conditions.

This book's opening arrangement thinks through time as a problem in relation to Blackness. It takes the question of Blackness in relation to time and centers it at the foundation of a larger question about what it is to be, live, and think while Black in this anti-Black world. Two things have to happen: We have to trace the problem in relation to the way these questions have been taken for granted or inadequately addressed thus far, and we must propose a corrective to this problem. Following this arrangement of narrative fragments, the next chapter will engage Michelle Wright's *Physics of Blackness* as a way of opening into a discussion about how thought—in and outside the academy—takes time for granted, and wields Gayl Jones's *Corregidora* to begin to uncover the problems that taking-for-granted veils.

We pursue how Gayl Jones's novel on the one hand recognizes the violent incoherence of Black temporality, and on the other hand explores questions of what this violent incoherence does to Black attempts at creating or "making." The final chapter of this arrangement continues the exploratory work of *Corregidora* to thoroughly map what characterizes the relation between Blackness and time, drawing from David Marriott's *Haunted Life*, namely its afterword and its introduction of the concept of "deathliness," and reading Octavia Butler's *Kindred* to expand upon the consequences of this revised understanding of time.

While I do not know when or how else to begin, I *do* know that each and every Black fragment matters.

Here are the entangled arrangements of the ones I could collect, the ones I hold the closest. I sit with all the bits that I can bear, listening and looking with intent.

Fragment 0[1]
LOOPS

Jasmine Darwin is slammed on the ground in a place of teaching.

Shakara is slammed and flipped and tossed and dragged on the ground in a place of teaching.

Dajerria Beckton is slammed on the ground in a place of teaching, outside of a pool because everywhere are the pavement, the fresh-cut grass, the chlorinated waters and saltwaters, the asphalt, the wood, the linoleum, the earth, the Earth, the grounds for teaching.

A repeated concussive force of Black girls and women slammed to tile, grass, pavement, and earth produces the percussive rhythm behind the over-and-over again shock and gasp at what we knew we knew and know we know and yet learn again each time. That thunderous breath and boom bumping, bumping anew on a loop letting loose the lessons of a particular curriculum, the ones and twos of which roll, and roll, behind a sam-

---

1. In advance, every fragment's number throughout the course of the project is a number that has some personal significance to me. The lack of sequential ordering and the lack of a definitive range of numbers also fits into how I imagine these fragments as being impossible to fully count or account for, and how arranging them does not adhere to conventional notions of linear or neat ordering.

ple of final words of Octavia Butler's *Kindred*, "And [she] screamed and screamed,"[2] on repeat.

Boom-bap go the Black bodies and the beat bangs, don't it? The way the cadence drums up the sinister meanings of the hieroglyphics on their flesh[3] mixes well with the staccato flow of the narratives that compose that flesh's text. The dependability, the constancy, of the concussive force, the theft of breath, break of bone, and boom of body, provides a portion of the key to a "praxis and a theory, a text for living and for dying, and a method for reading both"[4] as it pertains to delving deeper into the Blackness of the problem of time. The way this violence loops—typically as an expression of real, bodily, concussive force against/of Black women's bodies—and that it loops at all unsettle certain assumptions about the linearity and progressiveness of time's movement. Instead of the proverbial timeline, plotted with neatly arranged events along the axis of befores, nows, and afters and composing something called "history," time is looped, knotted, unwieldy, and impossible to so easily conceive.

Envision it.

Loops, circles, knots, tangles, and almost indistinguishable strands of events twist and turn into one another. How the loops circle back into or overlap with one another operates as a function of precisely how and how much these events repeat and resonate with one another. Dajerria's beat loops over and into Shakara's, and both loop over and into Jasmine's, and all three loop over and into the countless named, unnamed, and nameless beats that boom, bap, and bang the shared rhythm of what continues to emerge as

---

2. Octavia Butler, *Kindred* (Boston: Beacon Press, 2003), 261.

3. See Spillers, "Mama's Baby, Papa's Maybe," 68: "Undecipherable markings . . . hieroglyphics of the flesh."

4. This line—really, this whole "fragment" draws from and conjures Hortense Spillers's "Mama's Baby, Papa's Maybe: An American Grammar Book," which we'll dive more deeply into later in this chapter, and a bit in the next. Specifically, this line references a passage in the essay in which Spillers highlights the specificity of spectacular but quotidian anti-Black violence against "unprotected" and "ungendered" Black female flesh—"ungendered" because of the kinds of real and symbolic violence that transmute Black bodies into Black flesh, humans into property, and so gendered beings into nonbeings for whom the "genre" (pace Sylvia Wynter) or "ontic garb" (pace Calvin Warren) of gender does not normatively, if at all, apply. In my reading, Spillers attends to this specificity because it holds a/the key to deciphering the fundamental, constitutive elements of living and dying in the anti-Black world. Here, I posit that the "unprotected" Black women that have been percussively slammed to the earth, typically in spaces of education (e.g., schools), and the "rhythm" of that repeated violence, echo Spillers's claim and provide us insight into the problem for thought that is "Black time."

a pressing, peculiar, and singularly Black problem with time. In my mind, what this monstrous entanglement of bodies and brutalities "looks like" in the imagination becomes inconceivable.

The beat plods on. The rhythmic repetition of a specific, familiar strain of anti-Black violence beats and beats behind what fire time spits.

And it is so hot.

Fragment 35
LAPSE

My strained eyes aim at a blue light–filtered laptop display and stick, quiver, and move on the dash-cam and surveillance footage playing again and again. I search for answers that may not exist, or at least questions that might allow for deeper exploration into a timey-wimey problem for thought that continues to mutate with each viewing of this and countless other scenes of Black subjection.[5]

Video 1

Dashboard camera footage. Sandra remains unseen in her car stopped at the side of the road, but her presence is known and felt. Enter officer, screen left, approaching passenger-side window.

Suddenly, Sandra Bland finds herself stopped on her usual way to work. Suddenly the door is open.

Suddenly she is out of frame, but he is not. Where and when is her being? The void where she stands enraged and afraid only implies her being by way of his power, his gaze, his threats, his violence.

Suddenly she is in the frame, transmuted into carceral inevitability meant to satisfy his carnal needs.

And suddenly she is removed again. Where and when has she gone? He becomes two, then three—he multiplies as she disappears—rather, dissolves, into the disembodied and timeless fury of Black fire, manifest in a

---

5. I'm very deliberately conjuring Saidiya Hartman's *Scenes of Subjection*. The spirit of the text and of the word "scenes" strongly implies a demand to bear witness to a real, actual, and violent drama of subjection being played out across the times and spaces of Black experience and being.

voice, "All of this for a traffic signal! I swear to God. . . . Slamming me to the ground and everything! Everything!"

But suddenly, that, too, is gone. In another video of the same moments from a different angle, we see that she is pinned to the earth, thrown on the ground in a place of teaching, too. But we knew and felt the concussive force. We shudder to the familiar rhythm.

Scene.

Video 2

Surveillance footage. Enter and exit officers, overseeing the cells of the jailhouse.

Suddenly, a jail. She is invisible again, out of view. It is unclear if, where, or when we might find her, know her, or feel her again.

Hours pass, and silently, the routine terroristic surveillance of the officers, the exterminator, and the jail nurse persist unabated, the only indication of Sandra's life implied by the lack of disturbance in the routine.

Enter several officers, pacing, communicating something lost in the silence of the surveillance. Their movements might barely be interpreted as urgent; they appear to be frustrated—a sheriff outstretches his arms sideways in exasperation.

Suddenly, they are in her cell, where she hangs from a noose fashioned from a plastic, jail-issue garbage bag, strung up over a partition—and we only know this after the fact; we still do not and will not see, know, or feel her, here.

Enter another sheriff, screen bottom. She looks down the hallway toward the commotion, wiping her hands clean with a white cloth. Exit sheriff.

Suddenly, Sandra is gone.

Exit several officers, pushing a gurney on which medical equipment sits helplessly, silent in its failure to breathe life back into her Black body.

Scene.

All of that vacant time. All of those lapses between Sandra's life and her death. And all of the questions that remain unanswered or unanswerable, likely met with a silence as crushing and violent as the carceral silence of the surveillance footage. All of that ripples through me as psychosomatic tremors.

My left hand shakes while reaching for a coffee-filled TARDIS mug perched too close to the brink of my desk, and my right hand anxiously taps the pen against an otherwise blank page. Dots appear in disarray in the page's space, forming what I am only able to describe as a clutter of ellipses, littering the lines with a deranged array of the false starts, open ends, and loaded silences ellipses tend to signify.

Fragment 24
LOSS

I have had *Time: The Kalief Browder Story,* a six-part documentary series about Kalief Browder's wrongful imprisonment and ultimate suicide, paused on my computer for weeks, or months. I have displaced and ignored it. It lives, muttering in the background of open documents—this one included—peeking behind the edges of open browser windows. Time and time again, I switch to the media player and plan to watch. I know I have committed to bearing witness to the glimpses offered by the Black narrative fragments I have chosen to hold in my hands. But here I sit, hesitating to hold Kalief in my vision, to behold this horrifying bit of his existence.

I can hear his frustrated insistence as my thumb hovers over the spacebar.

They took over
three years of my life!
I'm never
Going to get those years back

He shakes his head and his eyes go elsewhere.

Never.[6]

I shake my head. I press play.

I immediately note the bracketing and interlacing of the narrative points the documentary traces. The gears of a clock spin before us during opening title credits of each episode, reaffirming that the aesthetic choices and audiovisual arrangements made by writers, subjects, researchers, and producers will be guided by a careful attention to the machinations and operations of time. Alongside the opening title credits' visuals, each interruptive visual cut within the episodes reminds we-who-bear-witness that time is unstable in the telling of Kalief's narrative fragment. Stylistic dramatizations of time passing, time rewinding, and time spinning out of control clarify the unpredictability of the violent movement of time around and upon the life of Kalief Browder. And they reveal the temporal violence experienced by Kalief, his family and friends, the Black folk who know of and feel the familiarity and horror of his narrative fragment, and of we who watch and rewatch the familiar horrors unfold over and over again in the documen-

---

6. *Time: The Kalief Browder Story,* "Part 1—The System," directed by Jenner Furst, 2017.

tary series. The visual gambit of the interruptive cuts aims at unsettling the viewer by visually announcing and repeating the temporal incoherence that characterizes what happens to Kalief: The hope, or the bet, is that these visualizations force viewers to recognize, to reckon with, and to feel the incoherence of time's movement here. We who sit and watch are meant not only to bear witness to the way time itself devastates Kalief, his family and friends, and Black folk, but also to bear that devastation in our own imaginations. We think and feel his subjection to time's unrelenting force.

I shudder to the rhythm of the moving gears of the clock. I pause again.

I lost my childhood. I lost my happiness.

In my imagination, Kalief remains insistent.

I'm never going to get those years back.
Never.[7]

Play.

I hear Kalief, and I see his face on the screen, at turns appearing defiant, despondent, enraged, disgusted, and lost, or at a loss. I feel that loss in my flesh and in my imagination.

Can't you feel it?

His is an insistence of his lost time and of the lostness of his time, vacant time. That it is lost, how lost, how it is lost, and above all that Kalief knows, embodies, articulates, and lives the dispossession of temporality for as long as he can bear—all of these pieces as well as the insidious kinds of in-betweens betwixt them that I remain unable to address. Both out of terror and out of a lack of available vocabulary, all of it collapses in me with immense density.

A gaping hole in me widens, engorging its massive absence with all the numerical and musical measures of Kalief's lost time and what they scream from within: just 16 years old when the theft of his time began; 1,110 days the wrongful incarceration on Rikers Island; over 800 cumulative days in the mad torture of solitary confinement; 31 court dates that came and vanished in the legal machinery of New York's justice system; 2 years of "freedom" haunted by the ghosts of all that lost time; 1 suicide; countless casualties in the wake of it all, most of all his mother, who "literally died of a broken

---

7. Ibid.

heart";[8] all of the other numbers and percentages that tell us fragments of the grand anti-Black story of mass incarceration; all the tick marks and tallies of the slave ledgers; all the years, all the bodies, all the unnamable, irretrievable loss.

Pause.

Tears blind eyes, liquid manifestations of the growing tear in me.

I feel like the whole point of me being on this show is just . . . to get my story out there.

I feel like this happens every day. This happens every day, and I feel like this gotta stop.

I feel like I had to fight.

I had to fight.

Play.

I am trying to do the impossible, typing the hard words while gently holding these fragments with care. The shards of their fractured Black lives seem attracted to one another; I can feel the push and pull of invisible tethers, a magnetic force suturing them together. I wonder about the texture, strength, and malleability of the unsettling homology, as well as the way it provides this force field of fragments its disturbing coherence.

Time loss. Time lapse. Time loops. Time lengths. Time emerges in these narrative bits as a problem for the Black lives imperiled by or subject to its peculiar and violent machinations. These parables of the perils faced by Black folk in time offer glimpses of what I understand to be a fundamental problem—a problem at the levels of being, feeling, and experience—between Blackness and time. Stories of the insidious sense that time seems to, at the very least, operate on a different register, with different resonances, and with different outcomes for Black living and dying in this anti-Black world.

After all, these are what I understand to be the stakes of holding, beholding, and being beholden to these and all the untimely Black fragments I am able to bear, and all the ones beyond my bearings: Black life and death themselves.

So here we find ourselves, invested in stories about Blackness and time. In this project's first section, we will delve into Gayl Jones's *Corregidora* and

---

8. Paul Prestia, the attorney representing Kalief Browder, and later the family of Kalief Browder, said this about Venida's untimely death.

Octavia Butler's *Kindred*, two stories of Black lives pushed and pulled by the forces of time in ways that will proffer an alternative conceptualization of Black temporality, one that more precisely and fully articulates the peculiar, perilous, and problematic nature of Black time glimpsed in these narrative fragments I bear. Donning Hortense Spillers's "Mama's Baby, Papa's Maybe: An American Grammar Book" and David Marriott's "Afterword: Ice Cold" as critical lenses, we will really see the problem of Black time in search of the machinations and (im)proper name of this problem.

Let us continue with our attempt at gathering and arranging the fragments, too late or too early as we might be.

11

Black Holes and Generations

> After having driven himself to the limit of self-destruction, the Negro is about to leap, whether deliberately or impetuously, into the "black hole" from which will come "the great Negro cry with such force that the pillars of the world will be shaken by it."
>
> —FRANTZ FANON, *BLACK SKIN, WHITE MASKS*[1]

MICHELLE M. WRIGHT shares some of my sentiment that prevailing understandings of temporality in general, and Black temporality in particular, remain dangerously imprecise. In her recent book, *Physics of Blackness*, she addresses a shared tendency in the humanities (and beyond) to take the concept of time for granted in a way that is limiting and exclusionary. "Mainstream"[2] thought and theory (and, I would argue, most thought and theory *not* considered "mainstream"), in and outside the academy, depends on a "mistranslation of Newton's laws of motion and gravity into [a] linear progress narrative" that depends on a "cause-and-effect framework."[3] To expand on said Newtonian laws, professor of anthropology Muhammad Aurang Zeb Mughal neatly describes Newton's theory of "absolute time" in an entry in *The Encyclopedia of Time*:

---

1. Fanon, *Black Skin*, 154.

2. I only use this word as Wright does throughout her text. I read it as an attempt to preempt any critique of her work that might zone in on what would otherwise be a blanket, generalizing claim that, in fact, would go against the motivations Wright expresses for researching and writing the project—namely, to move from a generalizing rubric to one that includes otherwise marginalized identities.

3. Michelle M. Wright, *Physics of Blackness: Beyond the Middle Passage Epistemology* (Minneapolis: University of Minnesota Press, 2015), 37.

> According to this model, it is assumed that time runs at the same rate for all the observers in the universe, or in other words, the rate of time of each observer can be scaled to the absolute time by multiplying the rate by a constant. This concept of absolute time suggests absolute simultaneity by the coincidence of two or more events at different points in space for all observers in the universe. So, absolute time has been discussed in two senses of absoluteness. In first sense, absoluteness means independent of events, while in second sense, it means independent of observer or frame of reference. . . . Newton regarded time as something absolute, true, and mathematical, of itself and by its own nature, that flows uniformly without relation to anything external, and by another name it is called duration.[4]

As Mughal describes him, Newton treats time as an *absolute* truth of the universe. Time acts as an independent feature or force of reality by structuring the order of events and defining the relation between event (as a temporal marker) and observer. This is a phenomenological relation as much as it is a structural one. In this framework, independent of how observers experience the structure of time, *all* experience of time is structured by the fact of time's defining characteristics: It "flows uniformly," independent of any "relation to anything external"; this is the notion of "duration." For Wright, this absolute understanding of time is central to how "all disciplines and laypersons organize knowledge as *progressive*,"[5] and all developments as moving forward—as chronological.

This characterizes Black studies writ large, "mainstream" and not. Specifically, it characterizes what Wright calls the "Middle Passage Epistemology":[6] a dominant historical narrative that moves from the violence of the Middle Passage, through the dispersal across the Atlantic, and to the still-unfolding histories of Blacks in the diaspora produced by this violent dispersal. All of the movement is forward, which means it is inherently progressive, and all

---

4. Muhammad Aurang Zeb Mughal, "Time, Absolute," in *The Encyclopedia of Time*, edited by H. James Birx (Thousand Oaks: Sage, 2009), 1254.

5. Ibid.

6. I would just like to address the fact that Wright addresses an earlier use of this term in the work of Henry Louis Gates Jr., while making sure she distinguishes her own take from it. My understanding is that while Gates only describes the Middle Passage epistemology as a system of knowledge, he does not dissect the spatial and temporal features of this system of knowledge in a way rigorous or suitable enough to meet Wright's criteria for analysis. Hence, her term *depends* on what she feels is a careful, meticulous attention to the temporality of the Middle Passage in relation to "collective identities" like Blackness (I will discuss my issue with thinking about Blackness this way later in the chapter).

developments along the continuum exist in relation to the origin point of the timeline (the "beginning" of the Middle Passage itself). While acknowledging the nuance and situational necessity of this epistemology, Wright reveals the limitations of the applicability and inclusivity of systems of knowledge that adopt a Middle Passage timeline to string together the thoughts and experiences of Black folk.

To unpack Wright's writing about time, we must attend to how Wright characterizes Blackness since her particular framing shapes her ideas about Black temporality. For her purposes, Blackness is a "collective identity" that is as constructed, "implicitly or explicitly defined as a set of physical and behavioral characteristics," as it is phenomenological, "imagined through individual perceptions in various ways depending on the context."[7] With this characterization at the foundation of her claims, Wright recognizes that binding the narratives of Blackness that inform academic and lay discourse to the finitude of a linear and progressive timeline with a fixed origin point inherently excludes identities that do not fit neatly onto this timeline. In Wright's analysis, the Western Black heterosexual cisgender male most often and neatly aligns with the rigid plane of the timeline. Blacks who identify any other way, with some other origin point or history, other geographical location, as a member of the LGBTQIA community, as a woman, are marginalized and cannot neatly—if at all—weave their narratives into the dominant thread. I find this especially to be prescient: In the most "mainstream" academic, activist, and lay discourse concerning the Movement for Black Lives (M4BL), proverbial slips of tongue often make overt references to a label for or list of Black (hetero, cis) boys and men and equally as often fail to pay equal (or sometimes any) attention to the cis and trans Black girls and women who suffer *at least* comparable orders of anti-Black violence and are the most vulnerable population among Black folk.

To answer her critiques of thinking that too easily accepts, if not completely reinforces, the absoluteness of a Middle Passage epistemology, Wright presents "epiphenomenal time," a more fluid time of the ever-shifting "now" that she draws from philosophy and quantum mechanics. The shift in visualization is key: Rather than a straight line or arrow, epiphenomenal time resembles "a circle with many arrows pointing outward in all directions";[8] the center of the circle houses the observer, the circle itself marks the shifting "now" the observer occupies, and the arrows move toward the many (possibly infinite) "times," past and future, inextricably bound to the shifting

---

7. Wright, *Physics of Blackness*, 4.
8. Ibid., 20.

"now." Wright's intention is easy to grasp if difficult to execute: Depart from the exclusivity of a limited understanding of Black temporality; seek out, or (re)create, and adopt a radically different temporality that can account for "the greatest number of Blacknesses that are possible and viable"[9]—that is, the most inclusive circle that can serve as the amorphous enclosure of a Blackness that is multidimensional, of different identifications, histories, and origins. This is why, of the thinkers she credits with being emblematic of crafting analyses dependent on a Middle Passage epistemology, namely Henry Louis Gates Jr., W. E. B. Du Bois, and Paul Gilroy,[10] she aligns herself most closely with the latter, who, unlike Gates and Du Bois, at least frames his understanding of Blackness as transitory, "rhizomorphic," complex, and fundamentally untethered from the fixedness of a single origin, identification, or destination.

At its most radical, "epiphenomenal time" eliminates the foundation for inherently exclusionary and limiting problems spanning at least "mainstream" Black studies discourse, academic and not. And at best, it turns on the genuine desire to include in the center of Black thought the otherwise marginalized "Blacknesses"—or, rather, it turns on the desire to disperse the notion of "center" altogether, refusing to cram all the complex "Blacknesses" into a limited space and, instead, scattering a multitude of centers, or temporal nodes, "now" nodes, from which the past and future might be interpreted through different Black lenses. This resonates with us. Wright's epiphenomenal time is a very timely concept, given the prescient issues of inclusion paralleled in Movement for Black Lives (henceforth M4BL) organizing and representation, and given the ongoing history of Black studies' inability or refusal to interrogate its limiting thinking about time. There is a real applicability of the spirit of epiphenomenal time to pressing questions being raised by Black folk about Blackness in the anti-Black world, whether those questions arise inside or outside mainstream academic and lay communities.

But I find Wright's concept to be too neat. Or if it is messy, it is too neatly and easily messy. In being so neat, the concept of "epiphenomenal time" and what Wright believes its implications to be mask certain unchecked assumptions about Blackness, time, and how they relate to one another that Wright

---

9. Ibid., 25.

10. She chooses their most famous works for analysis: Gates's *The Signifying Monkey*, Du Bois's *The Souls of Black Folk*, and Gilroy's *The Black Atlantic*. She categorizes all three as works of Middle Passage epistemologies, but she spends the most time and shares the most affinity with Gilroy's work for its attention to a "rhizomorphic" Blackness: one of many roots, outstretched in all directions.

must make in order to make the (quantum) leap to replace linear progressive time with epiphenomenal time in the first place.

What happens when we do not center "identity" in a way that displaces the structural position, or "political ontology"?[11] Differently, what happens when our analysis shifts its framework to a higher level of abstraction, from one that privileges intersectional analysis located at the level of "identities," collective or otherwise, to an analysis that frames those intersections and identities structurally, and does not forget the structure? If we understand that structure to be something like the universe, of which time is a force and a fundamental feature,[12] and we understand it to be as violently anti-Black as it is for Blacks everywhere and always, then what happens to time and our capacity to relate to it, let alone in a neat way? Put more sinisterly, if we understand Blackness as a structural position with a phenomenological relation to time's force, then what happens when time is a component of the universe's anti-Blackness—is anti-Black itself? Only time can tell, but what it communicates it encodes. And we require a way to decipher this time code, some form of key or cryptovariable[13] that would open a way to pursue answers to these questions we aim at Wright.

In 1987, Hortense Spillers published the groundbreaking essay "Mama's Baby, Papa's Maybe: An American Grammar Book," which will help us reconsider how time's force acts in relation to Blackness, and how Black folk bear time's force. By sifting through the temporal claims of Spillers's analysis, we will unnerve the limiting neatness of Wright's concept of "epi-

---

11. The best definition of political ontology I can think of comes from Jared Sexton's essay "People-of-Color-Blindness," *Social Text* 28, no. 2 (Summer 2010): 36–37. He writes: "Political ontology is not a metaphysical notion, because it is the explicit outcome of a politics and thereby available to historic challenge through collective struggle. But it is not simply a description of a political status either, even an oppressed political status, because it functions *as if* it were a metaphysical property across the *longue durée* of the premodern, modern, and now postmodern eras."

12. This is actually a topic of serious debate in the world of theoretical physics, and has been since the advent of relativity displaced Newton's notions of a rigid, absolute, and "pure" time.

13. The difference between "key," the language of lay and technical coding and cryptography, and "cryptovariable," the language used by the National Security Agency (NSA), is the overt reference to surveillance and state power not so deeply coded in the latter term. Since we are handling something cumbersome, spectral and violent, and since decoding what this force does to Blackness and Black folk in an anti-Black world might not just uncover, but also perform, its own violence—this is a twisted, but logical, extension of Saidiya Hartman's argument in "Venus in Two Acts," which we address later—alluding to an institution that performs anti-Black (state) violence in the form of surveillance/policing and all it produces, and to technologically advanced cryptography, seems timely.

phenomenal time." Of import is Spillers's characterization of the ceaselessness and repetitiveness of the symbolic order's "atomization" or "murder" of Black being "over time."

Spillers is "a marked woman"[14] with many names writing about markings. The many names and marks that converge on Black flesh in the name of a global project of ongoing anti-Black terror telegraph a more sinister problem. Spillers works to decode the signal of these sinister marks to better grasp the anti-Black violence of the structures or orders that govern and give form to the world: the "historical order," the "symbolic order," and the human[15] (as a political-ontological construct). We read her introductory gestures toward how these names and marks signal something structural and perhaps timeless as her way of beginning to "clear the field of static"[16] that has accumulated "over time."[17] And we interpret "over time" a few ways: "over" as in "during" the *longue durée* of Black subjection to the force of time, and to the force of social death, which is a more superficial reading; "over" as in "governing" or "controlling/defining" as an overdetermining feature of anti-Blackness, which is a recognition of the structural; and "over" as in "covering over" or "concealing," like a blanket, a mask, or a veil, which

---

14. From the introductory paragraph of legend, in which Spillers writes of the many kinds of names borne by Black female flesh, which opens us into the scope of essay's argument: "Let's face it. I am a marked woman, but not everybody knows my name. 'Peaches' and 'Brown Sugar,' 'Sapphire' and 'Earth Mother,' 'Aunty,' 'Granny,' God's 'Holy Fool,' a 'Miss Ebony First,' or 'Black Woman at the Podium': I describe a locus of confounded identities, a meeting ground of investments and privations in the national treasury of rhetorical wealth. My country needs me, and if I were not here, I would have to be invented" (65). There is so much in this passage, especially given how quickly and deftly Spillers introduces and entangles the central concerns her essay will explore—Blackness, gender, naming, marking, valuation, the "symbolic order" (68), and knowledge. Of profound importance is the way she explores this opening/entanglement as a set of problems that should be thought in terms of Blackness and time, Blackness over time, Blackness in time.

15. This specific point is drawn from Saidiya Hartman's take on "Mama's Baby, Papa's Maybe" in a roundtable discussion meant to revisit the essay and discuss its growing legacy; included in the discussion, entitled "'Whatcha Gonna Do?'—Revisiting 'Mama's Baby, Papa's Maybe: An American Grammar Book,'" are Spillers herself, Hartman, Farah Jasmine Griffin, Shelley Eversley, and Jennifer L. Morgan. Hartman's take is important to mine, and to the project of Afropessimism as a whole, as it reveals what concerns Spillers, the human as a metaphysical construct that can only be read via an analysis of the specific anti-Black violence that names, marks, and positions the Black woman (and she confirms as much in her response to Hartman's reading).

16. Spillers et al., "'Whatcha Gonna Do?,'" *Women's Studies Quarterly* 35, no. 1/2 (2007), 301.

17. Spillers, "Mama's Baby," 65.

suggests that part of what will be uncovered by clearing away the "static" is time itself.

For Spillers, Black women's flesh in particular provides part of the key we require to perform this "clearing away," this attempt at deciphering: "The materialized scene of unprotected female flesh—of female flesh 'ungendered'—offers a *praxis* and a *theory*, a *text* for living and for dying, and a *method for reading both* through their diverse mediations."[18] The particular vulnerability of Black women's "ungendered" flesh, the materiality and actuality of the wounds that divide and scar (read: "mark") that flesh, and the way gender does not "happen" on/to Black flesh the same way it does for all others,[19] as well as the "scene" of violence that frames it—so, Black female flesh in the context of gratuitous violence—is key. Not only does it reveal the "text," which is the flesh as a "primary narrative" composed of "undecipherable markings . . . a kind of hieroglyphics"[20] that must be deciphered, but also a praxis and a theory and a method to perform that deciphering. Spillers reads Black female flesh in order to examine the entangled historical, symbolic, and metaphysical orders in part because of the ways the academy and the world render Black women (and Black feminism) invisible or unthought, but also because the human being's inextricability from Black nonbeing, signaled by Black women's proximity to violence specifically,[21] had been unthought.

It is violence without end. The ceaselessness of this primary narrative and its orders of violence, as well as the undying need to decipher it "over time," appears to be a foundational problem passed "from one generation to another . . . [via] *symbolic substitutions* in an efficacy of meanings that *repeat the initiating moments*."[22] As Spillers writes:

---

18. Ibid., 68; emphasis mine.
19. Prior to this, Spillers writes of "pornotroping" (67) as a specific violence that reduces Black bodies with any defining "human" characteristics and relations to fungible flesh that can be accumulated and used however the anti-Black symbolic order see fit. It is this distinction, between "body," as a site at which gender might be applied, and "flesh [as] that zero degree of social conceptualization that does not escape concealment under the brush of discourse, or the reflexes of iconography" (67), that separates Black folk from all others (who are recognized as human bodies, or humans with bodies).
20. Ibid., 67.
21. Toward the end of the roundtable with Hartman, Griffin, Eversley, and Morgan, Spillers reveals the rage and the frustration that haunt every line of the essay and all its arguments, which, on a personal level, added a thickness to the essay's claims—for Blackness, for Black feminism, and for Black women.
22. Ibid.; emphasis on "repeat the initiating moments" mine.

> Even though the captive flesh/body has been "liberated," and no one need pretend that even the quotation marks do not *matter*, dominant symbolic activity, the ruling episteme that releases the dynamics of naming and valuation, remains grounded in the originating metaphors of captivity and mutilation so that neither time nor history, nor historiography and its topics, show movement, as the human subject is "murdered" over and over again by the passions of a bloodless and anonymous archaism, showing itself in endless disguise.[23]

Here, the interpretations of "over time" all seem applicable in describing the vexing relation between "dominant symbolic activity," "the symbolic order," the "dynamics of naming and valuation," the names and marks channeling those dynamics, and time. The "so that" implies a causal link, in which the symbolic order, and the naming and names it makes possible, at least influences, if not determines, the movement of time for Blacks and in relation to Blackness. The "primary narrative" of Black flesh is written in "undecipherable markings" and "hieroglyphics," and in the form of the flesh's "seared, divided, ripped-apartness, riveted to the ship's hole, fallen, or 'escaped' overboard,"[24] or "resting" burned and shot on a couch after a police raid (like Aiyana Stanley-Jones), or (s)lain on asphalt in Missouri sun (like Michael Brown), or bullet-riddled and overlooked (like Penny Proud). Names and marks are illegible in relation to the many orders of violence carving them onto Black flesh so that Black flesh becomes a Black (w)hole warping time (and space). In relation to Black flesh, time appears to stall and "show [no] movement," but really manifests as a series of repetitions, "over and over again"—time *loops*. By looping (and appearing to stall), this time murders Black human subjectivity: Time kills any "dimension of ethics, [or] relatedness between human personality and its anatomical features, between one human personality and another, between human personality and cultural institutions."[25]

Time provides "another angle on the divided flesh" or two. In one sense, it appears to act as a force through which the symbolic order and its dynamics "murder" Blackness's relation to humanity (Blackness becomes antithetical to humanness). In another, via apparent "textual" permanence (time showing no movement) and repeated inscription (the murder happens over and over again), it reaffirms the violence of the names/marks and the order(s) (structures) they telegraph. Through a series of "symbolic

---

23. Ibid., 68.
24. Ibid., 67.
25. Ibid., 68.

substitutions," time rewrites the "primary narrative" of Blackness on Black flesh into an apparent timelessness "over time." The "narrative" becomes an "anonymous archaism, showing itself in endless disguise," the undying past masked again and again in new names and with new marks, from "Dajerria" to "Jasmine" to "Aiyana" to "Penny" to "Shakara" to "Sandra" to . . .

The relationship between the mechanics and movement of time, the reduction of Black folk to fleshy objects, and the destruction of Blackness as a position with identifiable human features becomes a timelessly unethical one. At least part of what Spillers deciphers in this violent relation between Blackness, marked and named Black flesh, and the symbolic order is a problem between Blackness and time grounded in violence and illegibility. With this reading, we diverge from the neatness of Wright's "epiphenomenal time" in a more pronounced way. Such a name for time's unethical and violent relationship to Blackness, as well as all the attendant assumptions and meanings of Wright's concept, seems less and less able to capture the fullness of the problem Spillers exposes.

But we must also put pressure upon the limits of Spillers's conceptualization of time. Fully acknowledging that unlike Wright, Spillers does not base her whole project on the pursuit of an alterative theory of Black time, we must still reckon with how substitution, cycle, and repetition function in her characterization of time. If we recall the narrative fragments that compose the prelude prior to this chapter, we would concur that Spillers's characterization of the looped nature of Black time and the importance of Black women to understanding that looped-ness affirms what *we knew we knew and know we know but learn again each time. We shudder to the familiar rhythm.* But beyond the limits of what she writes about time in "Mama's Baby," we also wonder how Spillers might situate this form of unstable temporal looping alongside the temporal lapses and losses we know and shudder to the rhythm of as well. We approach the question of limits here differently than we approach the limits of Wright's epiphenomenal time, which appear to mislead us toward an identity-oriented conceptualization of what is really a structural problem. There, we prescribe redirection: Our analysis moves from a similar origin point, but with a different magnitude (political ontology instead of identity) and direction (toward a more appropriate sense of Black time). With Spillers's conceptualization of Black time characterized by symbolic substitution, which we interpret as loop-time, we prescribe supplementation: We extend and direct the vector of Spillers's astute observations about Blackness, gender, textuality, and loop-time so that it passes through and aligns with our knowledge of time lapses and losses. Including but also beyond the temporal implications of loop-time signaled by symbolic substitutions, we wonder about how to approach the mechanics of time's other, equally sinister forms. We ask: How might we (re)discover time's other names, and all of what their coded static scrambles and telegraphs?

The fragmented stories of Black folk subject to time's force remind us that Black stories about time might offer us more pieces of the key for which we sojourn. For Gayl Jones in 1975, "Black time's" name might be *Corregidora*. *Corregidora* complements the pieces offered by the pieces of Spillers's argument that called to us. The structure and mechanics of the force of time in relation to Blacks and Blackness grow and their shapes warp. *Corregidora* confirms the theories about time, Blackness, and Black flesh—Black female flesh in particular—seeded by "Mama's Baby, Papa's Maybe" while adding another set of menacing and unbearable questions[26] that help clarify our problem.

The fourth generation of a bloodline of Black women, Ursa Corregidora sings the blues in Kentucky from the mid-1940s to the late 1960s. Her "veins are centuries meeting":[27] the fleshy channels through which blood, the liquid lifetimes of the previous three generations of Corregidora women, interact with her own, laced with the undying force of the surname they share. The surname originates with a Portuguese seaman, slave owner, and whoremonger whose proper name becomes a mystery. He was the master and likely father of Ursa's great-grandmother and the father of her grandmother and mother, all of whom transfer his surname from generation to generation. This process of generational transference via generational (pro)creation becomes the subject and question of Ursa's lifetime, the intimate relationships that influence that lifetime (between and among the Corregi-

---

26. In the introduction to Frank B. Wilderson III's *Red, White, and Black: Cinema and the Structure of U. S. Antagonisms* (Durham: Duke University Press, 2010), Wilderson writes that the slave narrative is an "oxymoron" (41). Slave narrative is not just a genre of work specific to those works written by slaves in what most understand to be the "historical moment" of slavery, but also a designation of work produced by Black folk that might be considered to depend on or turn on "narrative," and a recognition of the problematic narrativization of Blackness in, or over, time. This oxymoronic status depends on the impossible application of a generalized equilibrium→disequilibrium→equilibrium-restored narrative progression to Black folk, who begin, and continue ad infinitum, in a state of disequilibrium. Narrative, as a temporal force, raises a question: "For if Slave narratives as an object field have 'no ontological status' . . . then what does this tell us about the ontological status of the narrating slave her/himself?" (41). The oxymoronic status of "slave narrative" reveals an ontological problem; it turns on the slave's nonbeing, such that Blackness and narrative become antagonistic to each other. The question, and what it reveals, *"is menacing and unbearable,"* and "the intensity of its ethicality" against an unethical temporal construct like narrative "is terrifying, so terrifying."

27. Gayl Jones, *Corregidora* (Boston: Beacon Press, 1975), 46.

dora women, between them all and Corregidora, and between the women and other men), and the way these relationships signal another level of horror at the intersection between Black flesh, time, desire, and creation.

Great Gram, Gram, Ursa's mother, and Ursa bear the name as a raison d'être: They must "make generations" in order to "bear witness" to the actual violence of enslavement, and the actual specificity of the trauma that constitutes their bloodline.[28] The (pro)created flesh becomes a conduit for the lifetimes traumatically bound up with and by Corregidora because it embodies "evidence" more permanent than the passed-down photograph of Corregidora. As Gram reveals: "They can burn the papers" or the photos, "but they can't burn conscious, Ursa."[29] How Jones entangles the flesh with consciousness is striking: To "make generations" is to make flesh that can "bear witness" by consciously accounting for the traumas of previous lifetimes telegraphed by Corregidora's name. The name is a loaded, telegraphic marker. The name marks the flesh. The flesh houses the mind. The mind houses the traumas—and each layer becomes inextricable from all the others. What is generated by this process is an entanglement between name/naming, flesh, and consciousness, all sutured by the timeless trauma of sexual violence and coercion, itself inextricable from the violence of enslavement. This entanglement is a series of interlocking and unwieldy loops: The process of "making generations" to bear witness to the sexual violence of enslavement is a way of symbolically substituting witnesses "over time" who can ceaselessly repeat the narrative of sexualized, gendered, and anti-Black terror. These generations loop into one another via their lived relationships with one another, and they also form loops with other folk, particularly men who violently produce echoes of the narrative to which the Corregidora women bear witness, and who are themselves the products of unknown traumas produced by being Black in an anti-Black world. As we imagine the shifting, unwieldy knot that this forms, it confirms and deepens Spillers's characterization of Black time as substitutive, repetitive, and looping.

Ursa bears the name and the complex duty of continuing to loop the loops, but the novel wastes no time jeopardizing this. As Ursa leaves Happy's Café after finishing a set, her drunk husband, Mutt Thomas, pushes Ursa, throws her, or otherwise causes her to fall (it is recalled differently throughout the text) down the stairs, hospitalizing her, causing her to miscarry, and ultimately resulting in a hysterectomy (all this before the first time we are introduced to the phrase "make generations"). We "begin" with

---

28. Jones, *Corregidora*, 10, 72.
29. Ibid., 22.

a "rupture" (pace Spillers)[30] of which we do not know the full implications until later. No longer able to "make generations" to continue to "bear witness" to Corregidora's horrors in the flesh (and blood), and perhaps never willing to do so to begin with,[31] the bodily and psychological trauma of Mutt's violence dislocates Ursa from her flesh-and-blood timeline as she cannot, via (pro)creation, give continued life and form to her family history in enslavement, and to the name (Corregidora) that telegraphs it. The flesh and blood of her womb removed, embodies, or "enfleshes," a temporal and familial rupture, rendering past, present, and future familial ties to traumatic history in the flesh and in the imagination impossible. The undecipherable hieroglyphics printed upon the absence of Ursa's uterus illegibly signals a loss of time, a timeliness interrupted and thrown into crisis. The possibility of an infinite lifetime for Corregidora, for his sexual violence, and for the brutality of enslavement his name signifies falls away, vacuumed into the void of her sex. This is a flesh-and-blood dereliction of the otherwise "neat" continuum between past, present, and future, opened into by the "door . . . between [her] legs," the black "hole" she "still got,"[32] a black hole in two senses, warping the time (and space) of those caught up in Ursa's orbit, and perhaps a portal to a traumatic nowhere. What had been the promise of another loop in a chain of looped witnesses breaks in the wake of violence, producing in the temporal loops' place an irreparable lapse in or loss of temporal coherence.

Because of Jones's attention to the sexual violence of slavery, the precariousness of physically intimate relationships for Black women, and Black intramural relationships in general, Ursa's black hole provides an opening into considering a set of problems with relationality, and how Ursa as a sentient, conscious temporal problem relates to the possibility of kinship between Blacks, to the possibility of a relation between Blackness and an identity or set of identities, and to Blackness and Black flesh related to creation. Specifically, I am interested in how Ursa (re)creates these relations, and how she creates (or makes or generates) in relation to them. All of these

---

30. In "Mama's Baby, Papa's Maybe," Spillers writes: "The symbolic order that I wish to trace in this writing, calling it an 'American grammar,' begins at the 'beginning,' which is really a rupture and a radically different kind of cultural continuation" (68). I wield rupture here in an echoic manner.

31. We learn this later on in the text: Ursa had, for some time, been questioning whether or not she would pass down this history of Corregidora to the next generation even if she were (able) to have children (60).

32. Jones, *Corregidora*, 41, 75, 100, 138. In each of these, someone—Ursa, Mutt, Corregidora, and then Ursa again—describes Ursa's vagina as a "hole," with the exception of the last instance, in which Ursa describes it as a "door."

are entangled with a lifetime, a bloodline, and a timeliness that have been mutilated. Examining the strings—here, through the lens of creation—will offer a deeper understanding of the nature of the knot.

Warped by the layered trauma that opens the novel, Ursa's voice temporally and sentimentally shifts. In the time with Mutt prior to the "fall," Ursa sings "songs that had to do with holding things inside you. Secret happinesses, a tenderness,"[33] songs of a serenity she hides somewhere behind the words she sings, "in the tune, in the whole way [she] drew out a song . . . the way [her] breath moved, in [her] whole voice."[34] Something vibes in the text of the song, and also in the praxis of the song's performance. Her performances place a demand on the method for reading (or decoding) her songs and their secrets, which perhaps ushers in, or at least requires, an alternative theory to frame how we (or anyone in Ursa's relation) might "read" the song. In an imagined conversation with her mother, she thinks that if only her mother "understood" her, she would "see [Ursa] was trying . . . to explain what was always there,"[35] the "secret happinesses" bound up with the traumatic, undying history of Corregidora "they squeezed . . . into [her]."[36] Her voice, the way she sings and breathes behind the words, and the songs themselves become their own sorts of "[texts] for living and dying," in which the timeless narrative of the sexualized brutality and violence of enslavement becomes entangled with the serenity Ursa hides with it.

It is an amalgamated temporality, one oriented through the stage presence of Ursa's blues in the "present" before the fall. Prior to the trauma that disjoins Ursa from her neater temporal orientation, the songs (as the novel's presentation of a relation between Blackness, creation, and time) seem to sing to the tune of Wright's argument. There is a fluid potentiality to Ursa's blues. Prior to the fall, her blues signifies Wright's unbounded Black temporality and relationality through its encapsulation of Ursa's unique identification with her "generational duty" to continue looping past, present, and future generations of witnesses, and through its shifting communicative form in the shapeless "now" of her performances, undulating between a secretiveness and an openness in what the songs speak to her audience. It is a blues full of breath and voice, life and creative possibility. To describe Ursa's songs before Mutt subjects her to physical violence with traumatic

---

33. Ibid., 154.
34. Ibid., 103.
35. Ibid., 66.
36. Ibid., 103.

effects for her imaginative and temporal positions, we will say that they are sung on an "epiphenomenal" frequency.

The trauma alters the motive behind Ursa's singing shifting the frequency and altering the "shape" of (the entanglement of) the song and its performance. During or thinking about a performance, Ursa thinks to herself: "I bit my lip singing. I troubled my mind, too my rocker down by the river again. It was as if I wanted them to see what he'd done, hear it. All those blues feelings. . . . That's what I called it. . . . My voice felt like it was *screaming*."[37] For Ursa, the temporal and relational break Mutt caused must be expressed and heard screaming through her singing in the strain on and in her voice. Something hardens in her voice, the frequency, the very structure of its expression, changing texture, tone, and color due to the interaction of multiple layers of violence and trauma in Ursa's imagination and flesh. Those for whom Ursa sings seem to key in on this loaded "hardness," recognizing it as a hardness that hurts as it is heard.[38] Ursa's trauma initiates a crystallization of her voice's essence from an airy, serene, secret "something" to a tactile, if cumbersome, more solid something else that is more capable of both damage and resistance. Her blues have become bluer, denser, and the screaming suggests an urgency to be heard paradoxically mixed with a defiant, insistent unintelligibility against which that urgency strains and grows in force.

There is an unwieldy blueshift in the blues Ursa sings; something moves closer, grows darker, warped by the gravity of the trauma initiating the text. In physics, a blueshift is the result of a condensation of wave frequency. In terms of light, it is the decrease in wavelength (and so increase in frequency and energy) of electric and magnetic fields traveling through space. Based on the frequency, which is a temporal measurement, the light exists on an electromagnetic spectrum between 4×10^4 Hz and 8×10^4 Hz, spanning what our eyes perceive as visible color, the former marking the red end and the latter marking the violet end. A blueshift is a change in frequency moving in the direction of the violet end of the spectrum. There are two kinds of blueshift: a Doppler blueshift and a gravitational blueshift. A Doppler blueshift is relativistic in a phenomenological sense: If the object in question moves at a relativistic speed toward an observer, that object should grow bluer to that observer; that it grows bluer at all depends on the relationship between object and observer. But with general relativity, gravity becomes an additional factor, generalizing the effect to being independent of observation.

---

37. Ibid., 50; emphasis mine.
38. Ibid., 96.

For example, when light particles (photons) fall into a gravitational well, especially a particularly massive one like a black hole, they gain energy and exhibit a blueshifting that happens whether or not it is experienced. This is a gravitational blueshift, and it is absolute.[39] The blueshift phenomenon and its mechanics finely complicate the structural shift in Ursa's voice and the phenomenological consequences of that structural shift. The blueshift of Ursa's blues operates both ways: It is both phenomenological, dependent on the relative experience of listeners, and also absolute, structurally occurring independent of one's capacity to see/hear it. This blueshift in frequency is "real" in relation to the gravity of the traumatic temporal dislocation Ursa enfleshes, itself enfleshed by the literal and figurative "Black hole" that she "still got." What her relation to time prior to the fall looks like—a neat, "epiphenomenal" temporal alignment of generations past, present, and future—warps in the violent gravitational tidal force of the black-hole-trauma. What might have been composed of decipherable hieroglyphics, legible markings/names (Corregidora, Great Gram, Gram, Mama) spaghettifies or atomizes[40] in relation to the black-hole-trauma, broken down into fragments of letters, or lexical symbols, or less; legibility becomes impossible. These atomized remnants stream into the black hole, squeezed and pulled toward oblivion. *This* is Ursa's creation, her new blues:[41] timelines shattered into a stream of illegibility caught up in the time warp of the gravity of unthinkable trauma, made all the bluer by a general blueshift of the "timey-wimey" bits that fall into her trauma. For others, this blueshift is relative, subject to their movement relative to her movement, their hearing relative to the frequency of her blues. How well they are tuned to her singing, which is described as sing-

---

39. For more on Doppler blueshift and redshift, see Theo Koupelis, *In Quest of the Universe* (2004), 122–23; for more on gravitational blueshift/redshift, see R. J. Nemiroff's article, "Visual Distortions Near a Neutron Star and Black Hole" (1993) in *American Journal of Physics*, 619–42. I'm drawing from these, but giving as cursory an explanation of the phenomena as possible (which is reductive relative to the detail of the research that analyzes these phenomena), accepting the limitations of performing something in a "cursory" fashion.

40. "Spaghettification" is the term that physicists use to describe what happens to matter and energy in relation to a black hole. Important to note in particular is that this is a particularly violent and extreme dying, one that reduces the flesh to its atomic constituents. I italicize "stream of atoms" because of the extremity of this violence on the flesh, and because I think this process best captures what Spillers means when she describes the violent metaphysical, actual, and symbolic reduction of Black bodies to (flayed, popped open, seared apart, and otherwise marked) flesh as "atomization" (Spillers, "Mama's Baby, Papa's Maybe" 68).

41. A friend and colleague, Nicholas Brady, is at work on a massive project concerning a theory of Black sound, which he calls "NuBluez." The work is unreleased but plays a heavy influence on how I'm imagining Ursa's work.

ing "with [her] whole body,"[42] and so how well they are tuned to her flesh and what illegibly springs from and marks it, determines whether or not the blueshift will be intelligible to them. This explains the general unintelligibility of the music in its essence, *as* the blues, and now as a *bluer* blues, to those who listen and look throughout the novel, or to those who fail to hear her.

Considering illegibility and unintelligibility, this blueshift in Ursa's blues also accounts for what the men who "listen" to her sing encounter when they gaze at her on stage, and "mess" with her "with they eyes."[43] They engage in attempts to decode her songs without really tuning to her frequency, exhibiting a reluctance to fall into the black abyss of Ursa's gravity. Max Monroe, the owner of The Spider, where Ursa performs after catching her second partner in the novel, Tadpole, cheating on her, describes her voice as "hard," and Ursa as someone "hard . . . to get into."[44] Her voice is phenomenologically hard in a double sense: crystalized, like a diamond, and impenetrable, resistant to the messing the men do with their eyes, and difficult, a problem and a quandary that produces a failure of both decoding and entry, which is prescient given that Max describes it this way after Ursa's resistance to his sexual advances. The "door" between her legs is closed to them and so is her voice. For Ursa, this reflects a resistance to being totally devoured by the looking and "messing" "eyeteeth"[45] of others, a challenge to the violent relationality imposed on her by the men who hurt her (Mutt, Tadpole) and the men watching/listening at Happy's or The Spider who want to sink their "eyeteeth" into her flesh. It is a counter-devouring, an unintelligible and illegible demand "behind the music" for a hearing and seeing that telegraphs a willingness to be devoured, a willingness to bear witness to the blueness of her blues, a willingness to fall into and for her, "to the bottom of *her* eyes,"[46] as she was made to fall.

In this reading, the ending of the novel becomes more unnerving. After twenty-two years, Ursa reunites with Mutt at the Drake hotel, where they once lived together, but in a different room; this is a very different time and space, a (blue)shifted context. Ursa's desire for an intimate reconnection lines up with Mutt's and she performs oral sex for him. In a moment

---

42. Jones, *Corregidora*, 50.
43. Jones privileges looking and looks throughout the text. In general, looks appear to be "warped" by Ursa's gravitational tidal forces—looks from other central characters like Cat, or Mutt, or Tadpole, or looks from audiences of men throughout.
44. Ibid., 96–97.
45. Ibid., 135.
46. Ibid., 51.

marked by a "split second,"[47] she realizes what she wants and needs in love and intimacy. It is a moment of overlapping entanglements, "a moment of pleasure and excruciating pain at the same time, a moment of broken skin but not sexlessness, a moment that stops just before sexlessness, a moment that stops before it breaks the skin."[48] It is an uneasy and monstrous intimacy that picks at the still-open wound that removed Ursa from, or at least crystalized Ursa's blue and cold antagonism to, the neatness of time. It is a "split second" outside of time that stops just before breaking, and maybe breaking open, the undecipherable hieroglyphics of trauma that constitute Ursa's flesh, and a "split second" outside of time that affirms, rather than denies, Ursa's desire.

This "split second" is a temporal entanglement: of Mutt with Ursa, of Great Gram with Corregidora, and of both relationships with each other such that Ursa cannot tell "how much" of the untimely knot of their strings belonged to any one part.[49] At the nexus of this "split second" is an unnerving bondage between death and desire, killing and love, "pleasure and excruciating pain" that forms the novel's final song. It is a short song, a duet. Mutt's "I don't want the kind of woman that hurt you," meets with Ursa's "Then you don't want me," repeated in a bittersweet refrain, culminating with Ursa, shaken and in tears, finally responding in kind, "I don't want the kind of man that'll hurt me, neither,"[50] and a final embrace. It is a bluer blues singing a shared willingness to fall (into each other's arms) into the abyss, grasp the full extent of the blueshift, and succumb to the tidal forces of an illegible, undecipherable problem, in flesh, blood, and being.

Returning to Wright, Ursa's time after the fall (and into the fall that culminates the novel) upends "epiphenomenal time" because it "adds another angle [to] the divided flesh."[51] There is no neatly messy relationality to be found, neither between Ursa and Mutt (her most intimately connected "other"), nor between Ursa and time itself. Ursa's blues drowns out the affirmations that may otherwise have come from the coherent relations and identifications promised by "epiphenomenal time." What we discover instead is a demand for a willingness to fall into the abyss. It is a traumatic fall, caught up in the immeasurable tidal forces of the black (w)hole of Ursa's Black flesh, into the illegibility and unintelligibility of the names, marks, symbols, and "narrative" constitutive *to* Black flesh, and into a violent warping of

---

47. Ibid., 184.
48. Ibid.
49. Ibid., 184.
50. Ibid., 185.
51. Spillers, "Mama's Baby, Papa's Maybe," 68.

time (and space) that is inescapable. "Time" becomes resistant to the ease of any definition beyond its violent relation to Black being and Black flesh, let alone one that claims to offer a more legible set of relations between Blacks and time, and Blacks and each other, and leaves us unable to present so neat a "solution" to the presumption that time is linear, progressive, and can be read as anything less than an antagonistic relation to Blackness.

We understand "time" as a force and a problem for thought in relation to Blackness that isn't wholly resolved epiphenomenally. At best, we might only be able to think of time as "wibbly-wobbly, timey-wimey, [n-word, -word] stuff," a phrase we borrow from "Blink," an excellent episode of *Doctor Who* that describes time in the same way (we inject Blackness through the brackets).[52] However unsatisfying, this still-not-quite-nameable time begs a question of (pro)creation in relation to this temporality: How might we create songs, words, desires, relations—how might we make generations—in the ceaseless wake of the violence of enslavement that lives on in, on, and as our flesh, and the repeated and new traumas that crystalize that ceaselessness? And how might we hear, or read—or develop a method, a theory, and a praxis for reading—those (pro)creations? *Corregidora* provides some insight, but also reveals the inescapable abyss of this line of questioning. Rather than offer the certainty of reprieve or reconciliation, Jones demands we fall deeper, and bluer, into illegibility, unintelligibility, and impossibility.

We must pursue these questions more deeply. We must go to where and when time is *at its most violent* in, and to, the gravitational singularity of Blackness, where/when it melds the time and violence of enslavement (Great Gram and Corregidora, and sexual violence) with the time and violence of its wake (Mutt and Ursa, and the "fall"), desire with hate, unknowable pain with irresistible pleasure, and killing with loving, into a "text for living and for dying," an undecipherable arrangement of marks inextricably entangling death and life in Blackness. We must go deeper into the deathly nature of the violent entanglements that happen when we no longer understand time's relation to Blackness as linear, neat, easily thinkable, relational,

---

52. I borrow this from two places. In reverse order: I use this phrase in a piece also entitled "Black (in) Time," which won the *Indiana Review*'s nonfiction contest of 2015 and takes a more accessible approach toward opening us into thinking about this problem of Blackness in relation to time. The piece draws from a much more diverse range of media (manga, film, television, and "current" events—namely, police brutality cases involving Black bodies being subject to the gratuitous violence of the police force); one of these is the sci-fi television program *Doctor Who*. In the season 3 episode, "Blink," the Doctor (David Tennant, at the time) describes time from his perspective as a time-and-space-traveling alien known as a Time Lord. The original phrase is "Time is like a big ball of . . . wibbly wobbly, timey wimey stuff." I add "n-word, n-word" to "blacken" the idea.

and so on—when, instead, we understand that there is an unthought, and perhaps unthinkable, antagonism between Blackness and time, a relation that is violently untimely. At the bottom of the well, or at least moving toward it, expressing a willingness to fall into crushing the abyss, we might find and face what we seek.

Down the deathly rabbit hole, we brokenly and boldly go.

III

Untime

> But this is not the sun about to rise in "the sky of history,"
> more the intermittent flashes from an underworld of images
> *that happen and keep on happening....* My belief is that what
> is being witnessed here—the scene recalls Louis Rutaganira in
> Kibuye—is a death that cannot ever die because it depends on the
> total degradation and disavowal of black life. Ipso facto: death
> emerges as a transcendental fact of black existence but without
> transcendence (similarly, black existence is one condemned to
> live without the possibility of being). This is no longer death
> but a deathliness that cannot be spiritualized or brought into
> meaning. This is death as nothing, less than nothing; as such,
> this death is never assumable as possibility or decision, but
> remains *the interminable time of meaningless, impersonal dying.*
>
> —DAVID MARRIOTT, *HAUNTED LIFE*[1]

DAVID MARRIOTT writes about deathliness and its untimeliness in "Ice Cold," the afterword to *Haunted Life,* his dark tome on Blackness and visual culture. The temporal implications of deathliness as an endless or interminable dying will help us narrow the course of this journey toward a more precise name for and understanding of a Black form of time. "Deathliness," with its attendant temporal implications, is another signpost en route to a more phenomenologically and political-ontologically precise theory of Black temporality that accounts for the epistemological, social, psychological, political, environmental, and metaphysical violence that characterizes Black existence. Further, by placing some pressure on the way the interminability of deathliness both occludes and signals some of the temporal features of Black existence to which we have already borne witness—in a similar form

---

1. Marriott, *Haunted Life,* 227, 230–31; emphasis mine.

of augmentation to the work we did with Spillers's looped conceptualization of time—we aim to transmute it into the conceptual material we require to fit this piece into the proverbial, if "timey-wimey," puzzle before us.

Dissecting a letter Fanon sent from his deathbed to his friend Roger Tayeb, Marriott meditates on the relationship between Blackness, death, and time. In his letter, Fanon writes, "Death is always with us." Death acts as an interminable, spectral presence ethically framing the possibilities of "the life of the mind, the life of reason."[2] "Life," and all its features and capacities, must be "answerable *to* death," and "political thought," rather *all* thought,[3] bears an "ethical responsibility" to the "nonrepresentable, *working* of death"; death frames, binding "life" itself, and death works through the "workful" life, demands that life work with and within its haunting "presence." This is an interminable presence—"always with us"—characterized by Blackness's "endless proximity" to death: "endless," a spatial recognition of boundlessness and immeasurability like the unimaginable vastness of the ever-expanding cosmos, and "endless," a temporal designation of ceaselessness, or timelessness, and so untimeliness. If "life" and "thought" are to be redeemed ethically ("in the end," or, "at the end of (one's) life," as Fanon's letter embodies), it is *with* death.

The distension of the temporality of death in relation to Blackness secures an entanglement between Blackness, life, death, and time: Death stretches from the static position of a moment or an event, even one with an imposed finality (death is/as an end) or transitional quality (death is a passage into a different/better/higher state of existence), into a permanent condition of Black being (i.e., death never abandons us). In Marriot's reading of Fanon's letter, death is inescapable; it is temporally entangled with Black life, "always" and forever. When we more carefully consider the mechanics of this interminability, however, deathliness proves to be more complex than Marriott's description suggests. A simplified interminability would suggest

---

2. Marriott, *Haunted Life*, 228–29.

3. This is a claim derived from Jared Sexton's "Ante-Anti-Blackness: Afterthoughts," which follows up his essay "People-of-Color-Blindness" (2010), originally published in *Social Text*. He opens by reading a passage from Lewis Gordon's "Theory in Black," extending it into the following two-part claim: "I am guided in the following task by a two-sided idea derived from Gordon's arguments: 1) all thought, insofar as it is genuine thinking, might best be conceived of as black thought and, consequently, 2) all researches, insofar as they are genuinely critical inquiries, aspire to black studies. Blackness is theory itself, anti-blackness the resistance to theory." It's a claim with paradigmatic implications: It places Blackness at the foundation for all genuine inquiry, all thought, in an academy and a world that refuses to think Blackness at all, with violent consequences.

an endlessness that only depends on linear continuation: Deathliness equals death that is endless, meaning death that continues in the future forever and ever. This would be inadequate to describe Black temporality, since it inheres in a linearity similar to the kind we have known to be defunct from the outset; plus, we can recall Spillers's phrasing and our reading of it here as a reminder that the appearance of a particular temporal movement (for her, it was stasis: "*shows* no movement") can occlude a more complex set of operations (for her, it was the loop or repetition of "symbolic substitution").

Knowing what we know and knew about loops, lapses, and losses in time, we recognize that if Marriott's identification of interminability stands alone, it does not wholly describe some of the key elements of our problem without sufficient transmutation. Death cannot merely continue endlessly, and deathliness cannot be a death that merely continues toward infinity. Death must also endlessly loop through Black life. Perhaps this is what Marriott meant to signal with the language that opens the epigraph at the top of this chapter when he describes the "intermittent flashes" that "keep on happening"—imagine death like a thread coiling forever into an ever-growing knot. Death must interminably interrupt Black life, creating repeating, unpredictable lapses in Black experiences of temporal continuity and coherence—imagine that same knot composed of several severed threads that keep getting severed as the knot becomes more and more unwieldy. And death must ceaselessly void Black life, causing losses of time—imagine whole sections of the already segmented knot vanishing unexpectedly. Taken together, we conjure a more complete interminability than Marriott's writing expresses, at least directly, and we recognize that the endlessness that extends death into deathliness is not only temporally violent by way of continuation, but also by way of continuous interruptions, destructions, and repetitions that never stop happening.

Death haunts Black life.[4] It is the ghost in the shell of Black life and time. The orders of violence it practices and the array of Black experiences of that violence (as loops, lapses, losses, etc. of time) cause a problem with meaning and nothingness. The defining feature of haunted living is a timeless truth: "that black life is meaningless and so black death is meaningless—a legacy

---

4. I want to reference the title of Marriott's book, *Haunted Life*, of course, but also Saidiya Hartman's term introduced in *Lose Your Mother*, "the afterlife of slavery" (6), as well as Christina Sharpe's concept of "the wake" from *In the Wake*, but I suspend a thicker engagement with these ideas until the next section, the Second Arrangement, in which a reading of Toni Morrison's *Beloved* stages a chance to expand the temporal implications of the phrase into thinking about memory, or "rememory."

in which death is nothing."[5] This is a meaningless death that structures and works with and through a meaningless life, so the "ethical obligation" to think and live in "endless proximity" to death becomes impossible to make meaningful; living becomes bearing witness to an impossibility at the level of meaning. What is made in place of meaning is the product of a negation: This is not a zeroing of the meaning of Black life and death via a deathly time or an untimely death, but instead a multiplication of the meaning of Black life and death by a negative, rendering it less than nothing. The product of deathliness, with all its attendant temporal consequences, and Black living and dying is a meaning with negative value; this is life and death inextricably entangled with a negative time, a negated time, an irredeemable time with less than no meaning.

Together, Marriott's two most compelling contributions to our understanding of Black temporality create an interesting, arithmetic tension between endlessness, or infinity, and less-than-nothingness. How they add up when placed next to one another stokes an apparent, conflicting indeterminacy at the level of value; deathliness, were it to be quantified, would simultaneously be infinite, so unquantifiable by definition, and have negative value, less than nothing. The product is an infinite negation, or a negative infinity, whose value remains indeterminate by being unquantifiable. For Marriott reading Fanon, this infinite, "indeterminate negation, a negation without end"[6] creates a state of being Black that is being "*without* time."[7] Thus, Marriott concludes, deathliness signals the absence of time, or the inability to take possession of time, which would also suggest the inability to make time. Put differently, deathliness positions Blackness, Black life, death, and people as atemporal.

Bearing witness to the fragments we struggle to bear, we recognize that Blackness is bound up with a time crisis. For this reason, we do not neatly align with the particular horror of atemporality: Black being in, or against, or subject to time's operations through deathliness suggests a more sinister problem than "being without" or "being that lacks" time. Instead, Black temporality seems to indicate a radically different form of temporality that acts as a force that functions independent of any notion of possession or lack. What is unethical about Blackness's relation to time is the complex knot of violence deathliness weaves through Black life and death, which suggests that being without time does not quite capture what it means to exist as beings subjected to the violent, deathly, and disorienting machinations

---

5. Marriott, *Haunted Life*, 230.
6. Ibid., 238.
7. Ibid., 240; emphasis mine.

of time. This is why a theory of Blackness's time, and also a praxis, and a method for reading time, comes with an "ethical obligation" to this same, impossible-to-redeem, bearing witness to death. The deathliness that haunts us, with which we are compelled or forced to work, mutilates, or telegraphs a mutilated, temporality characterized by infinities and impossibilities, by arbitrariness and gratuitous violence, which differs from a time that is violent by way of its absence or lack. Rather than an atemporality, Black temporality resists naming in the indeterminacy to which Marriott so imperatively draws our attention; it can be absent-time or no-time, but it appears to also be something else.

It manifests in ways that, at least, telegraph its mechanics. Through the everyday murders of Black folk by police force[8] we bear witness to the way, time and time again, Black death repeats. The all-too-familiar stories of anti-Black police violence telegraph death's infiniteness as a series of randomly violent and interruptive repetitions. Rekia Boyd. Aiyana Stanley-Jones. Oscar Grant. Michael Brown. Yazmin Vash Payne. Anna Brown. Trayvon Martin. Penny Proud. Dionte Green. Tamir Rice. Eric Garner. Renisha McBride. Nephi Arreguin. Sandra Bland. Stephon Clark. Willie McCoy.[9] And . . . and . . .

Via subjection to the constant disavowals of Black life that create an atmosphere, a miasma, of imminent destruction for merely being Black, a shroud of death's presence that is always in waiting, we bear witness to the elongation or distention of death's time across all ages (in all senses of the word)—sleeping on a sofa in one's home in Detroit at age seven, playing in a park in Cleveland at age twelve, knocking on a door for emergency assistance in Dearborn Heights at age nineteen, or defending one's home from forced infiltration in Atlanta at age ninety-two, or, or . . .[10]

Through the familiarity of each interruptive intrusion into life and thought, through the feeling that these many times rhyme, we bear witness to the sense that death's time does not appear to move, which telegraphs a deathly time in stasis, frozen, cold. Time, for Blacks, is dead and yet undying, a zombified force and feature of Black being, thinking, and living in an

---

8. For a full discussion, please see my essay "Black (in) Time" published in the *Indiana Review*.

9. There is no way to name them all here in due time; they've been reduced to nominal exemplars, which is disturbing, and seems to be a consequence of medium and imposed time more than my own desire to at least "mark" the deaths of the many slain that go overlooked and underthought, or unthought. For the minimization of life and death into "example," I have to, irredeemably, apologize.

10. In order: Aiyana Stanley-Jones, seven; Tamir Rice, twelve; Renisha McBride, nineteen; Kathryn Johnston, ninety-two.

anti-Black universe, which, to us, is a dead zone, an "underworld," a cosmos of death.

Time loss. Time lapse. Time loops. This is Black time: dead, undying, and deathly time. Black time is deathly unethical in its essentiality to the deathly orders of violence to which it subjects Black folk. It is unquantifiable, an infinity multiplied by a negative, and so wholly indeterminate, unknowable and unpredictable. In its deathliness to Black existence, it is essential,[11] an unwanted but perhaps unavoidable companion to being Black, here and now, always and wherever. Through their prefixes, these adjectives provide a guide to what appears to be a more appropriate name for Black temporality than a term like, "atime," for example, which has a prefix that suggests the absence of time. It must also be more precise than "antitime," which suggests that the characteristics and mechanics of time behave in a way that is antithetical to the way they should or could, and that there may be a form of time that does actually behave ethically. In this reading, such a prefix would absolve time of the unethical essence of its regular operations, and also facilitate desires for access to, entry into, or inclusion in the "better" or "ethical" time that occlude the horrifying truth: that the unethical deathliness one would hope to escape is actually essential to how time functions in this cosmos—worse, that it is whole cosmos, and not the "bad" time, that need be "escaped."

What we arrive at instead is *untime*: a Black, unethical, deathly, unquantifiable, unknowable relation to time. Black life and death are untimely, subject to the singularly violent operations of time. And we must wallow in the contradictions that comprise untime. Untime is as the states of water: It is cold and shows no movement, frozen; it is also ceaseless, infinite, and ever shifting via its repetitions, fluid; and it escapes seeing and hearing, resists the tactility of definition, and obfuscating, like a mist, a vapor—but all at once. In all, and together, unwieldy, untime becomes another telegraphic name encoding the mechanics and characteristics of Blackness in relation to time, but also inherently incapable of "fixing" time in a double sense: "fixing" time as in binding it to the singularity of definition, securing it, and "fixing" time as in remedying the deathly indeterminate relations traced here (a distinction from Wright's epiphenomenal engagement).

What's in a name is anything but salvation. In the imposition of new vocabulary is only a clarification of the full shape of the problem for thought, life, and being, *as* a problem; there is no solution. Our ethical obligation is

---

11. Ibid, 241: "Only by turning toward absence or loss can we grasp the gaze that petrifies and arrests at the very point of experiencing it, the *essential deathliness of black experience*: the irony and perversity of a haunted life"; emphasis mine.

to bear witness to the unethicality of this force and feature of the anti-Black universe in its undecipherability; this is what it is to heed Ursa's call, to see what she's singing, to leap into the abyss, the black hole. Neither as a form of agency or resistance to manageable forces, nor as a fatalistic and helpless sacrifice to the unimaginable powers that be, but as a form of bearing witness, as listening and looking, as taking account of and surveying what is *as* (blue as) it is, and of when and where we "be" in relation to it. To brokenly leap into the untimely abyss is to go with the flow of gravity's tidal forces, is to break (atomize, spaghettify) into the the black (w)hole of the Black position (its where and when).

Armed with what might be the key we've been looking for, we will continue to venture into stories about Black time, untime, for a fuller picture of the problem. I understand untime to be the unnamed[12] force at work in Octavia Butler's *Kindred*. How Butler mechanizes this force, and how her protagonist, Edana (who calls herself and is called Dana throughout), a Black writer living in California in 1976, experiences this force might offer us a deeper understanding of the phenomenological and structural features of untime.

While moving into a new apartment with her husband, Kevin Franklin, Dana unpacks and organizes boxes of books into a bookcase—"fiction only." Kevin joins her, and Dana places a stack of nonfiction in front of him—to his disgust—but, as she playfully goes to push another box of it toward him, she bolts upright: "I began to feel dizzy, nauseated. The room seemed to blur and darken around me. I stayed on my feet for a moment holding on to a bookcase and wondering what was wrong, then finally, I collapsed to my knees. . . . The house, the books, everything vanished."[13] Dana's being pulled back in time.[14] Dana's disorientation marks the effect of the tidal pull: The force denies a stable relation to reality; the untimely destabilization, or disequilibrium, precipitates in dizziness and nausea for the Black being pulled by its force; reality blurs and darkens, or becomes illegible and Blackens, as the interruptive force of untime takes hold of her capacity to orient to the room and world around her. In place of the time of her present in her California apartment, darkness and disorientation enter, creating an open

---

12. Butler, *Kindred*, 17. After returning from her first violent passage into the time of chattel slavery, Dana says, "I don't have a name for the thing that happened to me." The "force" at work remains unnamed throughout the novel—though, it seems, naming it seems less and less pertinent to Dana's survival.
13. Ibid., 13.
14. "Dana's being" both ways: "Dana is being" and "Dana's *being*."

temporal (and spatial) void, like a black frame between scenes of a film, a black cut severing continuity.

In the vacancy enters another spacetime: the time of chattel slavery on a Maryland plantation, owned by Tom Weylin. Over several compulsory passages—she has no control over being pulled "back" in time—Dana discovers that Tom's son, Rufus, is her ancestor, and that every tidal pull is a "call" of sorts: Rufus finds his life endangered, often by his own foolishness and arrogance, and instinctively "calls" for help across time to Dana; a "hole" in the universe opens, through which Rufus's conscious or unconscious need reaches, manifesting as the disorienting "pull" that brings Dana to him to save his life. To which Dana is obligated since, if time exists on a causal continuum, her existence presumably depends on his survival (at least until he procreates the next person in her bloodline).

Not only is the pull a force over which she has no control—frustrated, helpless, she repeatedly remarks on how she doesn't "have any control at all"[15]—but it is a force contingent upon the life and desire (to live) of the master. Time's force becomes a "power"[16] tied to the master's conscious and unconscious desire to continue to exist, another "power" inexplicably inherent to mastery, and is wielded to subject Black folk to an inescapable, dizzying contradiction: Cease to "be" by allowing the master/ancestor to suffer and die, preventing your own existence, or continue to "be" by securing the life of the master/father, and by willfully occupying the position of the slave (which is to willfully accept one's nonbeing) to do so. Dana's is a choice between never having existed or not *being* "while" existing. In either case, her feelings that this force is outside her control and that "it could happen again any time"[17] reflect a sense that Dana belongs irreducibly to this untimely force, and to the mastery of which it is an appendage.

This contradiction produces a problem Dana must negotiate as she is pulled into chattel slavery for ever-increasing durations. In the form of a ghastly and ghostly question that haunts the whole of the text through her: What is the distinction between Dana's Blackness in 1976 and her Slaveness across the multiple spacetimes of slavery to when and where she's yanked?

---

15. She first remarks on this on page 23, and then on 49, and throughout the novel. On page 247, prior to the final action of the novel, Dana asks herself about how she returns to the present: "Is the power mine, or do I tap some power in him?" Neither the force of the pull nor the force of the push (until the final sequence of the novel) has anything to do with Dana's "agency," which, from the beginning, is destabilized, if not outright denied.

16. Butler, *Kindred*, 247.

17. Ibid., 17.

Dana begins to confront this question by refusing the imposition of Slaveness onto her being. During her second passage to the time of the Weylin plantation, Dana converses with Rufus about his understanding of her presence. Recounting Dana's first visitation, Rufus relays to Dana his parents' confusion about her inexplicable existence; to Rufus's mother, Dana might have been best understood as a "ghost," an apparition of "some nigger"—some "strange nigger"—that "she had never seen before." Rufus casually imposes his mother's logic onto Dana's existence: His repetition and casual acceptance of her claims render Dana's being spectral, unreal, and suture that unreality to *being* "some nigger," to having one's being relegated to the namelessness that characterizes Slaveness. Dana contends Rufus's imposition, claiming she is "as real as" he is, that she *is* "a black woman," and that, because she saved his life, he should "do [her] the courtesy of calling [her] what [she] wants to be called."[18] Her attempt at a corrective signals a resistance reminiscent of the resistance built into Ursa's new blues that tries to undo the erasure of her name (Dana) and her identity (Black women), a resistance to the dissolution of her being via Rufus's disavowal of her "realness" (she is ghostly) into the unreality of being "some nigger" (some slave). And she positions her demands as a debt that must be repaid in this symbolic fashion: He owes, should owe, her his continued existence, and so she demands being—telegraphed by a right to "name" and name herself[19]—in suit.

What gives Dana's demands cohesion and legibility is the perceived temporal distance between her California apartment in 1976 and the spacetime of the antebellum Weylin plantation, which marks a temporal distance between Dana and the slaves Weylin owns. Temporal distance for Dana founds what she believes is the difference in political-ontological position. We see Dana transmute this logic into her language. To her, the matter of surviving on the plantation requires "playing the part of a slave."[20] Slaveness for her is just performative, a deceptive guise or act derived from a need to survive, to go unnoticed as a "strange nigger." While captive to the force apparently under Rufus's control, Dana understands that she is "*supposed* to be a slave,"[21] and draws from an index of gestures she is "supposed

---

18. Ibid., 24–25.
19. Spillers, "Mama's Baby, Papa's Maybe," 67. Spillers considers the power to name and the power of names to be a crucial part of the symbolic order, the anti-Black grammar that organizes thought and being. Dana's desire to resist this, to invert it, stands as a radical resistance codified in a demand for this power.
20. Butler, *Kindred*, 79.
21. Ibid., 66; emphasis mine.

to" perform to avoid the particular violence that tends to meet "strange niggers." Dana's language reveals a conflation between the performative and the political-ontological, between the performance and the position, of the slave. She transmutes this conflation into what she believes is a dual-layered defense. One layer consists in the performance itself, crafted under the assumption that the more precise the performance, the less likely the gratuitous violence. Withholding knowledge from and placating Rufus; attempting to derive a mathematical function describing how whipping, pain, and punishment relate to work and exhaustion;[22] keeping her eyes low as a sign of deferential obedience—Dana marshals these performative strategies to don the slave's garb in service of minimizing the bodily trauma she would endure while bound to Rufus. The second layer supposedly shields the cohesion of Dana's existence, which she maintains under the destructive order of slavery if and only if she identifies her Slaveness as a performance; this would be a defense of being, an attempt to escape the obliterating pull of the black hole.

At this point, it's worth clarifying that "black hole" describes a structure with variable forms, each with different characteristics. The shared, defining characteristic of "black holes" is the event horizon, which, simplified, is a point of no return beyond which escaping the tidal forces of the black hole's gravity becomes impossible—neither light nor any other, slower-moving, object can escape obliteration. Whether this is an absolute or apparent structure—whether the black hole is eternal, so the event horizon always marks a boundary, or the black hole is temporary, so the event horizon is as well—remains a topic of heated debate. The latter stems from Stephen Hawking's theorization that black holes emit radiation over time, eventually evaporating entirely, which has certain implications for what happens to the "information" of the objects devoured by the black hole (more on that below). In this latter case, which Sabine Hossenfelder suggests we might

---

22. While the moments don't always center on Dana, as other slaves are routinely punished in unique and horrifying ways (e.g., Alice, Nigel, Sam), I'm specifically thinking of her relation to the overseers of the plantation, Edwards and Fowler. Two moments stand out. The first is when Edwards threatens Dana with a "real" whipping when she attempts to defy his orders; he demands she do the wash, and Dana attempts to wield Rufus's name as a way of avoiding the work, to which Edwards responds by calling her a "lyin' nigger" and threatening her with violence. She complies. The second comes after Rufus's father dies. Rufus blames his death on Dana's refusal to help him and her desire to see him dead, sending her to work in the fields as punishment. Fowler takes her to the cornfields to work, where she must chop down stalks and collect them. Her inexperience immediately draws his whip's lash, which becomes a staccato rhythm to her day.

call an "apparent black hole,"[23] there is a small possibility that the object beyond the horizon might eventually escape if moving at the speed of light because, as Stephen Hawking writes, "the absence of event horizons means that there are no black holes—in the sense of regimes from which light can't escape *to infinity*," suggesting that there are "apparent" black holes, in the sense of regimes from which light can't escape to a point, and can and might escape at some other point.[24] This appears to characterize Dana's denial of a political-ontological overlay or entanglement between her Blackness and the Slaveness she believes she merely performs. If this is how we characterize the essence of her predicament, the black hole seemingly inescapably pulling her toward the crushing singularity[25] of that entanglement is merely temporary: Rufus's relevance to her existence, and so her need to "play the part of a slave," which is an obligation to be pulled—by him as master, and by the political-ontological force threatening to make her a slave—will, at some point, evaporate. At some point she will *be* and be able to escape, should she move fast enough (at the speed of light)—should she, in her mind, "play the part" well enough—for long enough. While perilous in its illusoriness, Dana's apparent belief in her capacity to perform her way away from total obliteration is an understandable fantasy meant to secure her psychic and psychological cohesion under calamitous conditions. Her denial of her political-ontological status as slave serves as a fraught strategy for try-

---

23. See Sabine Hossenfelder, "If It Quacks Like a Black Hole," posted on BackRe(Action), a blog devoted to physics that she shares with her husband, Stefan Scherer. Sabine Hossenfelder is a theoretical physicist, and the assistant professor for high energy physics at Nordita, the Nordic Institute for Theoretical Physics. Stefan Scherer is a physicist in the field of heavy ion physics, working in the field of scientific publishing.

24. Stephen Hawking, "Information Preservation and Weather Forecasting for Black Holes," arXiv:1401.5761 (Winter: 2014), 3.

25. I need to clarify that a singularity, as it's thought in terms of a black hole, marks a site at which classical physics can no longer mathematically predict what happens. In theory, this is where quantum gravity might come into play, having the explanatory power to remove the singularity. Right now, however, the singularity seems to be a source of a paradox, as it suggests that information is lost after a certain point. If the black hole evaporates—since black holes appear to evaporate—what happens to that information? This "information paradox" surrounding what exactly happens to the information that "goes into" a black hole is the subject of an ongoing and unresolved "debate" in physics, having a number of proposed solutions (the cited Stephen Hawking paper stirred the pot a bit, portending a solution of its own, but one that is neither "new" nor groundbreaking), but no single, proven answer. Central to the paradox is its inherent conflict with the laws of quantum mechanics and general relativity, ultimately creating a situation in which one or the other is incorrect, and throwing a proverbial wrench into any foreseeable attempt to unify the two. This is a(n over)simplification of the profundity and complexity of the issues at hand.

ing to orient herself to her situation and survive long enough to achieve the super-light-speed performance that would allow her to escape.

But Black folk, like most objects, do not and cannot move at, let alone faster than, the speed of light. Dana spirals toward this fact the less her performances seem like performances. The language shifts and the distance begins to collapse. As Rufus ages and his animosity waxes, his treatment of Dana increases her proximity to Slaveness. His preferential treatment of Dana as a "strange nigger," one "better than the ordinary niggers,"[26] rapidly dissolves in a progressive confirmation of the illusoriness distance between Dana's position and her "performance" of Slaveness. Dana's ability to wield the performance as a role in and out of which she might slip as she feels needed—most often to attempt to manipulate Rufus's behavior—falls away because the fact is, as slaves of the plantation remind her, she's "still a nigger." "Still" denotes an ugly temporal element to this fact: "Still" suggests continuity, the position persists from some prior point in time; "still" suggests stasis, the position persists and is unchanging, bearing the same essence (Blackness) of the same name "nigger."[27] The untimely nature of her being as "nigger" has existed, continues to exist, and will presumably continue to exist so long as her predicament persists; the time of her Slaveness-named-"nigger" continues endlessly. And this untimely position remains essentially unchained, the stillness of her Slaveness-named-"nigger" fixing her in spacetime, frozen (ice cold) in it. The untimeliness is apparently ceaseless, appearing to "show no movement." It appears the black hole that pulls her might have a more permanent event horizon, promising a more absolute (as opposed to apparent) relation between Dana and the obliterating singularity of Black nonbeing marked by the slave.

An important question seems to lie with the indeterminacy of the "beginning": When does Dana cross the event horizon, or, if Dana's "*still* a nigger," since when? The text offers no direct answers, but if we understand "beginnings" as violent, inaugural ruptures (pace Spillers), and as "tears" in reality that mark "the end of traceable beginnings,"[28] we recognize, without the possibility of reckoning, that this indeterminacy afforded us by Butler signals an irreparable and untraceable loss of one's bearings. "Still" reveals a temporal impossibility because Dana can no longer orient herself to time in a deterministic way, and the untimeliness extends her Slaveness-named-

---

26. Butler, *Kindred*, 164.

27. In a conversation on "the n-word" on CNN, Marc Lamont Hill defended Blacks' use of the word as a singular representation of what he describes as "a collective condition known as 'nigga.'"

28. Brand, *A Map*, 5.

"nigger" indeterminately, so immeasurably, "backward." The temporal distance between Dana and slave collapses into indeterminacy, and Dana can no longer maintain the political-ontological distance. The strain against the tidal forces becomes too much to manage in the face of waxing terror and domination on the plantation; this appears to be a correlative process, the escalating gratuitous violence Dana experiences inversely correlating with the capacity to "maintain" a distance between Dana's perceived position and the reality of the Slave position, however illusory it might be. Dana's awareness of this produces a vertiginous disorientation: "Now, there was no distance at all. When had I stopped acting? Why had I stopped?" A loss of temporal bearings codified as a loss of reason comes with Dana's recognition. The recognition produces a vertigo that signals Dana's critical misrecognition of the political-ontological distance as distance at all, which is a misrecognition of being (a slave, or "still a nigger").

Butler sutures this misrecognition to a fundamental misrecognition of the flesh (and all its illegible markings). Carrie, who cannot speak and communicates in gestures, clarifies as much to Dana after she speaks on the resentment she feels from other slaves who might consider her proximity to Rufus being alive or just being by association: "She came over to me [Dana] and wiped one side of my face with my fingers—wiped hard. I drew back, and she held her fingers in front of me, showed me both sides."[29] Dana cannot understand; the performance is singularly ("for once") unintelligible to her, even after Carrie repeats it. Nigel translates: "She means it doesn't come off.... The black. She means the devil with people who say you're anything but what you *are*."[30] While intended by Nigel as a dismissal of the possible perceptions of other slaves, it reveals a fact that previously remained illegible to Dana.

The fact of her Blackness, codified in the permanence of its marking(s) on her flesh, was masked by Dana's fantastic alchemy, her meticulous transmutation of her various fantasies of both temporal and political-ontological distance from being a slave. She transmutes the temporal distance between 1976 and antebellum enslavement into the illusion of a political-ontological distance between "Black" ("Black women," specifically) and "nigger" (as a name for Slaveness). Gratuitous violence from masters (e.g., Rufus Weylin and his overseers, Edwards and Fowler) and communication of the fact from slaves (e.g., Carrie and Nigel) shatter the mask of distance, revealing the fantasy for its fantastical nature, and the political-ontological distance dissolves,

---

29. Butler, *Kindred*, 223–24.
30. Ibid.

revealing the reality of a horrifying overlay between "nigger" and "Black," between "slave" and "Dana." Time becomes untimely in its two layers of indeterminacy: The indeterminacy of the origin of the overlay between Dana and slave, and the arbitrariness of the violent passages Rufus coerces Dana to make. The only remaining certainty is the illegible fact borne in/as Dana's flesh, and the flesh of all Black folk, on and off the plantation. After being brutally whipped, and while recovering, but in agony, Dana thinks to herself, *"See how easily slaves are made?"* But she is terribly mistaken: With no traceable beginnings, and only the fact of her Black flesh, it might not be that she was ever or easily *made* a slave, but that, as far as anyone was concerned, she always already was.

This resonates with Fanon's "The Fact of Blackness" on multiple frequencies. One of the key resonances resounds the moment Rufus, following Dana's second passage to the past, and so when he's a (White) child, casually names Dana a "strange nigger"; it appears to be Fanon's "Dirty Nigger!" manifest in another disguise (however thinly veiled). We will parse the parallels between Dana's treatment of the imposition of this fact of her Blackness and Fanon's careful dissection of his own psychic negotiations of that fact. Fanon maneuvers through an array of meticulous refusals of the "dark and unarguable"[31] Slaveness-named-nigger and the "reason" buttressing those refusals.

Fanon, like Dana, attempts to affirm the legitimacy of his existence and selfhood as a way of confronting the imposition of Blackness-qua-Slaveness onto his being. Against the "unreason" of anti-Blackness fixing him to his spatial and temporal "coordinates,"[32] against the "crushing objecthood"[33] in which anti-Blackness seals him, Fanon asserts the wholeness of a "corporeal schema" under the moniker, in intentional majuscule, "BLACK MAN."[34] He attempts to name and solidify himself against the "disappearance"[35] of his being into the position of the "dirty nigger." Almost conjuring this Fanonian moment, we recall Dana's immediate reaction to Rufus's casual imposition of the name and position of "strange nigger" onto her being, and her asser-

---

31. Fanon, *Black Skin*, 88.
32. Ibid., 84.
33. Ibid., 82.
34. Ibid., 87.
35. Ibid., 84. I encountered a recording of an interview with author Kiese Laymon about his novel *Long Division*, growing up in Mississippi, and writing for Black folk. Of the many topics he addresses, he brings up the problem of being "disappeared" in relation to being Black. The impetus behind his novel, his essay collection, *How to Slowly Kill Yourself and Others in America*, his writing in general, and his teaching, is a sustained resistance to the "disappearance" characterizing Black "life" in an anti-Black world.

tion of her identity as a "Black woman." The initiating discovery of and violent encounter with the fact of Blackness encoded in the imposition of the variously modified name, "nigger," reveals a crushing dislocation of this sense of being (a Black "person"), and that being is concurrently fixed to the unchanging coordinates of "nigger" in the flesh (Fanon describes this as a "racial epidermal schema"[36]). Fanon and Dana—or, perhaps, Dana channeling or paralleling Fanon—attempt to orient themselves by trying to reason against the unreason of the dislocation, and attempt to "retain" a name and an awareness of the wholeness of their flesh against the violence of this force.

But this discovery is really a rediscovery[37] of a fact "seated in the chair in the empty room"[38] before either Fanon or Dana arrive. As opposed to an initiating imposition of fact, the imposition telegraphs a "definitive structuring of the self and of the [anti-Black] world."[39] In this instance, rediscovery implies a temporal relation: The anti-Black world structure exists outside of and "before" the Black folk it positions as "nigger"; the Black is *always already* a "nigger" in the eyes of the world (because the world is always already anti-Black), and thus in the eyes of Whites (masters) and non-Blacks (junior partners, who are adjacent to but not quite masters), "the only real eyes"[40]—the only eyes allowed to "mess with" Black flesh. Fanon's and Dana's attempt to "retain" or (re)assert some alternative position is always already compromised; worse, there is no alternative position or name, or, at least, one that could displace the factuality of the position imposed by the structure and the gazes of its agents.

This places the disequilibrium as preexistent and permanent, with an indeterminate temporal "beginning" beyond the fixedness of the flesh. Disequilibrium does not merely inaugurate the escalation of Fanon's and Dana's encounter with anti-Blackness (and by extension, his chapter and Butler's novel as "narratives"). Fanon, Dana, and Black folk are perpetually "too late"[41] because the anti-Blackness of the world is anticipatory. It

---

36. Ibid.
37. Ibid., 99. This is also a way Spillers, in "Mama's Baby, Papa's Maybe," describes how the resurgence of even familiar trauma, in or outside discourse, never dulls trauma's terrible force: "I might as well add that the familiarity of this narrative does nothing to appease the hunger of recorded memory, nor does the persistence of the repeated rob these well-known, oft-told events of their power, even now, to startle. In a very real sense, every writing as revision makes the 'discovery' all over again" (68–69).
38. Brand, *A Map*, 25.
39. Ibid., 83.
40. Fanon, *Black Skin*, 87.
41. Ibid., 91.

preemptively prepares a position characterized by a fixed disequilibrium for Black folk who "arrive" into the world. Whatever trauma Rufus or the unnamed child Fanon encounters telegraph is constitutive as opposed to (solely) intrusive. The imposition of the fact of Blackness and the traumatic dislocation companion to it only "intrude" insofar as the intrusion is a violent reminder of the fact that Black existence is always already constituted by a vulnerability to being intruded upon. The untimeliness of the fact and its ensuing trauma is permanent and repetitious, appearing to "show no movement,"[42] no matter its disguise, no matter its context.

This leads us into rediscovery's second, equally menacing implication: In both Dana's and Fanon's "narratives," neither the articulation of the violent imposition of anti-Blackness nor the Black resistance with which it is met occur just once. The "initiating" trauma produces an indignance that manifests in an attempt to name and in a demand for explanation. The world counters Dana's and Fanon's assertions of subjectivity with another form of violence. Fanon remarks on this directly, expressing frustration over the escalation and evolution of the world's responses to how he responds to its violence: "Thus, my unreason was countered with reason, my reason with 'real reason.' Every hand was a losing hand for me."[43] Like Dana's resistance to Rufus's violence, discursive (her demands to be addressed on her own terms) and performative (her preemptively protective attempts to arm herself with knives between passages), which Rufus meets with escalating gratuitous violence (beatings, whippings); like Fanon's psychic resistance in the form of indignant verbal outbursts ("Kiss the handsome Negro's ass, madame!"[44]), or reasoned analytical dissections of unreasonable claims against his own (his attempt to disavow Sartre's patronizing misreading of *négritude*); like the "perpetual reversals and retreats,"[45] a more forceful assault meets every attempt at a strategic defense. Black folks' "rediscovery" provokes a counterattack by the anti-Black world. It signals a reinvigorated resurgence, one that reemerges with undaunted, if not increased, force when met with resistance. The untimeliness of the fact does not "move," but demonstrates greater and greater force, more and more violent resilience, the more Black folk resist its factuality. After each encounter, Black being and Black flesh return "sprawled out, [and more and more] distorted" than the previous instance, in what is an escalating reduction of Black being, as well as an increase in the depth and number of markings on the flesh. Whatever

---

42. Spillers, "Mama's Baby, Papa's Maybe," 68.
43. Fanon, *Black Skin*, 101.
44. Ibid., 86.
45. Brand, *A Map*, 29.

remains of being and flesh violently shrinks; the undecipherable markings grow in number, and illegibility becomes all the more impenetrable.

What, then? Is it all an exercise in futility? Is the logic, buttressed by the unwieldy evidence of experience and untimely facts, inevitably fatalistic? What to do with/from such a pessimistic position? I suspended a version of these questions at the outset of this section because attempting to map the violent entanglement between untime and anti-Blackness is essential to an engagement with them, and because Butler (through Dana) and Fanon (and Marriott's reading of him) lay the foundation for an intervention. Which is also why I suspended an engagement with the other side of untime. As Rufus arbitrarily wields untime's force to drag Dana through time, Dana must also and repeatedly "return"[46] to 1976 California. An examination of the mechanics of this "return" rends open our way toward a fuller, if more devastating, understanding of untime.

Concurrent with Dana's negotiation of the fact of her Blackness and that fact's effect on her relation to (un)time—or, perhaps, more quickly than that—Dana constructs a theory of her "returns" by testing a hypothesis early in the text. During her second passage, and after encountering Alice at her shack in the woods for the first time, Dana goes to retrieve a blanket Alice left outside while being threatened and nakedly exposed by a slave patroller looking for a runaway. The patroller, returning to the shack as Dana does, blindsides her. Dana counters his assault by fleeing, and, when this fails, wields a tree limb to forcibly, if temporarily, end the encounter. Battered, bruised, and fearing that he might kill her should he regain consciousness, Dana experiences a darkening dizziness before "returning" to her apartment and Kevin's company. They discuss what happened, and what, between her passages, catalyzed her "return." Kevin helps her realize that her own "fear of death sends [her] home."[47] But Dana objects to the utility of this hypothesis, even if proven correct: Since her vertiginous passages take "time" to complete, these moments leave her especially vulnerable, even more so if the danger must be deadly enough for her to begin to "return." As she rightly sums up her dilemma: "Seconds count when something is trying to kill you." Butler presents this as a problem stretched between compromised and absent control: Either Dana has absolutely no control over her passage across time, or she does, but at risk of harm or death. This might

---

46. With each "return" returning her flesh and psyche to her more "distorted" by trauma than the last, "the returns" might best be understood as incomplete inversions as opposed to agential reversals; the former recognizes the way violence persists in the flesh and in the mind no matter the "return," and the latter inheres in fantasy.

47. Butler, *Kindred*, 50.

explain why the first few "returns" occur in the wake of unexpected violence: Dana's unwillingness to accept the risk that is elemental to embracing the proximity and imminence of death makes the possibility of "return" arbitrary, such that it appears out of her control.

But as the violence against her escalates, giving the fact of her Blackness and its subjection to untime greater force, her willingness to seek out violence and death grows. Two "returns" interest me in particular. The first: Dana attempts to flee the plantation with Kevin after a long separation, but Rufus, armed with a rifle, refuses her departure. Desperate for a reprieve from the violence of his presence and recognizing Rufus's willingness to shoot Kevin in order to coerce her into submission, Dana throws her body between the barrel and Kevin's body. When she hits the ground, the darkening dizziness has been triggered and a temporary "escape" is imminent. And the second: After Rufus hits her for protesting his sale of a slave, Sam, in front of his weeping family, Rufus commands her to return to the house. With resolve, citing a violation of an "unspoken agreement—a very basic agreement,"[48] Dana instead makes her way to the cookhouse, where she warms some water, walks upstairs to the attic, and, in the water, slits her wrists in order to "return." These passages demonstrate Dana's development of a desperate and resolute willingness to embrace a proximity to death, corporeal death, in order to assert some form of control over untime's force. And it is precisely that: a proximity to corporeal death, a risk with sentience at stake. Should she fail, mistime, or misjudge her actions, she risks death in the conventional sense.

But "return" in this fashion leaves Rufus alive, and Dana must ultimately relinquish even the illusion of control to the arbitrariness of his will. Though Dana risks her corporeal life in both instances, Rufus lives on, which ensures that her subjection to untime's force persists. It is only after a final escalation on Rufus's part that Dana raises the level of abstraction and stakes of her actions. Rufus attempts to rape Dana, which is an absolute refusal of consent, and so an absolute disavowal of Dana's claims to her own flesh, let alone how she names or identifies it. Rufus's willingness to finalize his position as master through rape of his slave violently raises the stakes.[49] Pinned to the bed, but armed with a knife, Dana must choose between submitting to "crushing objecthood," specifically the pornotropic reduction of

---

48. Ibid., 238.

49. For an essay that examines the need to center "racial rape" in our development of a Black studies that radically examines and challenges the anti-Black world, see Joy James's "Afrarealism and the Black Matrix: Maroon Philosophy at Democracy's Border," *The Black Scholar* 44, no. 2 (2014): 124–31.

her being to sexualized flesh, which *might* allow her to continue to "exist," but as a sentient "object" that has been unimaginably violated, or using the knife to kill Rufus and defend herself from the specificity of sexualized anti-Black violence, which risks her ceasing to exist, or never having existed.[50] It is a choice that raises the level of abstraction and stakes from corporeality to political-ontology: from physical death, a loss of sentience, to a death of being, a negation of existence. The choice is impossible to make, but it must be made. Dana chooses to kill Rufus. She chooses to leap, or tumble, toward the black hole. As he lay dead before her, his hand still clenched around her forearm, a corporeal echo of their struggle, the darkening dizziness burgeons, and Dana "returns." Rufus's hand never unclenches, and Dana's arm, from the point of his grip and below, remains with him; her arm looks as if it has merged with the wall of the apartment. To loose herself from the wall and his grip, she pulls back a severed limb. She screams in agony. She "frees" herself from his grasp and the crushing objecthood of the wall, losing a bit of herself in the process.

To better grasp the import of Dana's decision to risk her own existence in the name of definitively violently eliminating Rufus, we will do well to return to Fanon. Against the deathliness that characterizes a Black existence that is subject to the arbitrary and gratuitous violence of untime's force, Fanon appears to believe that such violence might "be redeemed . . . by black revolutionary violence."[51] Fanon might describe this Black revolutionary violence as an "explosion"—that is, on the one hand, a characterization of the overwhelming, unrestrained nature of that violence, and on the other, a willingness to embrace obliteration in order to produce or make a violent "upheaval." If Butler's work resonates with Fanon's thoughts, what Dana chooses to do, and what consequently happens to her seems to be Butler's speculation on what happens when we choose to risk nonexistence by embracing its facticity. Butler's epilogue appears to be the structural expres-

---

50. Two things. First, I am aware that—if we consider time to be linear, which we do not—Dana "never having existed" would create a paradox, since it turns on having existed long enough to choose to kill Rufus in the first place, perhaps, as so many science-fiction films, novels, and television shows have suggested, "destroying the space-time continuum." Second, I am aware that at this point in the novel, Hagar Weylin, the next ancestor in Dana's bloodline, has been born, possibly rendering Rufus's continued life meaningless if not dangerous. At no point is this connection, or Dana's line of reasoning behind it, presented as a certainty, though; there is no guarantee that Hagar's existence will end this predicament. This is perhaps most evident in the fact that although Hagar has been born and Dana has "returned" to her time, Rufus calls her to him once more.

51. Marriott, *Haunted Life*, 231.

sion of a question based on this embrace: "What might happen if/once we embrace untime's force, and willingly risk not only corporeal death, but absolute nonexistence?"

In the epilogue, after what's left of Dana's arm heals, she and Kevin travel to Maryland searching for confirmation of the reality of all that Dana and the slaves of the Weylin plantation suffered. On the surface, this looks like a recuperative search on a few levels. On one, it is recuperative in that they seem to believe that "historical" confirmation would somehow preserve their sanity. On another, it is decidedly optimistic in its futurity: Dana and Kevin are on a shared journey despite the political-ontological rift between their positions, Kevin as White/master, Dana as Black/slave. This ending is recuperative insofar as it subtly reconciles irreconcilable positions via a shared experience, and also in that it attempts to fill in the constitutive blanks in the historical archive, the many "What happened?" questions about the whereabouts and well-being of the people Dana encountered. This would recuperate continuity and cohesion, which would fly in the face of "untime" and its constitutive features (which are antithetical to continuity and cohesion). But in the novel's final line, Butler leaves a way to challenge this reading. Kevin remarks, "Now that the boy is dead, we have *some chance*"[52] of recuperation. The recuperation ("chance") that Kevin describes resonates with what Marriott reads in Fanon to be the redemptive feature of and impetus behind Black revolutionary violence, and also with reading Butler as suggesting a speculative possibility for redemption grounded in Dana's recourse to an explosive, Black revolutionary violence at the novel's culmination.

Black revolutionary violence does not promise redemption, but it might provide a way to render the irredeemable available to the possibility of redemption, without really offering a fixed or clear image of what redemption could look like. The deathliness that renders time untimely in relation to Black folk, that frames untime and all its constitutive features and effects, might make legible the possibility of its own redemption via Black revolutionary violence that has, as its stakes, being itself. Taking the risk means making the leap or taking the plunge into the black hole, means embracing the inescapability of the tidal forces emanating from its central singularity—the anti-Black imposition of the *fact* of Blackness.

Fanon describes this black hole as "the zone of nonbeing," a derelict spatiality and temporality, "an utterly naked *declivity* where an *authentic*

---

52. Butler, *Kindred*, 264.

upheaval might be born."[53] Only "here" and "now," or "there" and "then," along the downward slopes of the "zone," or the inward funnel of the black hole's gravity well, an "authentic," which might mean "redemptive," upheaval might become available to thought—might be conceived, carried to term, and brought into being (born). The "zone of nonbeing" or "black hole" is the only site for the (pro)creation of redemption via an embrace of obliteration, but it is also an "arid and sterile region," constitutively infertile, or at least, resistant to the redemptive creation that stages or embodies "authentic upheaval" in the form and wake of Black revolutionary violence and its attendant risk of political-ontological obliteration. To heed Ursa's call, to leap into the black hole, to enter into the dereliction of being, is to fall into unimaginable contradiction in the form of an unresolvable paradox.

If Black revolutionary violence, as a form of untimely, authentic, or redemptive (pro)creation, is what we might make, and if that is constitutively contradictory to the only spacetime at which this violence and (pro)creation can even ever occur, what might our (pro)creations look like? How might we read or engage (pro)creation, understanding what is at stake—Black being itself—when, because of untimely fact, of *being* Black, we don't have time to do either?

These are the questions that frame our opening, tenuously holding it open. This is when we've arrived, and given that (un)time is of the essence, we might do best to (t)read carefully, but quickly, as we make the leap toward utter destruction.

There is no time for anything else.

---

53. Fanon, *Black Skin*, 2.

SECOND ARRANGEMENT

The Untimely Works and Worlds of Impossible Stories

IV

Prelude

Trauma Work

> Your imagination can't save you.
> —JEROME DENT

WE ARRIVE bearing a series of claims: (a) Black time is untime and so Black life, death, and creation are untimely; (b) Black forms of creation conjured in the name of "authentic" revolutionary "upheaval" depend on an embrace of this untimeliness and the violence it signals; and (c) these forms of untimely creation thereby embrace the impossibility of redemption-as-recuperation as essential to their work. We might think it fair to ask: What now, or what do we make of this, or how can we work with this set of claims? What do we do with and through the untimeliness of our position? What *can* be done? And we ask for a number of reasons, the first being that this line of questioning from academics, activists, or students, be it laced with venomous dismissiveness, utter despair, roiling rage, or genuine curiosity (or some mixture of them all), almost always follows the deathly theoretical claims that emerge from the Afropessimist framework.

Even as we begin this entire project by building our claims out of the lived experiences of Black folk in the anti-Black world, conscious of the high level of abstraction of the analysis and claims, when faced with somewhat abstract claims about impossibilities, leaps into black holes, and loops, lapses, and losses of time, we inevitably wonder about the applicability of the ideas presented. We ask what we are able and supposed to do with all of these ideas if we take them seriously; we ask, "So what?," "What now?," or "And . . . ?" Whatever the impetus for the inquiry, we recognize the energy such questions offer us; they give the vector of our exploration more momentum and direction. I often explain the utility of this line of questioning and this set of untimely claims to my students this way.

> *Memory Fragment—October 2017*
> *I am teaching two courses this semester, one entitled "The Black Fantastic" that traces a "tradition" of Black speculative creation across works of Black science fiction, fantasy, and horror, and the other entitled "Black Otherworlds" that explores a similar set of works, but centers literature that more explicitly grapples with trauma—these are texts I consider to be "Otherworldly" in the ways they create speculative spacetimes (or otherworlds) that hold space and make time for Black folk to confront trauma. In both courses, we spend the first few weeks much like the first few chapters of this book: theorizing Black untimeliness to found our questions about how to do the work of Black speculative creation given the conditions of our existence in this cosmos. During the fifth week of the course, after intellectually surviving the theory gauntlet of the first few weeks, and trying to capitalize on the rawness of their flitting imaginative energy, I pose the above set of questions to the students. And after I ask, I carefully scan their faces, catching glimpses of the jagged arcs of electricity glinting across their eyes.*

One of our questions—"What *can* be done?"—is a question of possibility given the facts: what are we able to "do," given our relation to an unethical and violent time, or when our relation to time is so derelict that we occupy a position of "nonbeing" that destroyed, destroys, and promises to continue to destroy us? As we ask them, these questions about what we do or how we work with our untimeliness is a question of practical, theoretical, imaginative, and ethical necessity: If we know what we *can* do or what kind of doing is *possible*, given that this is a tense matter, and only a matter of time, what *have* we done, what *do* we do, and what *might* we build *toward* doing?

We must think about what work means to us. To move forward, we must work through work, which forms the terrain of our approach to even shards of answers. We must map work's terrain and examine what gives it depth and form for us in order to understand why it is meaningful to our need to creatively "make a way out of no way." And we must plot the conceptual landmarks and waypoints so that we might deliberately trace the best route.

We think about work in two key ways: work as a process and a practice, and also work as a product of those processes and practices. When we think of work here and throughout this writing, we think of *a* work, what it means to do or put in work, how working or a work *works,* and how working or a work might work out. These are questions of mechanics, aims, and possibilities. In terms of Black literature, these questions open a route to thinking critically about the motivations behind, stakes of, and possibilities for Black imaginative creation given our untimeliness. Thinking about work in these terms draws our attention to the gravity of Christina Sharpe's archetypal conceptualization of "wake work." The way Sharpe maps the motivations, stakes, and possibilities for all Black work, including literary work, is crucial to her two projects on the subject of "wake work." We will trace the thread of her thinking in order to pursue a clearer idea about what "work" should mean to us as we move forward in the analysis.

We will think about creative work, work and works that are generative in a way that draws from the abstract reservoir of the imagination. Part of what resonates from Sharpe's formulation of "work" is the way she relates it to thought and imagination. Sharpe describes "Black Studies: In the Wake" as "a call for, and recognition of, black studies' continued imagining of the unimaginable: its continued theorizing from the 'position of the unthought.'"[1] Work and works do not merely emerge from the imagination. Instead, "imagining" and "working" overlap: To work is, at least in part, to imagine. The work of Black studies is imaginative work, the product and process of the working imagination of Black folk who imagine from their own "unthought" position—who routinely *do* the unthinkable while also *being* unthinkable. This is the imaginative work of Black creation. Black creating is working in at least two ways: It is a working like a kneading of dough, like a shaping of clay, like the making of a construct, and it is also like a machination, an inner working, a fundamental component of a being, a thought, or a machine. It is both the acts of thinking, writing, and singing that produce Ursa's blues *and* the blueshifted voice that becomes essential to making Ursa's blues singularly hers. It is both Dana's existence-risking act of revolutionary violence *and* the untimeliness of her political-ontological existence that necessitates that act.

The unimaginable machine of Black studies in the wake does deathly, untimely work. We cannot disentangle the work we do, the Black work with which we pose the questions that animate this chapter, from the untimeliness we traced in the opening arrangement of this project; the conditions that temporally dislocate Blackness from "life" and subjectivity (recall *Kindred*'s Dana), snake their tendrils into the very fabric of Black work. How Sharpe translates this entanglement into a question of caring for Black folk

---

1. Sharpe, "Black Studies," 59. "The Position of the Unthought" is an interview between Saidiya Hartman and Frank B. Wilderson III, in *Qui Parle* 13, no. 2 (2003): 183–201.

under such conditions uniquely balances the realities of untimeliness and deathliness to which Black folk remain subject with the belief in and necessity of work that vies to care for Black folk. Inspired by M. NourbeSe Philip's call "to defend the dead,"[2] Sharpe asks:

> How do we who are doing work in black studies tend to, care for, comfort and defend the dead, the dying, and those living lives consigned, in the aftermath of legal chattel slavery, to death that is always-immanent and imminent? How might theorizing black studies in the wake—and black being in the wake—as conscious modes of inhabitation of that imminence and immanence (revealed every day in multiple quotidian ways) ground our work as we map relations between the past and present, map the ways the past haunts the present?[3]

Working and imagining are animated, on the one hand, by the untimeliness of Black existence, and on the other by a need to protect and nurture Black folk—to "defend the dead"—who exist at various points along death's orbit. The imaginative work of Black creation inheres in a tenuous balance between recognizing the untimeliness of Black folks' existences and, impossibly, making or taking time to care for Black folk under untimely conditions. Sharpe's volley of questions exposes the central conflict of doing and imagining wake work: We must work toward care for Black folk that the violent conditions of the anti-Black world render otherwise impossible; we must make and take time to care for Black folk when time itself is a violent problem for we who are untimely. I take this set of obligations as a pedagogical principle as much as an essential problem, both grounded and abstract, at the heart of Black and untimely work.

Memory Fragment—Spring 2014
They don't really speak, and they don't really listen, and they aren't really here. Their presence seems destabilized and their attendance is less here-and-now than it is elsewhere-and-then. Above the quivering quiet, dogs bark distant, playful barks. Looking out of the second-floor window behind the half-moon of my students' nine desks, I see people and dogs frolic on the campus's main green.

"So what's good? Did anyone do the reading? Y'all know we can't sit in this room staring at each other. We need to do our best to stay on schedule." I punctu-

---

2. M. NourbeSe Philip, *Zong!* (Middletown: Wesleyan University Press, 2008), "Zong 15."
3. Sharpe, "Black Studies: In the Wake," 60.

ate the admonition by plopping my bag onto the desk before plumbing its depths for my book and my laptop.

Quiet. Dogs barking. I pull up the essay we're reading as a companion to Toni Morrison's *Beloved*, turn the book to the appropriate pages, and exhale a sigh into the classroom's void.

Before I can begin, a student speaks, "Something happened on Friday before we left for spring break." I listen.

She explains that at a welcome event organized by current Black students for incoming Black students, a White student tried to intimidate attendees by standing just outside the quadrangle where the event was being held and cracking a very real whip, smiling. Having sought out help from administrators, they and all the Black students who were shaken by this person faced what many Black students face in the wake of traumatic, anti-Black experiences: a lack of care, effort, and work on their behalf. Beyond not doing much to mete out a punishment for the whip-cracker, administrators advised students to seek counseling. Unhappy with the lack of representation among counseling staff, the students requested alternative avenues for help while highlighting the need for Black counselors able to deal with the fallout from nigh-inevitable experiences like this. According to my students, administrators told them that if they were unhappy with the available resources, they would do well to find help elsewhere or take an academic leave of absence.

Quiet. My eyes meet all of theirs. Dogs bark in the springtime sun.

"You know what? Let's go get some air."

At least once every semester, the university hosts an event called "Heavy Petting" on the main green, inviting community members, students, and staff to bring their dogs as a form of playful therapy for students who need a release in the midst of midterms and final exams. Outside, we find dogs of all sizes lumbering by on too-small leashes or tumbling over one another in the grass.

"Let's talk in about twenty minutes," and the students fly.

I make my rounds to each group and we talk a bit about how they felt about the absence of discernible care they experienced in the wake of whip-cracker's whip-cracking. Some described their disillusionment. Some, their rage. Some described feeling like, between the rigors of school, the demands of extracurricular activities, and the regularity of experiencing anti-Blackness on and off campus, they just never had any time to breathe.

I can only empathize with each student, sharing a story from my own undergraduate life and really feeling with and for them in their struggles. I can only pull from the curriculum and from the spirit of the moment and say something like, "Well, sometimes, while we can't call this healing or redress, moments like this— we can take this time and catch our breaths a bit. And that's important. And we have to. And we have to. For ourselves. For each other."

> *Quiet. A few nod in understanding while we stand in a circle around two corgis wearing sweaters.*
>
> *I spy a dog bigger and heavier than I am. I run over and ask one of my students to take a picture of me with the large, 180-pound black Pyrenean mastiff. We inspect the photo, and I look delighted, excited to be next to such a mythical creature, and to be there and then with and for them.*
>
> *We break for the day. I remind them to remember to breathe.*

For Mackala Lacy, recalling a workshop on care led by Sharpe, this is a question of what Sharpe calls "aspiration": of the capacity to draw breath, and, to extend phonetically, the capacity to rhythmically produce language as and through exhale. This is not aspiration as healing or as breathing either since "a corpse cannot ever 'breathe'"—a socially dead being cannot (re)inhale social life, through music, art, or otherwise. Instead, aspiration is an intentional intake of that which nourishes us as we occupy a deathly position. Lacy describes aspiration as a means of being purposeful toward survival—aspiration that energizes the exhausted flesh, mind, and spirit—and toward a form of rising, a rising to the occasion, distinct from "traditional idealizations of achievement or . . . upward mobility,"[4] that turns on physical, psychic, psychological, and spiritual nourishment. For Lacy, this might look like routinizing meditation; crafting a "conscious pattern of breathing or mantra"; beginning or developing a bodily and spiritual practice like "yoga, running, or dance"; or "making time" for interactions with loved ones, including the self, the living and the dead, and the named and the unnamed—"whatever feeds [one's] soul." The aspirational feature of "wake work"—of our work—is that it must nourish one's being; it must do so in order to ensure one's fitness for not only surviving, but continuing to do the "wake work" Black folk must perform with and through every gesture. In a world in the wake of slavery, sustained by its need to imperil Black being, this individual and communal aspiration appears to be a part of what is so unimaginable and impossible, and yet absolutely imperative, about working in the wake.

In Sharpe's most recent project, *In the Wake: On Blackness and Being*, she elaborates upon "aspiration" in a way that affirms Lacy's interpretation of the concept, and also lays bare the stakes of holding close this component of our imaginative work in the "untimely" wake of enslavement. Not only does aspiration describe the process of drawing breath, a process that for Black folk is disastrously imperiled by the anti-Blackness of the hold, the

---

4. Mackala Lacy, "Wake Work—Self Care for the Black Community," *Out of Nowhere*, February 18, 2015.

ship, the water, the weather,[5] and the world constructed upon and around us, but aspiration also signals a desire and a demand for *"keeping* and *putting* breath in the Black body."[6] This is aspiration as the process of drawing breath, and aspiration "as *audible breath,*" the breath "that accompanies or comprises a speech sound."[7] When Sharpe writes that this work and "wake work," as theory and praxis, "*sound* an ordinary note of *care*"[8] for Black folk against and from within the extraordinary conditions of Black life and death in the world,[9] we understand that the imaginative work we attempt is not just the work of facilitation but also the work of articulation and protection: We must make time when Black folk can draw and expel breath, and we must secure that capacity to take and hold breath. Further, our work must articulate in a way that ensures that both of these aims come to fruition.

Articulation, the production of sound, the sound of a note of care, of an audible breath, propagates through the air as a disturbance of it, as a pressure wave producing vibrations through the fluid medium into which one articulates—think air, water. Articulation is also a function of time: Sound waves propagate at a particular frequency, which, as I understand it, can be considered a numerical value attached to the level of disturbance the pressure produces in the medium over time. In our reading, Sharpe's aspirational wake work sutures care-for-Black-folk to Black breath to sonic-temporal disturbance; caring and breathing while Black is a sonic and temporal disturbance. Wake work is aspirational in that it produces pressure that disturbs the medium through which it passes or against which it careens, and in that disturbance of the medium—the air, the water, the wake, the world—aims to both facilitate the passage of breath into and out of Black bodies and secure breath in those bodies. Our work must vie to facilitate and secure this nourishing disturbance and disturbing nourishment.

For the socially dead, we who intimately know deathly, untimely disaster, the practice of Blackly creating breath-giving and breath-securing disturbance is as essential as it is unimaginable, at least as a form of redress. This seems to be the importance of the word "ordinary" in Sharpe's articula-

---

5. For more on the concepts, "the hold," "the ship," and "the weather," please read or revisit the second, third, and fourth chapters of Sharpe's *In the Wake: On Blackness and Being,* the whole of which is profound in the way it theorizes and puts into practice "care" that both recognizes the immeasurability and singularity of Black suffering, and attends to the glimpses of something-like-"life" scattered throughout the archive.

6. Sharpe, *In the Wake,* 129; emphasis mine.

7. Ibid.

8. Ibid., 132.

9. She dubs these conditions "the weather" in her theorization of the wake, and this weather is disastrous—anti-Blackness as climate itself.

tion of her book's purpose, especially when placed in relation to larger and more overwhelming words like "disaster,"[10] which Sharpe returns to dozens of times, and "overwhelming force," which Sharpe includes in a refrain that repeats throughout the whole text. We are, as she is, interested in fragments and making arrangements without holding fast to impossibilities like redress, reassembly, repair, return, resuscitation, or resurrection. Rather, we are committed to the "ordinary" work of disturbance in the form of care and Black breathing against the extraordinary conditions of Black life in an anti-Black cosmos. Our concern must be for the mechanics of this process of imaginative work-as-aspirational-disturbance: What is essential to how this creative, disturbing process happens? How can we play conduit to the untimely fact of Black subjection in a way that produces the caring, imaginative disturbance we need? If we put this disturbance-as-breath back into Black bodies and keep it there, what might that look like?

Memory Fragment—December 2017
Above the blue-lit hum of the projector, the stilled image of a small coffin, just a silhouette in the parlor room that only the muted light of the sun mutters its way into—barely a whisper or a gasp of sunshine—looms in the center of the screen. It mirrors us, we twenty-seven or eight, as we sit, ready to reflect.

"I remember . . . the first time I watched this I cried," and behind closed eyes fixed upon the memory, the urge wells up again. "I'm not sure I can articulate why exactly—there certainly isn't one feature on its own. The confluence of all of it . . . I think the lyrics, the piano, the build, his voice, the children—the children, and their dancing!—I think all of it, really, really just moves through me in a strange way." My tongue doesn't know what to do here. The hum overtakes the room, the soundtrack to electric thoughts whirring in the dark. "Which is why I wanted to show you this today. I want to trace that movement, for us to consider that movement. Especially in the midst of the dancing dead." I press play.

"Never Catch Me" opens quietly over the wistful sigh of chimes playing over the image of the coffin as the camera retreats, showing us the blue-black emptiness of the room, and then the sepia emptiness of the pews and pulpit in the next room. To begin with emptiness beckons a recognition of the lack and the loss the coffin announces in its hushed blackness, right at the center, right at the outset. And to begin with the wistful sighs of chimes lightly chiming, like a soft song to signal the departure of the dying, conjures whimsy and magic tinged with sorrow. It is death, not quite presented as stillness and quietness. It is death, lightly unsettled, mysterious, laced with wonder. The wide, attentive eyes of my students suggest as much.

---

10. Sharpe, *In the Wake*, 5 and throughout.

We cut to a funeral service about to begin. To a piano melody that continues the wistfulness of the chimes over a snare drum tapped with stick and shuffle-scratched with wire brush, a woman in a black dress with a large black hat leads us into and through the chapel where mourners sit, posturing differently beneath the weight of whomever they've lost. The drums pick up, and Kendrick begins, seemingly at a sonic distance—he's more nasal, and he sounds distant behind the soul-jazz beat—and after we've seen the pews filled and the pastor preaching at the pulpit, we arrive at the altar strewn with small white candles and photos of the two children, maybe brother and sister—maybe even twins—and make the discovery of who and why we mourn here. The classroom stiffens a bit. Someone sniffles. Maybe it's me. I can't quite remember. One minute, thirteen seconds in, and the drums pick up, and Kendrick is louder, closer, now.

And then we see her, from the neck down only, a brief, perhaps intentional inversion of the urgency with which Mamie Till prioritized showing Emmett's mutilated face. We wonder with worry at her expression. Her small hands rest on her chest, folded across a single white tulip pressed against the sky blue of her sequined lace dress. Photos show us her laughter. They show us her body mid-dance.

And then we see him. Eyes closed. Until they aren't. The drums punctuate the moment and signal a change. The tap-scratch of the snare shifts to the conjuring magic of quick claps between Kendrick's volley of bars; something magical is happening; something wondrous is being conjured. Our ears readjust; our eyes follow suit.

One minute, twenty-six seconds in, Kendrick begins to fire his lyrics rapidly as the camera retreats to the center aisle between the pews, and the children rise from their coffins in sync as Black folk clad in choir garb clap-clap-clap-clap with their heads down, caught up in the rhythm of the ritual. The air quivers in anticipation as the children unwind and unravel before leaping down from the raised stage and darting toward one another.

At one minute, forty-three seconds in, their energy cannot be quantified. This is all so electric. Their movement is the choreography of complete release replete with a frenetic kinetic momentum that just seems to buildandbuildandbuild as the sense of awe does in the classroom. Hot-stepping, fire-dancing, and their movement is explosive.

But the mourners—all adults—cannot see the small big bang blow up before them. Their moods remain unchanged, their eyes everywhere else, and their bodies still. They dance without the imposition of a gaze because they and their joyous departure are unseeable.

Just over two minutes in, an electric bass erupts in a convoluted arpeggio as the children's movements crescendo. But the music suddenly calms and the choir joins Kendrick to sing the soft hook of the song as the children, backs straight and eyes toward the doors, run out of the church in slow motion. At two minutes, twenty-two seconds in, the boy looks back at the caskets, smiling the titular lyrics of the chorus: "Say you will never ever catch me / No, no, no."[11]

They run through the empty rooms from before. They form dynamic silhouettes crashing across blue curtains. They laugh and laugh and leap over empty parlor pews. Just the clapping now, and the playful synth that begins to wind its way toward the musical foreground signals another transition.

It builds and builds with the electric bass as we enter into the sunshine with children playing Miss Mary Mack and jump-roping, and the children we came to mourn prepare to explode again. A synth bass drum overtakes the snare and the clap as the children fully let loose. In the blurred foreground, a little girl with beaded braids in a purple shirt faces away from us, looking on, and while we can't be sure, we suspect she sees them for all their joy and energy.

The tears well up in my eyes. This nexus of light, movement, joy, innocence, play, rhythm, and death rattles something loose again deep in my being somewhere. I feel the room sharing in the shaking; I notice some of the students caught in this strange moment of happiness, mourning, and wonder.

Finally, in the break of the beat, the children leap into the open back of a parked hearse—the hearse that likely delivered their coffins—climb into the driver and passenger seats (the girl drives), and pull away. The children that were playing chase after them, full sprint, to see them off, the energy of their movement and the resurgence of the beat suggesting nothing but celebration at their departure. In the final moments, we only hear the rush of the air passing over the hearse, and we only see the little boy, eyes closed and mouth agape in a wide smile before we cut to black.

We sit in the dark together for a moment before I can make out the silhouette of a raised hand.

"Did they come back to life?"

"I'm not sure that's precisely what happened."

"Yeah, I don't think so either—it seemed more like they died and went somewhere happy."

"But it wasn't, like, the 'ending' kind of dead; they had energy, they had life, right?"

"Or like Kendrick said, 'life beyond your own life,' so, like something else"

"'Something else . . .' But still dead, just not still dead, you feel me?"

"So, if they were dead, and they didn't . . . they weren't . . . filled with life, but with something else, what was really happening?"

"Yeah, and . . . where were they going?"

---

11. See/listen to Flying Lotus, "Never Catch Me," featuring Kendrick Lamar, https://www.youtube.com/watch?v=2lXDovv-ds8.

> *In the quiet that came after the outpouring of questions, I couldn't even hear us breathing. Something else and someplace else, and joy and sorrow, and dancing and death, hung in the air in the dark. Just for a moment, and for all eternity, and never ever.*

When we imagine what putting disturbance-as-breath back into Black bodies looks like, we imagine how our bodies get filled, how and how well they can hold what pours in, and what occupies our vessels. Part of the aspirational work of Black imaginative creation depends on carefully thinking about our bearings. Keeping the breath, the nourishing disturbance, put into Black beings is a problem of capacity and sustenance, of how our beings can bear or hold that breath while also bearing the traumatic aftermath of being subject to the untimely force of anti-Blackness that governs this cosmos.

Consider the note of care Sharpe repeatedly returns to as a guiding, grounding mantra that bleeds and breathes through *In the Wake*, reminding us what is essential to the ongoing project of Black creation. When Sharpe writes this refrain, "We are constituted through and by continued vulnerability to this overwhelming force [of untimely terror in the form of anti-Blackness], but we are not only known to ourselves and to each other by that force,"[12] she attempts to work through—and by venturing to do so, compels us to follow suit—a certain paradoxical problem of Black work in the wake of enslavement. What we know about ourselves and our relation to one another is framed by this doubled bearing of disturbing-sustaining breath and of the anti-Black violence that necessitates and frames that breath. While we know ourselves in ways that are in excess of that violence, that violence is also part of what we know and bear, and with which we must contend. We remain unable to imagine fully the mechanics, possibilities, and consequences of Black breath speculatively and spectacularly nourishing Black bodies if we do not also consider how untimeliness also occupies our bodies. While we have spent text and time considering the workings of our breath and how we might bear it or create ways to bear it, we must also turn to how this breath will work with the trauma that the anti-Black cosmos deposits into our vessels.

This means that in order to imagine scenes of Black breathing, or of the dead rising and dancing away, we should investigate the mechanics of trauma and how it plays out in and on our beings. In their 2013 essay, "The Violence of Presence: Metaphysics in a Blackened World," Patrice Douglass and Frank B. Wilderson III offer us a way forward by meditating on what

---

12. Sharpe, *In the Wake*, 134.

it might mean and what it might take to think through a Black "metaphysical violence."[13] They demand Black work rooted in a metaphysics disfigured (or atomized, or spaghettified) by its entanglement with the singularity and unthinkability of "the violence that enables black (non)being . . . of blackness-qua-violence."[14] In the first instance, this disavows the prevailing tendency in conventional philosophical inquiry to forget, forego, or otherwise turn away from an engagement with what founds, and, in more ways than one, breathes life into all thought as such: anti-Blackness, and the Black breathlessness[15] it demands and ensures. In the second, it offers a thought vector that travels away from this fundamentally anti-Black tendency, moving the movement of thought toward the crushing abyss of Blackness—in other words, it seeks to Blacken the very foundations of thought and wield them as what, elsewhere, Jared Sexton describes as the work of "genuine inquiry."

We turn to Douglass and Wilderson because, from our vantage point, their prescription for a metaphysics of violence depends on analytical claims that deal with both the singularity of Black subjection to overwhelming violence and how this subjection is bound up with one's capacity to imagine from a Black position. Their argument depends on an examination of the metaphysical problem of violence and Blackness, and how that problem materializes as a dereliction of the capacity of Black folk to craft relational narratives about themselves because Black folk have an untimely relation to violence and trauma. Tracing their argument will help us continue building our theory of Black imaginative work performed under untimely conditions. Their argument composes two complementary critiques that will both affirm our approach thus far and propel us deeper into the abyss. First, against Jasbir Puar, who in *Terrorist Assemblages* "deploys anti-black violence" in and as "critique" of state violence that, by way of an "anxious intent to sidestep blackness"[16] altogether, leaves the anti-Black structure it fails to consider intact. Douglass and Wilderson center Saidiya Hartman's *Scenes of Subjection: Terror, Slavery, and Self-Making in Nineteenth-Century America*, an

---

13. Patrice Douglass and Frank B. Wilderson, "The Violence of Presence: Metaphysics in a Blackened World," *The Black Scholar* 43, no. 4 (2013): 122.

14. Douglass and Wilderson, "The Violence of Presence," 117–18.

15. I conjure the murder of Eric Garner on July 17, 2014. In the video of his murder, Garner, who is asthmatic, cries, "I can't breathe," as officer Daniel Pantaleo employs an illegal chokehold, strangling the life from him. His words become a refrain for the ongoing Black Lives Matter movement. The reference here conjures the specter of his death as, like all Black death, it haunts every word and thought, here and beyond.

16. Douglass and Wilderson, "The Violence of Presence: Metaphysics in a Blackened World" 118–19.

unflinching, "world-shifting" meditation on Black existence in an anti-Black world. Different than the nameable, "direct relations of violence as a traceable force" (e.g., the violence of the state) that limit Puar's attention, what Douglass and Wilderson demand through Hartman is a Black philosophical inquiry that relentlessly thinks with and through "the infinite refractions of violence at the level of being and existence in the world."[17] We will turn toward these infinite refractions in the following chapters, but for now, this demand is for a paradigmatic shift, and it opens a route toward fully facing the untimely Blackness that girds the capacities to be and think, and also to be rendered unthinkable and antithetical to being, in a reality that has its fundamental features distorted and mutilated by Blackness and like Black flesh. Put in the terms of our work thus far, it is a shift that, like Ursa's blues, demands we examine creation that emerges or might emerge from being and thinking entangled with Blackness and violence.

Specifically, Douglass and Wilderson situate the being and thought of the titular violent, Black "presence" in a question about what it means to suffer. In their second critique, they put pressure on the assumptive logic of Elaine Scarry's book *The Body in Pain: The Making and Unmaking of the World*, which examines the metaphysical violence of torture. Scarry attends to what violence (e.g., the extreme violence of torture) seeks to destroy: "The violence deployed in acts of mutilation and the infliction of pain . . . attempt to annihilate metaphysical presence."[18] Such violence rips open a metaphysical void (where one's being might once have been) available to being filled with "fiction": on the one hand, the "fiction" of being, of world, of being in/of the world the victim must create in order to maintain (even an illusion of) cohesion; on the other hand, the "fiction" made available to the torturer that turns on the lie that anything other than being itself (e.g., information) was the "actual" target of the violence.[19] For Douglass and Wilderson, Scarry's intervention is doubly important: It attends to how "torture destroys the victim's capacity to know herself as a relational being," and it opens us up to a question about what might be the nature and purpose of "fiction" or "fictions" that necessarily, if not desperately, emerge in the wake of such terror and destruction at the level of being. Scarry delineates the political-ontological parameters of overwhelming violence against human subjects and forces us to consider the relationship between that violence and imaginative creation.

---

17. Ibid.
18. Ibid., 120.
19. Ibid.

But for us, the most generative elements of Scarry's intervention really emerge from some of her core assumptions about the status of the subject that enters the torture room. To make her claims about the psychological and metaphysical destruction of the tortured subject, Scarry works from an assumptive logic that automatically considers the tortured subject a subject to begin with. As Douglass and Wilderson describe this problem, Scarry presumes that "all sentient beings who are tortured are relational beings; and that all victims of torture enter the chamber with the capacity for psychic integration."[20] To counter Scarry, they turn to an essay I wrote in 2013, entitled "Smile Undun, *Django Unchained*," and we revisit that piece here to consider why Scarry's analysis, based on her assumptive logic, crumbles when Blackness and untimeliness enter the torture chamber. In the essay, I read Frantz Fanon's "Dirty Nigger!" moment to dive more deeply into the darkness and horror of what Fanon gestures toward in chapter 5 of *Black Skin, White Masks*, "The Fact of Blackness." As I describe it, Fanon's account, or recollection, of the infamous hailing "Dirty Nigger!" or "Look, a Negro!"

> will be told and dissected as a piecing together of fragments, performed by another Fanon, one that is split from and yet internal to Fanon (BSWM, 89). Clarify further: He recognizes this on the train, almost jokingly, and familiarly, noting that this other him that is also him, the first person Fanon reflecting on the third person Fanon (which, I wager, alters the understanding of perspective when asking who wrote this account—I believe it to be both Fanons, simultaneously first and third persons)—noting that this other him collapses/splits/shatters/breaks again, "no longer in the third person but in triple," and, the joke in the visualization of it, that "in the train, instead of one seat on the train, they left [him] two or three" (92).[21]

This reading zones in on the temporal features of Fanon's metaphysical and psychic destruction. The Fanon writing the recollection, distinct from but containing or contained by the Fanon that is being hailed and seen (and so destroyed) in the recollection, appears to be the product, perhaps the "work," of a metaphysical and psychic "breach" that fragments his being, negating his ability to recognize his being as cohesive. It is a violent split that, on the surface, as the authors recognize, appears to be analogous with Scarry's reading of torture; violence breaks Fanon's being, and this breaking

---

20. Ibid.
21. Murillo, "Smile Undun, *Django Unchained*."

precipitates in a traumatic loss of bearings that denies him the capacity for psychic integration.

How Fanon shatters differs from how Scarry's torture victim breaks. In the previous arrangement, I dissected the temporal features of Fanon's encounter with the fact of his Blackness alongside our engagement with *Kindred*'s Dana. I described the "Dirty Nigger!" moment as a "rediscovery" of a fact that is always already factual, prior to and independent of Fanon's (or Dana's, or anyone else's) entrance into the room where the fact waited, waits, and will continue to wait. The crucial difference between Scarry's torture victim, whose metaphysics are broken by an encounter with the psychic, physical, and metaphysical trauma indexed by "torture," and the Black being, whose metaphysics are always already shattered prior to any encounter with "torture" or any form of trauma that might signal back to the fact of Blackness, is at once a temporal and metaphysical difference with consequences for how we negotiate our relationships to time, to being, and, by extension, to any work we try to produce.

The metaphysical difference between the entanglement of Black being, time, and trauma, and that of human being, time, and trauma plays out upon the relationship between Blackness and narrative. Scarry's torture victim moves from a metaphysical status of "equilibrium to disequilibrium" with the "promise of a third stage: equilibrium restored,"[22] but Black folk occupy a metaphysical position inextricably entangled with disequilibrium, which only appears to be magnified by each encounter with antiblackness. Black folk do not have access to what Douglass and Wilderson term "narrative progression." Our metaphysical relationship to violence and its traumatic aftermath, which turns in part on our untimeliness, upends any neat relationship between Blackness and narrative to the point that the terms become oxymoronic, if not outright antithetical because of a particular relationship to violence and trauma.

What interests us about this is the set of relations more implicitly addressed by Douglass and Wilderson's analyses: the importance of and consequences for "narrative" and "fiction" that the trauma of living (which is really "no life at all"), being (which is really a state of nonbeing), and creating (which is a form of "work") while Black. Their reading of Scarry in relation to my writing on Fanon affords us the opportunity to consider two new points of interest: Narrative, as inherently progressive, is impossible for, if not antagonistic and antithetical to Blackness, and the fictions we (must) create to fill the metaphysical, psychic, and political void violently vacated

---

22. Ibid., 121.

by trauma are, on the one hand, the direct, fantastical, and creative products necessitated by our traumatic and untimely positions, and on the other, inextricable from the violent and destructive fiction(s) of the anti-Black world. Trauma and violence bind our creations, literary and not; further, *they are the constitutive forces that animate our creations, rendering them possible to begin at all*.[23]

We have been in orbit of a troubling contradiction: The anti-Blackness that renders Blackness unthought and unthinkable through any combination of forgetting, sidestepping, silencing, slicing, popping open, and shooting, or otherwise stealing the very breath from our flesh, imaginations, and beings, produces and reproduces the trauma that untimely and breathlessly positions us in the universe, and the untimely violence of that trauma is constitutive to what breathes nourishment into ("animates") our wake work and works. Black flesh, imaginations, and nonbeings become the conduit for the untimely force that positions them, and our work channels that force into "works"—literary and otherwise. This line of thinking positions trauma as, in one way, an unstable, raw material, the "stuff" we must work with and through in order to conjure our many creations, and in another, the electromagnetic attraction that allows what we produce to cohere, a connective force composed of energized threads humming, buzzing, and vibrating between the fragments we've strained to arrange.

Understanding the way trauma infiltrates and binds our creative endeavors, Black creative work, if it is "wake work," should and must purposefully, imaginatively, and unimaginably "care" for the physical, psychological, and metaphysical well-being of Black folk who do and encounter this work. In terms of the literary at least, this is a demand to caringly narrate Blackness, for which narrative is somewhere along the spectrum between impossible and antithetical. With, in defense of, and *for* the variously dead and dying, this would be Black literature that channels the force of untimely trauma toward ordinary notes of care; this would be a Black literature that is the textual and aesthetic conduit of deathly and untimely force, for the sake of the unimaginable, disturbing, and caring aspiration(s) of Black folk.

Literature that might operate as a conduit for performing "wake work" must engage the untimely persistence and repetition of trauma, which suggests that we will benefit from an examination of the mechanics of Black

---

23. This line of thinking will heavily inform our reading of *Beloved*. It also represents a serious departure from much of the scholarship I have encountered that reads *Beloved*, as that scholarship tends to hold the novel as a story that represents an overcoming of or resilience in response to trauma. We take as principle the way trauma animates creation without leaping toward ideas of resilience, recuperation, and redemption.

memory in relation to trauma. Let us consider memory as a means of bearing, hyperbolizing, and even materializing trauma; memory as an example and product of untime, and a consequence of the way untime collapses the past, present, and future. Literature that might also create untimely spacetimes, "worlds," or "universes" must do so in a way that relentlessly channels the force of trauma—that takes the leap into trauma rather than flies from it.

This section of the book will work through Toni Morrison's work: her magnum opus, *Beloved*, as well as her Nobel Prize lecture. These works explore memory, forgetting, and trauma and provide insight into the capacities and limitations of language to embolden what is essential and nourishing about encounters with remembered and forgotten trauma. This section will also move through Kiese Laymon's *Long Division* in relation to his essay on Trayvon Martin, love, and reason to explore questions about what an "untimely universe" might look like if explicitly driven by an "unreasonable," unimaginable love, or desire to love, Black folk.

In orbit, we return to the opening set of questions, having traveled a revolution around the abyss they telegraph. A journey toward the unknown of nowhere demands copious preparation, or at least a decent map with some semblance of a key. With aspirations of love in the untimeliness of death, and our work never finished, we must go deeper into the dark. There is no rest or shelter here, and our imaginations have yet to save us.

V

Of Shadows and Diamonds

WITH A careful attention to the way trauma asserts and reasserts itself in the psyches of the traumatically Black and Blackly traumatized, Toni Morrison tears rifts to untimely universes where and when we might imagine how trauma positions us and what trauma might teach us. Differently put, Morrison's novels generally, and *Beloved* specifically, are cartographies of the kinds of ways trauma and Blackness entangle.[1]

Memory Fragment
On the first and second-to-last days of my "The Black Fantastic" course, my students and I task ourselves with collectively meditating on the mechanics, stakes,

---

1. I want to elaborate upon the acknowledgment I made in the introduction regarding the ample collection of writing about Toni Morrison's *Beloved*. Based on the assumptive logic and generally accepted claims shared by much of that writing, I deliberately chose very different academic guides to help us wade through the beautiful difficulties of Morrison's novel. I have determined that engagements with this material will send us on detours that will only distract from the *specific* reading I will perform of the novel from what is and has been a primarily Afropessimistic framework. I am also uninterested in sustaining individual critiques of scholarship that did not ground this analysis as the goal here isn't to be polemical with regard to any supposed canon of Morrison scholarship, but instead to offer unique insights from an alternative perspective in a way that advances *this* project toward its central goals regarding Black time, space, and creation. Several of the works are categorized by the kinds of readings I interpret them to be, and are listed in the introduction's footnotes.

and aims of Black speculative work—literature specifically, but our concerns extended from street to page. We think carefully about the extremes of imaginative invention that gave the Black speculative work we encountered its "speculative" name and qualities. For guidance, we turn to the sagacious Toni Morrison and searing Saidiya Hartman, and we spend the class period and assigned readings pondering the nature of invention.

In fall 2014, Toni Morrison read her 1987 novel, *Beloved*, for the first time.[2] The novel is a multiplied entanglement of historical and imaginative temporalities: Moments in time knot together, history's strings intertwining with the narrative threads of Morrison's imaginative invention. One segment of *Beloved*'s entanglement spans the thread of Margaret Garner's fate. The fragments of archival information about Margaret Garner are the originary material from which Morrison began stitching together the story that would become *Beloved*. In an office at Alfred A. Knopf, Morrison's longtime publisher, she spoke of her amazement with the horror of Margaret's story after coming across it in a magazine from the Reconstruction era.

A slave from the pre–Civil War era, Margaret fled from Maplewood, a plantation in Boone County, Kentucky, pregnant with a daughter, in a party consisting of her husband, Robert, her children, and other relatives. Once the group reached the home of Margaret's uncle in Cincinnati, the party disbanded, and Margaret, her children, and her husband remained while the other slaves escaped to Canada via the Underground Railroad. The Garners, awaiting movement to a safe house outside the city, were discovered by US Marshals and slavers, and attacked. Robert attempted to return fire, and Margaret, refusing to return her children to slavery and its horrors, killed her two-year-old daughter with a butcher knife and wounded the others, preparing to kill them as well. In Morrison's novel, Garner's story pauses in time here. Morrison does not wish to adhere to the historical narrative beyond this point. She leaves Garner in temporal stasis as a means to be generative, the orders of physical and social death tearing an opening into a void that calls for creative invention:

> I really wanted to *invent* her life. I had a few things. The sex of the children, how many there were, and the fact that she succeeded in cutting the throat

---

2. In a 2014 interview with Stephen Colbert on *The Colbert Report*, she claimed she'd only read *Beloved* for the first time weeks earlier, and had only done so by chance—someone mailed her a copy to autograph, and in the process, she read the text.

of one and that she was about to bash another one's head up against the wall when someone stopped her. The rest was novel writing.[3]

Morrison's desire to "invent" life for Margaret Garner aspires for a fiction that might fill in the void created, sustained, and widened by the traumatizing violence of the moment (of Margaret Garner's historical situation) and of the archive (that limits what can be accessed by imaginations). In the wake of the destructive force of the "afterlife of slavery," in the rift, Morrison "invents" the second segment of the string, the "narrative" time of Sethe as a temporal echo created by Morrison, as the product of a process haunted by Margaret Garner's story.

Memory Fragment
My students and I pause at imaginative "invention." The language floats, suspended in the air.

We need to examine Morrison's recourse to imaginative invention in relation to the fact of historical (and political-ontological) destruction or incompletion, and we can do so through Saidiya Hartman's vision. We will pivot between Morrison and Hartman, conjuring a conversation between them, across genre, time, and medium. These nodal points form a circuit of thought about the limits of Black invention when untime, trauma, and language are our primary materials. Walking with them through their somewhat conflicting ideas about what we can and should do with these materials will allow us to build a bit more of our own theory about the stakes, mechanics, and aims of Black creative work, given the available materials and ongoing conditions. To devise a working sense of what we can or should do with or make of the fragments around us and what they reveal, we must unpack what "invention" means and how it works; as always, we worry about the mechanics and stakes.

In "Venus in Two Acts," Hartman writes honestly about the desire to "invent" from or with the ongoing history of anti-Blackness, and the problems that such desire, and any subsequent invention, reveal and create. Venus is a ghostly presence in the archive—offered as a glimpse of enslavement—who is captured only in death, "as a *dead girl* in a legal indictment against a slave ship captain tried for the murder of two negro girls."[4] Countless Black girls and women—"hundreds of thousands,"[5] Hartman writes, but

---

3. Toni Morrison qtd. in Darling, Marsha J. Tyson; emphasis mine.
4. Saidiya Hartman, "Venus in Two Acts," *Small Axe* 12, no. 2 (2008): 1.
5. Ibid., 2.

we know the horror of the likelihood of underestimation—share her "name," and share the consequences of losing their "proper names"[6] to Blackness and time. The various Venuses do not have "stories" of their own, only stories in orbit of them; for them, narrative is impossible. They are glimpsed in the periphery of "the violence, excess, mendacity, and reason that seized hold of their lives, transformed them into commodities and corpses, and identified them with names tossed-off as insults and crass jokes."[7] Their "name," which is an insult, and really signifies being violently unnamed, displaces them from the center of the "narrative" of history, relegating them to the margins of time. Their story is untimely, a "death sentence" and a "tomb" that both kills ("over and over again"[8]) and suspends the dead in place.

Hartman wants to "save" this incarnation of Venus, to detail and resolve her vague and unresolved death; she desires to flesh out the ghosts that haunt the elisions and fictions of the archive. But if to even "read the archive is to enter a mortuary,"[9] to enter its deathly, deadly untimeliness where "the unimaginable assumes the guise of [the] everyday,"[10] what might, or even can, we imagine to, to whatever degree, give "life" to the unimaginable dead? Slavery shatters time's relation to Blackness and unnamed Black folk. Untime deadens history, demarcating the boundaries set by Black bondage, rendering "newness" and so invention similarly unimaginable, unthinkable, impossible. What Hartman wants to imagine—and I imagine, what my students, what all of us, want to imagine—"a free state,"[11] a spacetime "for mourning where it is prohibited,"[12] is impossible.

The methods of available discourse (academic or otherwise), the symbolic order that sanctions them, and the imaginations that struggle to read and invent in relation to the archive deny us access to the "conditional temporality," the time of "what could have been." Retrieval and redress, whether in finding the names or reviving the dead or giving voice and sound to the silenced, is impossible. There is no way to breathe life back into the dead killed by the moment and the archive. Thus, the questions become more "menacing and unbearable":[13] Is there a way to be made (even out of no way)—rather, is defending, caring for, comforting, and tending to

---

6. Spillers, "Mama's Baby, Papa's Maybe," 75.
7. Hartman, "Venus in Two Acts," 2.
8. Spillers, "Mama's Baby, Papa's Maybe," 68.
9. Hartman, "Venus in Two Acts," 4.
10. Ibid., 6.
11. Ibid., 11.
12. Ibid., 8.
13. Wilderson, *Red, White, and Black*, 41.

the dead impossible, too? What might it mean, how, and why, to write or "tell impossible stories,"[14] then?

Memory Fragment
I see my students' faces. Some dejected; some confused. All eyes lost in thought.

If we keep moving with Hartman through her thinking here, to write or tell impossible stories is to "(strain) against the limits of the archive . . . and, at the same *time, (to enact)* the impossibility" bound to it; further, it is to "*amplify* the impossibility of the telling."[15] To do this requires "narrative restraint, the refusal to fill in the gaps and provide closure," as well as an ability to play with and rearrange "the basic elements of the story, by re-presenting the sequence of events."[16] To do this demands a recognition of the position of Blackness in time, as untimely, and an ability, or at least a desire, to amplify the defunct relation between Blackness and time by playing with it. Invention under these constraints plays with what is by testing and clarifying the violence of the boundaries set by enslavement in order to imagine, from this position, what could have been and what could be. In other words, the imaginative work it performs and produces ventures to cross the event horizon into the abyss, seeking to work with and through destruction, and reckoning with not only the inevitability but the possible utility of the destructive force that gravitationally calls to and positions us. What Hartman desires to do (and very likely, what we as Black folk desire to do)—fill in the blanks, recover the lost, "breathe," and "breathe life into" the dead—stands in relation to the "ethical responsibility" we bear to venture into the absences and screams of the archive, to read the absences, the fragments and the screams as they are, *and to amplify their status as absences, fragments, and screams.*

Before we turn back to Morrison, we should pause to consider how this amplification should work. This language is key in Hartman's insight, but it is not wholly clear *how* it plays out in the "playing with" and "rearranging" fragments Hartman describes. We must ask ourselves how playing and amplifying—if the two are synonymous or, at least, entangled with one another—with fragments happen in the mechanical sense: How does one amplify a silence, wholly behold and hold a fragment, or articulate a scream? What kind of play would not only accept the absolute quiet of silence, the brokenness of fragments, and the unintelligibility of screams,

---

14. Hartman, "Venus in Two Acts," 10.
15. Ibid., 11; emphasis mine.
16. Ibid.

but enhance them such that their meaning, or their failure to mean anything (anything we could articulate in language, anyway), becomes clearer? And what does amplification sound or look like when we think of aspiration as Black breath-as-disturbance—by what means does one play with or amplify that disturbance? Finally, what is "amplification" in the first place—rather, what resonances does it have with other terms that may clarify its mechanics; is amplification akin to magnification and enhancement, the disturbance of particles in the air made more potent? And if it is, is that the production of a clarification of what the silences, fragmented utterances, and screams enunciate—because the volume's just a bit louder, or just loud enough, and we hear more clearly? Or is it amplification to the point of total distortion—because the volume's gone up too loudly and we can no longer hear anything other than the chaos of the noise? Or is it not "or" but "and," and to what end?[17]

Perhaps a clue in Hartman's language is the word "play." In 1992, sixteen years prior to Hartman, Toni Morrison thinks in ink about Black imaginative invention in *Playing in the Dark*. The "blank darkness"[18] Black objects collectively and individually create locates a vast opening, ready to be filled with the metaphysical, psychic, spiritual, corporeal, and limitless whims of non-Black imaginative invention—what Morrison calls "play," an inventive, pleasurable mastery. There are two orders of play, bound to the same darkness, one of masters writing themselves into life and light, and one of slaves writing themselves deeper into the dark to better understand the fullness of its depths and death. Does the latter hold the dangers of the first? Do we threaten the dead with new orders of violence when we spend time looking at and searching for them? These are questions that appear to haunt the relations between Blackness, narrative, and fiction that Douglass and Wilderson touch upon in their call for a Black metaphysics, and that haunt this writing as it ventures deeper into the void.

Unlike the play of masters that seeks to construct "a history and a context for whites by positing history-lessness and context-lessness for blacks,"[19] play that creates untimely stories for Black folk in order to make time for the human, the play Hartman seeks must not play with the dead in the same

---

17. In a different but resonant way, Marilyn Sanders Mobley affirms the importance of these questions from afar with a line from her essay "A Different Remembering: Memory, History, and Meaning in Toni Morrison's *Beloved*," which reads, "Each of their fragments amplifies or modifies Sethe's narrative for the reader" (21). We will return to her thought as an important jumping-off point in the outro to this project.

18. Morrison, *Playing in the Dark* (New York: Vintage, 1993), 38.

19. Morrison, *Playing in the Dark*, 53.

way. It must not *make* corpses by disappearing Black beings to the fictions and annihilating forces of history, and then dismember those corpses and all their defining features to distribute their parts to wherever and whenever they happen to be needed—a name mentioned here or there, a character removed from the plot then or whenever, a set of teeth in George Washington's mouth, an arm or a leg or a penis or a breast severed, a husk emptied of its soul and humanity so it can be stretched into the right canvas for all sorts of texts. Instead, this is a kind of play that plays with and within "narrative restraint," that chooses to recognize that it must remain coated in the ink of reality and the timeless horrors of its names and stories in order to imagine the impossible. In our analysis, playing in the dark this way is creative only insofar as it might make a way *to* what lurks in the Black hole that continues to threaten us with total annihilation.[20]

Memory Fragment
Weeks pass and their breathing has shifted.

In an assigned blog post posted to their procedurally updated course blog prior to beginning Beloved, *a student writes extensively about playing a video game called* Limbo. *A haunting outing by suitably named studio Playdead,* Limbo *tasks players with traversing levels and solving puzzles as a young boy searching for his missing sister. Absent motive, context, dialogue, and music, and with only the most minimalistic control scheme (there are only three button controls for "move," "jump," and "action"), the game's narrative and mechanics act like silhouettes or vague outlines or "shadows" that must be "filled in" by the player's own imagination. This parallels the remarkable aesthetics of the game: The game is a two-dimensional side-scroller composed only of grayscale backgrounds, characters, and objects; the "nameless boy" protagonist of the game, the grotesque spider that chases him through parts of* Limbo's *forest, and the few other people the player encounters throughout the game are best described as shadows or silhouettes with small, white eyes.*

---

20. Something to consider here is the difference in discipline and identification between Morrison and Hartman and how one could read into that distinction as a way of drawing some sort of line between the kinds of play one does as opposed to the other, Morrison being a novelist and Hartman being a historian. I think it's more generative to think of them as doing heavily overlapping work despite the avowed difference in discipline; collapsing the divide between the inventive narratives of Morrison and the derangement of the fictions of the archive performed by Hartman is useful. In *Speaking in Tongues and Dancing Diaspora*, Mae G. Henderson speaks to the utility of this collapse, remarking that the work of this novelist and historian, when it comes to thinking about historical recovery, "does not differ" (80).

The student wrote about Limbo *as a way of connecting the experience of "playing with the shadows" of the gamescape with Morrison's ideas about playing in and with the dark. As a response to the student's supposition that the player must "fill in the blanks," the shadows signify throughout the game in order to discern the "real" content and course of the game's narrative, the nameless boy's motivations, and the strangely abrupt but moving ending, I only posed a single question: "But remember what we arrived at through Hartman:*

"What might happen if, instead of 'filling in the blanks' as we, Morrison, Hartman, and so many others can admit to wanting *to do—what might happen if we, as a first principle, embraced the namelessness and shadowiness and blankness/blackness of the boy and the game—and, even further, 'amplified' that namelessness, shadowiness, and blankness/blackness?"*[21]

We arrive, sort of, "not quite in a hurry, but losing no time"[22] back in time to Morrison's desire to "invent" or play with Margaret Garner's life from the fragments of her untimely story that have been scattered throughout the archive—the magazine articles, abolitionist periodicals and speeches, hints from Cincinnati's archive, the slave ledger with Garner "accounted for," all things *about* (in orbit of) her but not about *her* (her origins, her "life," who she was—so, her being). We must wonder if *Beloved* is an impossible story that restrains itself from the fantasies of escape or of bursting forth. We must wonder if it seeks to do defensive, caring, and comforting "wake work," or if it performs some other order of violence against the variously dead and dying. Does it amplify impossibility? Does it play in the dark of the unknowable, the unthinkable, and the unimaginable position of Blackness? Might it shed light from the brightness of her desire, and our desires, to save Black babies, girls, women, boys, and men, queer, trans, cis, dis/abled—all Black lives—and reveal something we've yet to spy in or in orbit of the Black (w)hole?

As noted earlier, Beloved and *Beloved* warp time in at least two ways. The first collapses the time between the text, the ghost, and Margaret Gar-

---

21. Two quick points: First, once the semester ended and my brief teaching opportunity at California State University, Dominguez Hills (CSUDH) ended, the blogs and the course page became inaccessible, so I cobbled this together from a few notes I made and from a conversation this student and I had during office hours sometime after their initial post. Second, upon its initial release I played this game as well, which is why I was very interested in parsing out the connection the student made between "playing with shadows" and "playing in the dark." Also, this is a great video game, so if that's your cup of tea and you haven't tried this yet, please do—and make sure to support independent publishers; they are the best.

22. Morrison, *Beloved*, 22.

ner's archival fiction, positioning Margaret as the "haunter" haunting the text. She acts as a ghastly, ghostly reminder of the "actual" horrors of slavery. Margaret's haunting is that of the "afterlife of slavery."[23] The second shares or translates that haunting in to the ghostly flesh of Beloved, who haunts House 124 with the histories she wears in her name and in the flesh, and who simultaneously hides and reveals Margaret Garner's initial haunting:

> I wanted that haunting not to be really a suggestion of being bedeviled by the past, but to have it be incarnate, to have it actually happen that a person enters your world who is in fact—you believe, at any rate—the dead returned, and you get a second chance, a chance to do it right. Of course, you do it wrong again.[24]

The past moves and is sentient, at least like a ghost is sentient: It is the "living," wa(l)king dead, a paradox in at least time, and a direct (and logical) product of the untimeliness of Black folk. In its "new skin, lineless and smooth,"[25] skin that defies age and the ages or, as we might best imagine it, flesh that is timeless, are the stories of "whens" that precede, and so exceed, the boundaries of the experienced present. Written in the "undecipherable hieroglyphics of [her] flesh"[26] are moments passed that are no longer located (just) in the past, but interrupt the present. There is something unsettling in Beloved's very emergence into the world (of the novel, of the reader's or the writer's imagination); Sethe, Paul D, and Denver experience this over and again throughout. The lie of her smoothness and "the newness of her shoes,"[27] the strangeness of her simultaneous oldness and youth, the problem of her aliveness in relation to the shared knowledge of her deadness: She is a disturbance of the illusion of temporal cohesion in and outside House 124, and in and outside the world of the novel. They and we all feel it, and what it shows.

Beloved's conceptualization as a ghost is violent, both in the temporal interruptions it creates, and in its embodiment of the violent untimeliness of Sethe and Margaret Garner (specifically) and slavery (more generally). She is a force of and forced confrontation with the dead. In essence, she is an opportunity to enter the "tomb" of the archive: to in a literal and literary

---

23. Hartman, *Lose Your Mother*, 6.
24. Morrison, in Rothstein, 17.
25. Morrison, *Beloved*, 61.
26. Spillers, "Mama's Baby, Papa's Maybe," 67.
27. Morrison, *Beloved*, 63.

way look death back in the face, to watch it watching us. More than that, she is the terrifying possibility of an engagement with the impossible, "a second chance" at something less or at least other than redemption or renewed life. She is something different than a form of imaginative invention that would save or resuscitate Sethe, Paul D, Denver, or even Beloved, or Margaret, or her children, or us.[28]

Morrison's desire to invent telegraphs an aspiration toward "wake work" that offers not the lie that harms through falsely filled-in blanks, but instead the opportunity to care for, tend to, play with, and defend the dead. If into the mausoleum of the archive, the space and time of death, we go to meditate and play, what words and worlds might emerge in the silence? In lieu of our desire for fantasy and given a second chance, if we do not fantasize away the darkness that occludes what happened to Venus or what Margaret Garner lived through, but instead listen to and work and play with the blanks, what might we make from our endeavors? I think these are the central questions animating Morrison, *Beloved*, and Beloved. With regard to the titular ghost, these questions prime our attention: The reading practice we engage in as we read *Beloved* becomes a search for the ways Beloved speaks to this specific kind of creation with absence, this making from/with fragments and the spaces between the shards. Of particular interest will be how Beloved compels us to think about the mechanics of this kind of creation; Beloved becomes the ghost in the machine of Black creation, and how she catalyzes Black creation will point us toward answers to these key questions the text raises.

Beloved works as a ghostly singularity, attenuating time and simultaneously vacuuming those with whom she interacts into the crushing gravity of

---

28. This point alone stands at odds with several entries in the rich collection of writing about *Beloved*, but some lines from Mae G. Henderson's "Toni Morrison's *Beloved*: Re-Membering the Body as Historical Text" specifically come to mind: "Against these forms of physical, social, and scholarly dismemberment, the act of (re)memory initiates a reconstitutive process in the novel. If dismemberment deconstitutes and fragments the whole, then rememory functions to re-collect, re-assemble, and organize the various discrete and heterogenous parts into a meaningful sequential whole through the process of narrativization" (*Speaking in Tongues*, 84). As these lines and the title of the essay suggest, Henderson reads "rememory," and so Beloved as rememory's catalyst, as being a means toward reconstituting or re-membering the dis(re)membered self. She writes from the premise that *Beloved* and Beloved are recuperative and redemptive, promising through memory the reassembly of broken Black life and temporality. In that vein, Kathleen Marks's reading of *Beloved* in *Toni Morrison's* Beloved *and the Apotropaic Imagination* as having "esemplastic" (read: reconstitutive) power and being "apotropaic" (read: protective; able to deflect misfortune) comes to mind as well. As I have written here, these trains of thought are fundamentally at odds with the ideas of amplifying the fragmented, brokenness of Black being that Hartman and Morrison lead us to consider.

traumatic pasts made present through memory and recollection. Black memory acts as the mechanism with which she performs her (at least imaginative) spaghettification of whoever's in orbit. Hers is a violent intrusion; she is a destructive, untimely Black force encapsulated in the ghostly form of a living-dead memory. Morrison mobilizes in her what she calls "rememory." Sethe meditates on "rememory" early on: "You know. Some things you forget. Other things you never do. But it's not. Places, places are still there. . . . What I remember is a picture floating around out there outside my head. I mean even if I didn't think it, even if I die, the picture of what I did, or knew, or saw, is still out there."[29] Sethe and/or Morrison's rememory stages spatial and temporal collapses (more on the spatial in the Third Arrangement). The time of the "pictures" of other times, summoned with or without thought, in and outside of a living or dead consciousness, persists. It both is and is not of the imagination: It is, in that it depends on the remembered pictures the imagination conjures from the past, whether or not they are actively thought by the one subject to their interruption, and it is not, or at least it is not just of the imagination, as it exists as untimely places "out there outside [her] head . . . not just in [her] rememory, but out there in the *world*."[30] The "place" she once was will always be "out there," undead because "nothing ever dies."[31] Rememories live, timelessly, undead, independent of the one most likely to run and "bump" into their ghastly and ghostly presence.

Beloved moves ghostly as rememory's singularity: the text, and everyone within and outside of it. She moves independent of the will and intents of the consciousness with which she becomes entangled, embodying, or at least sparking the reemergence of, the undead, untimely, and traumatic stories that haunt the residents of House 124. Her force materializes as language: Her presence speaks and she inquires and requests—or demands. Beloved asks Sethe, "Where your diamonds?" and the hardest of the hard crystals buried in her memory emerges. Then the pressure placed on memory in the form of a request/demand: "*Tell* me. . . . *Tell* me your diamonds."[32] In one sense, this is a doubly ocular demand: to show and to bear witness. In another, this is a doubly auditory demand: to tell and to listen to what's told. What must be told, what Sethe "and Baby Suggs had agreed without saying so . . . was unspeakable"—the unspeakableness of what the diamonds hide is itself also unspeakable, or at least unspoken—is an impossible story, with

---

29. Morrison, *Beloved*, 43.
30. Ibid.; emphasis mine.
31. Ibid., 44.
32. Ibid., 69.

its "hurt that's always there,"[33] its untimely hurt. Against Beloved's demand for the impossible, there is Sethe's resistance to the pain of telling, of traveling in time to revisit, converse with, and tell about the impossibly painful, and the unimaginably shameful. Beloved is seeing/showing and listening/telling demand to feel what breaks them and us through broken time: a story of birth (Sethe's) and death (countless other infants, *"without names,"*[34] thrown overboard) forcibly reborn, and all the blood and pain to go with it.

> *Memory Fragment*
> "Are the diamonds blue?" A glint flashes across Taylor's eyes as she asks. She cranes, looks left and right to her eight remaining peers, and her gaze glitters with obvious intent. "Blue diamonds. Like Ursa's songs. Making demands. Hiding pain."
>
> "Her voice was hard, too, right?" Alexis reads the lede that can't be buried, "Diamonds are the hardest material, right? So that makes sense."
>
> "Yeah, I think that's what I'm getting at, like, how Ursa's demands and Beloved's demands are both from trauma and violence, how they're both Black women, and how they're both trying to show you something but also not trying to show you something."
>
> "So are the diamonds, like, Ursa's screaming, then? What kinds of . . . jewels scream?"
>
> "Blue ones, I guess."[35]

Beloved performs (dances) this seeing/showing, listening/telling demand to feel without questions with Denver. The double demand: *"Tell me. . . . Tell* me how Sethe made you in the boat."[36] Another birthing reborn; another story of (pro)creation—of "making generations," so Ursa comes to mind here—of flesh, blood, bone, with a name. In Denver's mind: "Denver spoke, Beloved listened, and the two did the best they could to create

---

33. Ibid.
34. Ibid., 74.
35. This is a moment from the first literature course I ever taught, which was at Brown University during my graduate studies. Strangely, given campus demographics and attendance on the first day of class, my "Dark Matter: 20th and 21st Century Black Literature" course was home to nine Black students (after two weeks of students shopping and dropping the course based on its apparent difficulty). We read *Beloved* as the last book in this course, and we read *Corregidora* as the first. This discussion was toward the end of the course and, while not verbatim, is as closely adapted as possible from memory.
36. Morrison, *Beloved,* 77.

what really happened, how it really was."[37] To fill in the blanks, or, rather, to uncover what has been concealed and made to look blank—"blank blackness"—becomes an imaginative process. Through and with Beloved, Denver reveals what's there in the dark in this active or enacted process: Denver becomes the conduit for the force Beloved embodies, and she channels this force in the performance of an aspiration for or an attempt at—"did the best they could"—creation, at telling the impossible story. Perhaps it is the effort to perform and the impossibility of performing "well" or "right"—"you do it wrong again." Perhaps there is no do, and only try, when it comes to telling (and perhaps reading, writing, thinking, feeling, and doing) the impossible, or imagining the unimaginable. Perhaps the constitutive impossibility of this work done in the wake of many layers of trauma necessitates a ceaseless search, an endless attempt, an inevitably inadequate form of creation all for the sake of this engagement with untime and its archival secrets, without end or ends.

At the nexus of mind and body—rather, of imagination and flesh, rememory performs. Beyond the imagination, what Beloved "begins" (which is to say ruptures[38]) without end, bleeds out, "out there, in the world," and acts upon the canvas of the flesh just as it does the terrain of the mind. When Sethe closes her eyes and imagines her voice speaking a desire for Baby Suggs's touch, almost at command, familiar fingers lightly begin to caress her neck.[39] The touch Sethe summons—or creatively invents—seems to invert the relation between rememory/Beloved and Sethe (and Denver): Sethe requests, or creates, albeit silently, and rememory, or its ghostly embodiment, performs accordingly. She feels the sudden collapse of time in the familiar touch and crosses into memories of when "124 was alive," venturing into a dark sphere of time where she might find and look in the face of that "life."

But before long, the perils of wielding, or trying to wield, rememory's force in the name of imaginative creation or excavation, are felt: What appears to be the spirit of Baby Suggs begins to strangle her.[40] Rememory becomes unfamiliar; perhaps Sethe looked too long into the face of death, lingered too long in her memory's archival tomb. Perhaps there is a way to wield rememory that avoids suffering another deathly fate. Perhaps not.

---

37. Ibid., 92.
38. See Spillers, "Mama's Baby, Papa's Maybe," 68.
39. Morrison, *Beloved*, 112.
40. Ibid., 113.

Perhaps the question is "How often does one touch a ghost?"[41] and also "How long is too long to touch one when one does?" How would she or we know but by peril of trying? This imaginative work through the impossibility of healing that we are called to do paradoxically appears to necessitate endangering the imagination and the flesh to do so.

Trying and failing to decipher Sethe's bruised flesh in the aftermath will yield us insights precisely because we cannot easily read it. The incomplete strangulation leaves bruises that tell something of the dangers of this deathly form of imaginative creation, but the hieroglyphics of those bruises remain undecipherable beyond the event that wrote them. They tell a story only of the violence and the terror that produced them, but they cannot be translated or achieve legibility because "how," let alone "how often," does one "speak one's grammar" or to it? More terrifyingly, these markings—and all the others, the tattoos, the scars, the brands, the dips and folds where lost flesh could not have hoped to heal, and the bruises—help us consider the way rememory sticks to and indelibly marks the flesh. Hartman speaks to this, and I quote her at length:

> In this case, these traces of memory function in a manner akin to a phantom limb, in that what is felt is no longer there. It is a sentient recollection of connectedness experienced at the site of rupture, where the very consciousness of disconnectedness acts as mode of testimony and memory. The recognition of loss is a crucial element in redressing the breach introduced by slavery. This recognition entails a remembering of the pained body, not by way of a simulated wholeness but precisely though the recognition of the amputated body in its amputatedness, in the insistent recognition of the violated body as human flesh, in the cognition of its needs, and in the anticipation of liberty. In other words, it is the ravished body that holds out the possibility of restitution. . . . [W]hat is precisely at stake is the *body* of memory. . . . Breach triggers memory, and the enormity of the breach perhaps suggests that it can be neither reconciled nor repaired.[42]

The crises in time to which we gain access by way of rememory appear in traces on the flesh, so that Black time, rememory, broken flesh, shattered being, and the ceaseless undeadness of them all refigure Black flesh as timebearer. Borne on the ruptured flesh are the ruptures in time that manifest as corporeal and imaginative memories through which untime appears and

---

41. Wilderson, "Grammar and Ghosts: The Performative Limits of African Freedom," *Theatre Survey* 50, no. 1 (2009): 86.

42. Hartman, *Scenes of Subjection*, 74–76.

can be entered.[43] Performing rememory, and the violent time travel it promises, is to endanger oneself and one's community of the variously dead and dying, with the hope of caring for, defending, comforting, and tending to them, in imaginative memory, and in memory made flesh—broken memory in the broken flesh.

Recalling how Beloved triggered Sethe's "rememory" specifically—"Tell me your diamonds"—we encounter yet another peculiar, seemingly contradictory conceptualization: Black memory, if it can best be thought of in terms of rememory, is constitutively and irreconcilably broken, but Morrison selects the absolute hardness and preciousness of diamonds to symbolize the first materialization of the concept. As in this novel's staged encounters with the ghostly embodiment of slavery's ceaseless trauma, the untimely force of anti-Blackness operates such that not even the hardest hardness[44] of diamonds can resist the multiple and repeated orders of breaking that come with initial and repeated encounters with that trauma. That force might best be thought of as an overwhelming pressure, powerful enough to sever the powerful bonds forming the complex crystal lattice and fracture the structure of both the resonance (the traumatic memory scattered in "bits and pieces") and the imaginative, physical, and metaphysical relation to it (the capacity and desire to recall/reengage the trauma).

The diamonds that characterize the singularity of the trauma suggest that what's going to be told is a set of glittering fragments, refractory and precious, but broken and disorienting in the trauma(s) they crystalize. Recalling Douglass and Wilderson's reading of my reading of the opening passages of "The Fact of Blackness," this feels Fanonian, and Morrison's symbolism adds to the infinite horror of Fanon's recollection-cum-breaking-over-and-over-again a terrible preciousness and a strange hardness in order to explore what Black trauma might look like. And it also brings to mind the work of M. NourbeSe Philip (her most profound work, *Zong!*, partly the

---

43. There is a doubleness to this word, "entered," that can be felt and understood by recalling, or returning to, the first chapter's analysis of Ursa and her "black hole."

44. Hardness can be thought of in terms of scientific measurements: Scratch hardness (along the Mohs scale), indentation hardness, and rebound hardness (also known as dynamic hardness). While in recent years, diamond has been usurped in its status as "hardest known material" by a growing list of "ultra-hard" materials (e.g., Fullerite), at the time of Morrison's writing, diamond persisted in most discourse, for all intents and purposes, as the pinnacle of hardness. And, to date, the actual utility of ultra-hard materials remains difficult to measure due to manufacturing problems, specifically with the extreme pressures and temperatures required to make even small quantities of the material, though this is likely to change as scientists pursue alternative methods. At least in the realm of the symbolic, the absolute hardness diamonds telegraph remains unchanged.

inspiration for Sharpe's questions about "wake work," will be central to our discussion in the outro), namely, "Fugues, Fragments, and Fissures—A Work in Progress," which thinks, in fragments, about the unwieldy entanglement between memory and forgetting.

Philip organizes the essay into a series of journal entries, anecdotes, readings, lyrics, and lists of thoughts; her words compose a careful and sporadic meditation on the way memory is bound to forgetting, "w/holeness" to fragments. She considers the paradoxical way Black "w/holeness exists in the fragments,"[45] and the way Black "memory carries within it forgetting."[46] In her thinking, "the fragment is both/and: containing the w/hole while being at the same time a part of the w/hole—it compels us to see both the w/hole and the hole; impulse to memory and impulse to amnesia."[47] The fragment cannot be "static," even if its presence is constant. It moves and moves us, spurring imaginative movement toward the fissure where memory and forgetting/amnesia collide. It is this spurring toward the latter that is the "fugue" state of being, characterized as a potential flight from physical and/or imaginative space and time to elsewhere/when. This "fugue" state is akin to wandering into the depths and deaths of the fissure, the "tear in the world," that searches the fragment for w/holeness, and searches for fragments to explore.

How might we look into the Beloved eyes of death if we cannot, or not wholly, remember? If the "nation state can be described as a fugue state,"[48] if reality, and so time as a feature of reality, can be described as fugal states created by "the amnesia generated by slavery and colonialism,"[49] then how to explore the fissure if we cannot remember, or if memory and forgetting are constitutive to one another? Which is to say, if rememory might be tooled as a guide into the archive of the Black w/hole, how might we confront the "beginnings" and legacies of enslavement, the multifaceted and catastrophic traumas that ruptured all of time and collapsed fragments with wholeness, remembering with forgetting? How might we take this echo of Ursa's call to leap into the black (w)hole, and leap into what might be the "site of bottomless terror"[50] at the nexus of memory and forgetting? Philip suggests

---

45. M. NourbeSe Philip, "Fugues, Fragments, and Fissures—A Work in Progress," *Anthurium: A Caribbean Studies Journal* 3, no. 2 (2005): 3.

46. Ibid., 5.

47. Ibid., 6.

48. Ibid.

49. Ibid., 9.

50. Rebecca Ferguson, "History, Memory, and Language in Toni Morrison's *Beloved*," in *Contemporary American Women Writers: Gender, Class, Ethnicity*, edited by Lois Parkinson Zamora (New York: Longman, 1998), 164.

wandering in search of fragments: "And one of the ways to confront it is through memory—the *memory fragment.*"[51] This is a performance of broken memory, "the jazz of memory" that "riffs on absences and gaps" in order to "weave from a fragment"—or a collection of fragments—"a whole";[52] this is a broken memory that must move creatively, or move into creation (read: invention), that must "live," or at least be envisioned as "sentient." A correction, then: This is not a performance *of* memory, but a performance *with* a "living," or undying, untimely, and broken memory.[53]

In a journal entry from 2004, Philip allows us to visualize this search for fragments. At length:

Fragment

Journal—January 2004

I walk the beach almost every day—as is my custom I collect shells—if I manage not to pick up one then I can walk without picking up any—having picked up that first shell, or pebble, or piece of smoothed glass, I am then condemned to keep picking them up. . . . I find the fragments of shell more beautiful than the whole ones and today, reading a book on shells of the Caribbean, and again on the beach, am aware of preferring the broken ones and liking the challenge of trying to figure out the identity of the shell from the fragment.[54]

On the one hand, Philip's "quest" for fragments is the consequence of a condemnation to the necessity of at least a continuous searching; once the search begins, it must continue, with or without a foreseeable end. The work, or the play, of the search is essential. On the other hand, the search can be characterized as a search for beauty—or, rather, as inherently beautiful in its hope for multiple or repeated encounters with the broken; in fact, it might be even more beautiful than the presence or promise of an encounter with some prior or forthcoming wholeness. "Rememorial" encounters with the fragments of traumatic events produce a litany of questions that Philip articulates for and with us: "*–can fragments be an organizing principle . . . ? –how much of a shell can be lost before it is no longer a shell? –when does the fragment cease being a part of the w/hole? To become its own w/hole?*" What

---

51. Ibid., 7; emphasis mine.
52. Ibid., 4.
53. I think this characterization of rememory as broken memory really resonates with Rebecca Ferguson's thinking in "History, Memory, and Language in Toni Morrison's *Beloved.*" Unlike much of the writing about *Beloved,* Ferguson centers destruction in place of reconstruction or recuperation in ways that better parallel what we're thinking about here.
54. Ibid., 2–3.

we can take from her questions is that the search for fragments might be a search for w/holes, and that these w/holes might best be thought of as distinct in their own right, a departure from the privilege placed on the singular, restorative wholeness (e.g., "diamond") that Hartman challenges in her essay, and a recognition of the distinct wholeness of individual fragments ("diamonds"). Working with fragments in this fashion means trying to work with the wholeness of a fragment, a fragment in the totality of its fragmentness: the limited but open content of the fragment, the absences signaled by the jagged edges and incomplete utterances, and the circumstances of their breaking altogether try to show us what we need to see, and so are worthy in and of themselves of her search and our work.

Telling impossible stories demands that we reckon with impossibility. Philip's work recalls our engagement with Hartman's essay on "Venus," crystalizing some of the features and clarifying some of the conditions of possibility of how we might be able to create with absence, silence, lapse, loss, and the other irreparable forms of breaking that force us to do work that seems to be impossible. Placing Philip and Hartman alongside each other alters the demands imposed upon us as impossible storytellers, as creators who work with fragments. In terms of the archive, in terms of memory and forgetting, and in terms of imaginative creation, we are called to work with and through the absences, the silences and the fragments as they are. In the tomb of the archive, on the edge of a beach, or in the presence of ghosts, doing "wake work" in the form of imaginative invention must wholly attend to the fragments—of shells, of diamonds, of existences—as fragments. Philip extends Hartman's claims into the questions she poses, pondering what our work might look like if reckoning with silences, absences, and fragments as they are means of treating these "holes" as "wholes." The fragments of the shells and the fragments of the diamond become shells and diamonds in their own right. They are at once the pieces of an irretrievable and unknowable whole, and also a set of wholes arranged by the force of untimely trauma that produced and reproduces them; what defines the set as such is the spectral force that transmuted a singular wholeness into an arrangement of dispersed wholes. This affirms what we have done thus far and how we have built our work: We began in search of fragments of Black life and death that called out to us, searching to hold and behold them wholly *as* fragments, as *whole fragments*.

But if fragments/wholes can or should be our "organizing principle," a symbolic order or grammar for how we understand our untimely relation to the trauma of being Black/Black nonbeing, I think it's important to examine their structure to better understand how they might work and be made to work for us, and what imaginative invention or work a fragment-framework might make possible. Returning to our examination of the physical and symbolic properties of Sethe's diamonds will prove useful here. Specifically, the interaction between Sethe's diamonds and the force of trauma they interact with might be illuminated by a discussion of the highly refractive quality of diamonds.

Diamonds have a very high refractive index, a ratio that describes the relation between the speed of light, or any kind of radiation, as it moves in the vacuum (the space/air outside the diamond) versus the phase velocity of light in the media with which it interacts (the diamond's internal lattice). The incident light that comes into contact with the diamond's surface will refract inside and travel throughout the lattice via a series of internal reflections that will eventually direct the light back out of a different surface of the diamond. With such a high refractive index, this could result in a phenomenon known as "total internal reflection." For total internal reflection to occur, the incident light must strike the surface of the medium (diamond) at an angle that exceeds the diamond's "critical angle." If it does, the light totally (as opposed to partially) reflects internally, reflecting repeatedly throughout the medium, instead of passing through to the other side uninterrupted, or at a slight angle. This, in addition to the diamond's cut, determines the diamond's brilliance, or radiance.

If we understand Morrison to be symbolically telegraphing Sethe's past trauma through diamonds as a force, and if we understand this to position the diamonds as conduits that channel the waves or particles of this force, then our questions become ones about the optics of refraction. How, how much, and how well do the fragments of trauma—the peculiarly horrifying splashes infants make when flung into the water, the smell of blood in the freshness of open air, the fact of the namelessness of other babies, the parallel fact of Sethe's name—refract the total and absolute force of the traumatic event?

This is as much a question of radiation and radiance: Given the questions about how these diamonds/fragments play conduit to the force of trauma, what is the quality and character of the energy these fragments radiate? Thinking of this as radiation allows us to question whether or not this energy behaves like particles or like waves (or, as with photons and helium particles, indeterminately like both), and so helps us also consider what's being done with that force as Sethe, Morrison, Douglass, Hartman, Sharpe, Lacy, and the rest of us wield, and seek to wield, it. Reckoning with radiance homes in on the optical because it allows us to think about what these diamonds/fragments render observable to our varied optical systems. We see so that we might (a) consider what is observable in relation to what we see (e.g., Venus as a fragment of a life/time; Margaret Garner dead, underwritten and unthought) and want/hope to see (e.g., Venus and her friend dead, but together, at the bottom of the ocean; Margaret with family members, a backstory, and second chances), and (b) consider the ways the sensory input (e.g., seeing) and output (e.g., writing) that frame our encounters with fragments and trauma transmute into the imaginative invention we do and want to do.

As our work turns on literary analysis and narrative exploration, our medium is language. and our method has been a form of analytic experimentation during which we routinely "plug in" for the many variables that emerge at the intersections of the physical and the literary. Plugging in "language" as the variable for the radiation rememory's fragments produce feels appropriate. Thinking about how language works as what the shattered "diamonds" of our untimely existences reflect, channel, refract, and radiate will be generative: Thinking about how language interacts with the untimeliness of our trauma will give us deeper insight into how this process of radiation works and ultimately influences our creative work. Further, if rememory is a/the form of amplification or play that is necessary to tell the impossible stories we aim to tell, and language functions as the ghost in the machine of rememory/amplification/play, thinking about language should give us insight into the material we should try to play with, how we should play with it, and to what ends we should play with it.

In order to explore language further, we return to Morrison, but at a different location in spacetime. In 1993, Morrison told a story as she accepted her Nobel Prize in Literature, and I retell it anew here: An old, blind wise daughter of slaves lives on the outskirts of town. Despite, or because of, her blindness, she is clairvoyant—sight beyond seeing; a seeing not accountable to conventional understandings of sight. All in town know of her, which is, perhaps, why petulant young folk approach, apparently determined to disprove her ability and wisdom by playing/preying on her physical blindness. One of the group approaches her with a question: Is the bird in his or her hands dead, or alive? Morrison reads the question as one about language—is language dead or alive? If the hands were to unclasp, would they reveal language languid, wings crushed, dead? This is Morrison's Schrödinger's cat—Morrison Blackens Schrödinger's thought experiment into a story, and so an ensemble of questions, all grounded by a fundamental, guiding inquiry: What is the relationship between Blackness, space, time, and language?[55]

---

55. Building from a paper authored by Albert Einstein, in 1935, with Boris Podolsky and Nathan Rosen (commonly referred to as the EPR article), Ervin Schrödinger imagines a thought experiment involving a cat, some poison, a radioactive trigger, and a

The "I don't know"[56] this old, blind, wise daughter of slaves utters marks the young folk's question with an indeterminacy that is both an opening and a closing. The cat-become-bird-become-language occupies its own quantum superposition, the physical system concealed by clasped hands and moist palms—simply, the bird, or language, and the concealed space it occupies— renders it simultaneously alive and dead. This "and" presents a few possibilities: Language is as it reads, both alive and dead, as if "and" shares the same meaning as a plus-sign; or, the bird's status is greater than what we can grasp via addition, this alive-and-dead quantum state being more than can be accounted for by the mere sum of its "alive" or "dead" parts; or, finally, the quantum state, being totally indeterminate, leaves language neither alive nor dead, an unnamable state of flux that can only approach the realities of either life or death, as a limit approaches infinity in calculus, but only achieves one or the other once the hands open and the superposition collapses into one reality. An opening because in any instance, the hands remain closed and these possibilities and their collective indeterminacy remain possible. A closing because in any instance, the hands remain closed and these possibilities remain possible. Both, and so maybe neither, and so maybe more—whatever the case, the shared assumption remains: Not only are the possibilities simultaneously opened and closed by their posing the question, but the cat-become-bird-become-language must be concealed in the young folk's hands. Hence, what she says to the young folk: "But I do know that it is in your hands. It is in your hands."[57]

---

steel chamber. Essentially, the cat is sealed in the steel chamber with an extremely small amount of a radioactive substance that, once it decays—say, it takes an hour or some other measurable amount of time—will trigger a mechanism that will release the poison, killing the cat. Schrödinger suggests that if we understand and take seriously quantum mechanics' ideas about uncertainty, the outcome—whether the cat is dead or alive—is indeterminate until it is observed; the cat is simultaneously dead and alive in the meantime. The cat occupies a quantum superposition, existing in all of its possible theoretical states (dead, alive, or some unimaginable state in between) at once, until measurement or observation (reality) collapses that superposition into one of those states. Schrödinger means to press the limits of quantum mechanics' explanatory power by asking when this collapse occurs, as the implication of the thought experiment seems to suggest that the state of the system is observation-dependent, instead of operating based on the rigidity of prefigured physical laws, whether or not a measurement is taken—an implication both Einstein and Schrödinger vehemently challenged. However, emergent experiments in theoretical physics seem to seek to inhabit the indeterminacy that characterizes Schrödinger's famous thought experiment, so inhabiting this indeterminacy may prove generative.

56. See/listen to Toni Morrison's Nobel Lecture: https://www.nobelprize.org/prizes/literature/1993/morrison/lecture/.

57. Ibid.

But in deeper reflection, Morrison's wise woman thinks about the mechanics of the language and how they transform depending on the answer to the young ones' question, offering us entry into both, how Morrison thinks about language here and across her critical and creative writing, and also how we might frame our reading of language as amplified or amplifiable radiation. Facing the critical question posed by the petulant young folk, the old, wise, blind daughter of slaves (and, in my mind, theoretical physicist) considers the aliveness or deadness of language, and the conditions of possibility and implications for reality of each.

If language is dead, then language also deadens—spreads decay and death. In one sense, it operates from a static, paralyzed position that "actively thwarts intellect, stalls conscience, suppresses human potential," and is wielded to "sanction ignorance and preserve privilege."[58] It is the numbed, inflexible tongue of the subjugated, and the tool wielded by the tongues of the agents of the anti-Black world's systems of domination. "Menace and subjugation" replace language's "nuanced, complex, mid-wifery properties,"[59] killing the potential for intellectual and creative flight—this is the language of mastery. The language of mastery positions Blacks as antithetical to humanity by wielding "powers of distortion" that dismember and mutilate, and that gird not just language's content and expression, but the very grammar (or symbolic order) that organizes it. Blacks, as anti-Humans in the anti-Black world, bear a singularly "abject muteness"[60] in the absence of the "right to name and 'name'"[61] Black existence. In sum, language as the language of mastery, as language that deadens, acts as a recognizable force with recognizable consequences for Black folk and Black creation. And in another sense, language as dead language operates as if it is endlessly dying, as if "'murdered' over and over again," to recall Spillers, and as if subject to the gravity of "deathliness," to recall Marriott. Language, in this collapse of reality, behaves like an unstable particle, inevitably and continuously decaying into other elemental forms.[62] The radiance of language, in this sense,

---

58. Ibid.
59. Ibid.
60. Ronald A. T. Judy, *(Dis)forming the American Canon: African-Arabic Slave Narratives and the Vernacular* (Minneapolis: University of Minnesota Press, 1993), 89.
61. Spillers, "Mama's Baby, Papa's Maybe," 69.
62. Particle decay is the process of one elementary particle becoming other elementary particles, specifically an elementary particle with less mass along with an intermediate particle, the latter of which decays into other elementary particles. If these particles are also unstable, then particle decay can continue. In terms of language, this might begin syntactically: The sentence particle decays into the conjunction particle and the

marks a loss of data or information that decays or reduces toward greater and greater incompletion and incoherence.

If language lives, language's vitality might behave more like waves, which propagate. This is language as a disturbance, moving, or "[arcing] toward the place (and time) where meaning *may* lie."[63] Its incompletion inheres in recognition of the ineffability of what it attempts to telegraph, encode, or explain; "its *force*, its felicity is in its reach *toward* the ineffable." Language's waves approach the infinite, or at least extremely immense, gravitational force marked by the event horizon, and they do so aligned with the uneven power relation between language's explanatory power and the obliterating, untimely force of anti-Blackness that forms its medium. Language surges toward the unknown knowledge that "may" lie beyond the event horizon and at or within the singularity. In this way, "word-work is sublime . . . because it is generative . . . [and]it makes meaning that secures . . . the way in which we are like no other life,"[64] or, in our terms, like no imaginable life at all. Language propagates toward and through the deathliness that warps the time and space of our being, thinking, and inventing, and itself bends into the shape and quality of energy we might wield to create deathly and untimely words and worlds out of nowhere.

Considering both, but professing neither, the old, blind, wise daughter of slaves and quantum theorist leaves the young Black folk (and us) in the indeterminate dark. Language's radiance and language as radiation become uniquely generative in the simultaneous both/and-ness and neither/nor-ness of its aliveness/waviness and deadness/"particulateness." Language as the cumulative product of a decay toward incoherence and a propagation toward destruction and meaning; language as something unimaginable in between the poles of decay and propagation; language as some other unimaginable thing, unimaginably beyond the scope of either decay or propagation—beyond the limits of names and knowledge.

In the story, the indeterminacy tears an opening, a deep silence that, without available fictions, can only be filled with unanswerable (or impossible) questions, demands, and faithful assertions—questions about what constitutes telling and showing, demands to be told and touched, and assertions about the supposedly protective qualities that "only language" possesses. Here, though, reckoning with the peril elemental to encounters with untimely fragments—through rememory, through the archive—described

---

clause particle; the clause particles break down into the punctuation particle and the word particle; the word, into the phoneme and the semantic content; and so on.
63. Morrison, "Nobel Lecture."
64. Ibid.

by Hartman and experienced by Sethe suggests that, at the very least, we must qualify or curb what Morrison suggests here to be language as singularly, but not purely or wholly, protective. In fact, I think we will do well to reframe her reading of "protection" in terms of the nourishment that this imaginative invention, word-work, or wake work in question throughout the entirety of this chapter.

Returning to *Beloved* one last time, submitting to the burgeoning tidal forces of more and more untimely questions, I want to think about what Morrison ultimately suggests we do, having carefully considered the framework and mechanics of our doing. The final pages of the novel dwell in the indeterminacy on which Morrison meditated at a podium six years after *Beloved*'s publication. Of all that happens—of all the plot—it is the ultimate subjection of Sethe, Denver, Paul D, and all in the characters in the novelistic world of *Beloved* to forgetting that might best guide us to the next waypoint. *Beloved* ends with a lamentation about forgetting. Beloved exits House 124 and the lives of those whose trauma she telegraphed, and disappears to casual and deliberate forgetting. Being dis(re)membered, unclaimed, unnamed—her name is forgotten, or never known, or both—and "unaccounted for," Beloved both falls and is willed out of consciousness and the imagination in a way that relegates her to a different kind of ghostliness; she becomes figmentary. For all they know and forget, Beloved might have been purely the product of a collection of imaginative projections; she only voiced "what they themselves were thinking."[65] Her presence fractures like the diamond of a traumatic event/resonance, and the fragments that play conduit to her force—"the rustle of a skirt . . . the knuckles brushing a cheek," the shifting of a photograph looked at too long or too closely[66]—no longer signal the fact or fiction of her existence.

"It was not a story to pass on"—Morrison's refrain becomes an admonition modified by lamentation. Beloved laments being deliberately dis(re)membered, not being passed on. Beloved's "this is not a story to pass on" laments the present tense factuality of this dis(re)membering. And it appears to, if at a distance, admonish this deliberate forgetting as it eliminates even the power and utility of fragments in constructing and (re)imagining the kinds of trauma that form them and form us. The repeated admonition might also suggest that, contrary to the behavior of the characters that encountered Beloved, the language (what Beloved said) and the presence (Beloved's real or imagined existence) telegraphed a set of meanings and

---

65. Morrison, *Beloved*, 324.
66. Ibid.

images—a story—that one should not pass on, not avoid, overlook, pass over, pass up. In those senses, Morrison's narration/narrator really seems to be saying that this story, especially given the dis(re)membering that threatens it with absolute erasure, must be passed on, over time and space, carefully shared, or offered up and forth. This, with the apparent hope that it/this was/is not a story to—that will, at some point—pass on, fade, dissipate, die, or otherwise fall into disarray and disuse.

Morrison might also be warning us not to pass on—share, disseminate, and so forth—this text precisely because of the perils that come with repeated encounters and engagements with the fragments and force of trauma (e.g., Beloved's words, Beloved's factual/fictional presence). The perils of participating in and spreading the encounters/engagements with the trauma(s) of Black nonbeing are, maybe, too great, and so forgetting, as the characters of *Beloved* do, might be our way to ensure the sanctity of our individual and collective consciousness—to ensure that our shadows hold hands,[67] or that our hands transmute love and intent into touch.[68] For example, we encounter a version of this in discussions about repeatedly and uncritically sharing—or sharing at all—the images, videos, and sounds of Black death on social media. Whatever the case, the indeterminacy of the refrain opens us up into a question about what we might do with the arrangements of language and meaning—the structures, stories, that emerge when we channel the however radiant radiation of the fragments we collect, encounter, and take seriously—once we make them. What are they for? If they differently channel the force of trauma that characterizes being Black in an anti-Black cosmos, what do we do with these Black worlds? Are they too dangerous to engage, or to demand that others engage, and in that sense, should they be allowed to pass on or be forgotten? Or are they to be passed on and carefully shared as breath and nourishment? Or, given that indeterminacy generatively founds our journey, what is the shape and scope of impossible, dying, shareable stories, and what are the stakes, potentially dangerous, but dangerously necessary, and, hopefully, necessarily caring storytelling?

Memory Fragment
I scan the faces of my students across time. I see the faces of my students across time. Glint, glitter, and gold arc electric across their eyes. Lost in thought. Every breath a question, taken in, held, held, and then released into wind.

---

67. Ibid., 59.
68. Ibid., 322.

VI

Elliptical in Love Dot Dot Dot

MENACING AND UNBEARABLE, or at least troubling, as these questions might be, we find ourselves returning to the problem of and need for "care," care as theoretical foundation and as crucial praxis. With "care" as our framework, we might ask: What kind of care becomes possible—or, rather, what kind of care is rendered available by the untimely conditions of Black life and death? What we must grapple with is how the untimeliness of Black movement and creation in time allows us to approach what we will describe in this chapter as the "elliptical" problem of our dynamic life/death sentences, and how that elliptical problem appears to transform the available practices and products of the creative Black care work we are ethically responsible to perform.

    This chapter will briefly explore the concept of care and the names and forms it has been given by Kiese Laymon in an article about Trayvon Martin and in his first novel, *Long Division*; by Fred Moten and Stefano Harney in the joint text *Undercommons*; and by Keguro Macharia in his meditation on love. Our aim is to unpack the nature and mechanics of the unruly and unwieldy concept of care that remains tangled with our various threads of thought on Black untimeliness and creation. Our methods will be twofold: synthesis, as we try to build from the essays and scholarship a sense of what care for Black folk might look like, and distension, as we try to mutate or even mutilate what we build to adapt it to our considerations through our reading of Kiese Laymon's novel; reading the novel will put pressure on and push outward from the conceptualization of love we synthesize from Laymon's and Macharia's essays and Harney and Moten's book. Thinking about the way care works will help us understand the ways we perform our care work and sharpen our sense of the ends to which we perform that care work.

Thinking specifically about care, what is at stake in passing on or passing on stories, the *works* and *work*, of Black life and death under these conditions? Concerning care and "Da Art of Storytellin'," what kind of storytelling under these extraordinarily disastrous, untimely conditions, might, as Sharpe puts it, "sound an ordinary note of care?" When we understand that conceptualizing, let alone practicing, care for Black folk across time and space remains nastily entangled with the very conditions that necessitate that care in the first place, how do we understand the nature of the work, or da art, of storytelling? Further, what do we make of what Laymon means when he writes about and returns to "love" throughout his writing?

For Laymon, anti-Black subjection and love are the countervailing but inextricable parts of "our story," the story of all the stories of Black life and death in the wake. In a 2013 essay published by *Colorlines,* Laymon writes about the killing of Trayvon Martin while revisiting a question he posed to his students two weeks before composing the essay, a question aimed back at him by Wilson, one of his students: "How do you want to be loved?" Desire animates the inquiry, aims it. Like his students, Laymon must confront the nature of Black desire. He and they must interrogate what animates that desire—for example, the many catastrophic kinds of "lack" experienced by and imposed upon Black folk around the world that animate unimaginably or impossibly vast desires. He and they must question Black folks' relationship to desire as a construct in a world where desire's capacity for fulfillment depends on one's structural position, which, for Black folks, almost ensures the denial of the most fundamental desires (e.g., for nourishment, for knowledge, for space, for time) or even the smallest wants (e.g., for a bite to eat or sip of drink, for a book to read, for access to a pen or pencil or computer, for room, for "a minute"). And he and they must, menacingly as it might be, dissect their internalization of the anti-Black desires bored into their consciousness: internalizations performed deliberately as a mode of psychic and psychological, and even physical, survival; and also internalizations made accidentally or incidentally as part of the long process of "education" in the wake. All of the conditions that both precipitate in and undermine Black desire for any of a number of forms of love or care operate as part of the logic of the anti-Black world. For Laymon, this logic frames what is thought of as "reason," and so what is considered to be "reasonable" under these conditions. In his framing, the killing of Trayvon Martin, for example, is "reasonable." Against this, Laymon answers: "I want to be loved by an *unreasonable love*."[1]

Unreason animates the love Laymon desires; this unreasonable love—a refrain in the text—"lives" and acts as one name borne by the work of care for "Black life forms."[2] This is an unreasonable love that "refuses to accept . . . the poison of *reasonable* loving, *reasonable* liking, *reasonable* living, *reasonable* essays, *reasonable* art and *reasonable* political discourse,"[3] all of which compose and buttress the symbolic order that makes the killing of Black cis and trans men and women reasonable, that animates the classist, sexist, homophobic, transphobic, ableist, and racist logic that overlays the violent terror of anti-Blackness with reason itself, such that anti-Blackness is not only reasonable but, perhaps, reason itself. Against all reason—in refusal of all that can be thought to be "reasonable" in what Sharpe calls "the sadomasochism of everyday black life"—Laymon desires, and so invokes unreasonable love, love as unreason.

It is an insistent love, insisting on Black creation and community against intramural and structural violence; it is a love that insists on Black existence in the wake, one that embodies a collective insistence of "Black being into the wake."[4] It is an unreasonable love that unreasonably but seriously considers the glimpses of "Black life insisted from death."[5] It is an unreasonable love for all Black folk—all that we make, and all that we are, aren't, or might become—that is peculiar in its entanglement with all the "reasonably loving" features of an anti-Black world, and principled in its absolute refusal of anything less than a complete devotion to the unreasonableness and untimeliness of Blackness. But let us push harder than Laymon does in his conceptualization of how love-as-unreason works in relation to the anti-Blackness-as-reason of the world. Love-as-reason works best as a triptych. Indeed, love refuses the reason(ing) of the world; also, love simultaneously insists upon the Blackness of Black folk against that reason. Beyond Laymon's and Sharpe's language, unreasonable love for Black folk deranges

---

1. See Kiese Laymon, "Kiese Laymon on Trayvon Martin, Black Manhood and Love," *Colorlines*. December 30, 2013. https://www.colorlines.com/articles/kiese-laymon-trayvon-black-manhood-and-love.
2. Sharpe, *In the Wake*, 74. She draws this from the scholarship of Rinaldo Walcott, who coined the phrase.
3. Laymon, "On Trayvon Martin, Black Manhood and Love"; emphasis mine.
4. Sharpe, *In the Wake*, 11.
5. Ibid., 17.

or disorders reason. Just as untime signals a derangement of the order of time for Black folk, unreason, and so love, signals a similar derangement of reason. Less a corrective, and more an amendment, love for Black folk acts as Laymon's refusal of, Sharpe's insistence against, and a more pronounced and destructive derangement of reason.

Even with our amendment to Laymon and Sharpe, we only know love inferentially from what it refuses, what it chooses, and what it does, but we must consider more deeply how love operates and what it is or might be. We turn to another guide of sorts in Keguro Macharia. Macharia's insights in his essay "Love" help us more precisely aim our thinking. More accurately, Macharia offers insight into the way love might best be thought of as, referencing Kenneth Burke, "equipment for living."[6] For Macharia, love embodies an interruption in (or derangement of) "the ostensible distinction between the public and the private, the personal and the social";[7] this is what Macharia describes as a "sociogenic" framing of love, one that operates as an "interface," a mediating force between the "social and the psychic."[8] If it is equipment for living (or if it is unreasonable) and meant to be wielded unreasonably as equipment for Black living (or something like the disorderly insistence of Black life "from" death, something like the disturbance of Black "aspiration"), love operates as a convergence of the psychic and the social, the individual and the structural. This is love as a sociogenic principle, raised, tooled, or even weaponized against the "hygienic," reasonable kinds of love that violently disallow forms of Black creative, intentional care. In Macharia's reading, this means wielding love-as-unreasonable-equipment as "dutiful critique," as a "risk"—of life, of flesh, of possibility—taken in the name of "revolutionary persistence"—and here, we will do well to notice the resonance between "persistence" in Macharia's language and "insistence" in Sharpe and Laymon's.

Taken together, these thinkers offer insight into how love or care can animate the work we aim to do and maybe even "pass on." Through Sharpe's attempt at sounding an insistent, if "ordinary," note of care; Laymon's desire for and commitment to an imaginative, unreasonable love; and Macharia's conceptualization of a sociodiagnostic love, unreasonable love becomes a force, a tool, a machination in our hand. Love looks like the thing in the machine of Black critique and creation, and its capacity to derange inheres in its unreasonable insistence upon the necessity of care for Black folk. Absorbing love into our understanding of the complex work of telling impossible

---

6. Keguro Macharia, "Love," *Critical Ethnic Studies* 1, no. 1 (Spring 2015): 69.
7. Ibid.
8. Ibid., 71.

stories, we recognize that love is bound up with language, amplification, memory, and play; it operates as an essential mechanism in the work of Black creation. It is the tool or weapon that, when wielded, is likely the only way to perform the critical and creative work of caring about, for, with Black folk in the wake. Love, as unreason, as refusal, as insistence, as derangement, is the condition of possibility for wake work, the work of care. Love is nigh indistinguishable, or at least absolutely inextricable, from genuinely (to invoke Jared Sexton),[9] authentically (to invoke Fanon),[10] really-truly (to invoke my mother and grandmother) doing this work, in streets and on pages, in and on and as the relation between two or many more of "us," untimely and unreasonable as that work might be in a world that, horrifyingly, has all the time, and is always so very reasonable.

Even this positioning of love still remains a bit orbital, spiraling the Black (w)hole of what it might be beyond its relation to work or its status as work. The unreason of love for Black folk might be the Beloved/ghost-in-the-machine of work, but we have yet to tether the two concepts together. To build upon this, we will consider more deeply the feel of love through Stefano Harney and Fred Moten's collaborative 2013 work, *Undercommons: Fugitive Planning and Black Study*, through which they introduce the concept of hapticality. Understanding hapticality will help flesh out our still growing understanding of love. In the sixth chapter, entitled "Fantasy in the Hold,"[11] Harney and Moten consider the rise to dominance of "logistics" as the framework under which "work," here written interchangeably with knowledge production, becomes possible, legitimate, and meaningful in a capitalist society.

Put into productive practice, this "capitalist science," which is capitalist reasoning or reason, aspires to achieve the total thoughtlessness and subjectlessness of labor by eliminating the thinking subject from the subject-labor (or laborer-labor) relation. Logistics-as-science-as-reason strives to preempt the possibility of "human time" or "human error"—although, as a corrective, I would theorize that this violent imposition, or replacement, of one

---

9. See footnote 12 of the Introduction.
10. See footnote 53 of chapter 3.
11. This phrase has attained a certain amount of weight in the series of disagreements, often presented as fundamental paradigmatic distinctions, between Afropessimism and what Moten calls Black optimism. While Frank Wilderson wields the phrase to distinguish the reality of captivity and structural subjection embodied by the hold of the ship from the fantasies of escape, retribution, freedom, and life developed and held by the slaves in the hold, Moten reads the capacity to imagine or fantasize as a form, or at least in indication of, life in the hold. The line is fine, but clear, and if it remains unclear, I am more of Wilderson's mind than of Moten's.

temporality with another that is paradigmatically capitalistic or anti-Black is precisely an attempt at creating and generalizing a time that is *only* human time. I would position logistics and the labor it seeks to allow and disallow as reasonable, as human, constitutively against Black untimeliness. Importantly, Harney and Moten trace the origins of logistics in the Atlantic slave trade and recognize its precipitation in very recent history to the histories of slavery, thought by them as a history of the shipping (read: violent dislocation) of (Black) objects across Atlantic, Indian, and Mediterranean waters. To tailor their analysis to ours, the reasonable, human time or timeliness of logistics, of the logic or reason of "shipping," extends itself as an iteration of the afterlife, or the wake, of legal chattel slavery—all its deathly logics, and all its untimely consequences for Black life and death across the *longue durée*.

As I understand it, the work of logistics erases Black life from the equation. Put another way, work under logistics, the work of working Black flesh to death, the worked things or thingliness of work or things that work or don't—the commodities that could not even aspire to be laborers—depends on the total disavowal of Black labor as labor, Black work as work, or, thought differently, of Black work transmuted into functioning Blacks, stripped of the capacities for thought and consideration that might precede, precipitate in, and follow "work," if work is thinking production. This is part of the conditions of what Harney and Moten call "the logisticality of the shipped,"[12] a recognition of the "shippedness" and the "containerization" of Black folks over the course of the long, human time of logistics' proliferation as "capitalist science," and on both sides of the Atlantic, or, as I would prefer to think it, all regions of the cosmos (given both my own framing of the structure-as-universe or structure–as-cosmos, as well as the advent of what appear to be serious plans to colonize Mars and, eventually, inevitably, beyond). On the other side of this recognition, and as an extension of what Moten here and elsewhere characterizes as a "paraontological interplay of blackness and nothingness,"[13] is what Harney and Moten position as a counter-logistical "some/thing"—some fantastic work, some elusive conjuring, some silent uttering, something necessarily broken and lost in the hold of the ship between the dispossessed, between slaves, a glimpse at something like Black "social life" in both the literal and figurative structure of Black social death.

---

12. Stefano Harney and Fred Moten, *The Undercommons: Fugitive Planning and Black Study* (New York: Autonomedia, 2013), 92–97. This is the section entitled "Logisticality, or The Shipped."

13. Ibid., 96.

This thing appears to be hapticality, and it is a feeling. It is the feel. It is the sensation shared among and in the flesh of the dispossessed, the dislocated, the untimely, the denizens of nowhere, we who occupy the hold, who dwell in and as that distance of distances between structures—between the vastness and terror of the world beyond the hold, and the hold itself—who hold on to the absence of a determinate space and time, who are held in and by the immediacy of the feel of being untimely, who "feel through others, a feel for others feeling you."[14] In the flow of the ceaseless moment of the wake, this always yet to come mingling with the always already, we experience, know, and are this "touch," this interiority borne in the glyphs of/on our flesh, against the ruthless, cruel, deliberately arbitrary and arbitrary deliberate denials of the space and time to fully build and evolve the peculiar sentimentality that emerges among the singularly terrorized, the enslaved.

For Harney and Moten, this hapticality is the very "touch of the undercommons." Or, as I interpret their feeling riff, it is the very essence of the gestures toward "study," resistance, movement, and creation that might occur in the hold-as-site-of-social-life. We will do well to push back against this line of thinking because it is particularly optimistic, and the leap toward definitive affirmation, toward the recognition of the elusiveness of this sentiment not only as fact but as gift—"the hold's terrible gift"[15]—and as gift locating the presence of a present and, in their riff, unquestioned feeling "at home with the homeless, at ease with the fugitive, at peace with the pursued, at rest with the ones who consent not to be one" mark a flight toward the poetic that obscures certain fundamental questions elemental to the descriptors of "the feel" they choose here.

We would do well to think about what space Black folk can or would call "home" in the zone of nonbeing—and we do in the next chapter—or to think about what happens when "home" is always a haunted house, like House 124. We would do well to think about what kind of ease remains possible in the troubled time of fugitivity, or of the temporal or spatial distinctions between fugitive flight and innovation and fugitive terror—how do we locate an end to terror and a beginning of ease? Even assuming the cohesion of the relation among fugitive Blacks to remain constant, can it ever really be "ease," then? What of "peace"—when is Black life not in a state of siege or assault from the violent symbolic and material orders of the anti-Black world, the full force of which is mobilized against even the most peace-

---

14. Ibid., 98.
15. Ibid., 97.

ful of Black demonstrations and affirmations: marches, rallies, contesting solely that Black lives (should) matter? How do we understand the quotation marks I wield around the term here, recalling what Spillers says about them? In turn, how do we understand the too-optimistic lack of quotation marks around the terms as they appear in Harney and Moten's riff, as they indicate manifestations of the feel? What happens to hapticality then?

Hapticality as a conceptual name bearing the water of the work and the sentiment of love and/or care for, of, and by Black folk in the wake remains intriguing. Considering more carefully the nature of this guiding feel, this feel in, of, through, and on Black flesh and much more than flesh provides us with a conceptual guiding light to think about the untimely literary and otherwise imaginative worlds, or rather spacetimes, we choose to sculpt, or work, like dough, out of nowhere. Also, we likely decrease our orbital distance from the black, dense singularity of what precisely determines what makes a story that is or is not to be passed on, or felt, or dot dot dot;[16] or what constitutes language's aliveness or deadness as it is in our hands, like water to be borne and born; or what operates behind the "anagrammatical Blackness"[17] that mutilates the grammatical formations—clauses, sentences, punctuation, and all their possible permutations—allowed and disallowed in the grammar of suffering shaping the world's symbolic order in a way that alters the time of the arrangements we call "writing" (pace and arrangement, for example, change when Blackness works with, or deranges, the grammatical possibilities afforded in such an order).

While I repeat that what's in a name (or in a new vocabulary) is certainly not salvation, it does prove useful for thinking about what heeding Ursa's Fanonian call to leap into black hole looks like with and against the demand to make generations. We resist thinking about this as salvation primarily because the language and tone of Harney and Moten's description of the feel of this feeling, hapticality as the name for the sentiment work that wake work might be, or as the essential thing or ghost-in-the-machine—our Beloved machination—proves useful for thinking about what heeding Ursa's call to leap into black hole looks like with and against the demand to make generations. Basically, naming and knowing hapticality offers us a deeper insight into the why and how of the question, "What might we *do*, or how might we *play*, with untimeliness, especially as Black folk aspiring to destroy and create, destroy then create, destroy by creating?," and, I hope, shifts how we think about transmuting untimeliness into "equipment" for

---

16. From Kiese Laymon's *Long Division* (Evanston: Agate Bolden, 2013), throughout, which we will discuss below.

17. See Sharpe, *In the Wake*, "Chapter 3: The Hold."

making imaginary worlds where Black life, dying, and death can appear in careful and cared for ways.

While every work we have engaged and will engage, and many, many works we will not have the time or space to engage (care)fully, would offer us opportunities to explore how love, or care, or hapticality manifests in Black (literary) creation, I would like to return to Kiese Laymon. Specifically, I'd like to reconsider the responsibly unreasonable love he invokes. He describes his first novel, *Long Division*, as a "book about love and intimacy," one that, conjuring hapticality, teaches readers "about love and its relationship *to the touch*"—not of the undercommons, which is indirectly but wholly challenged as a concept in the next chapter, but of the imagined word-worlds carved out of the untimeliness of every moment and of the nowhere that is and is beyond every space we occupy.[18]

Long Division follows two strangely entangled stories about two protagonists, both named Citoyen "City" Coldson, as they explore what it is to love, live, die, make "dynamic sentences," and time travel while Black and country. In the 2013 iteration, fourteen-year-old City becomes a YouTube sensation after his defiant comments during the nationally televised Fifth Annual Can You Use that Word in a Sentence go viral. Before being sent to stay with his grandmother in Melahatchie, Mississippi, where a young Black girl named Baize Shepard recently disappeared, he encounters a book with no author in his principal's office entitled "Long Division." *This* iteration is set in 1985, and it follows City's parallel iteration and Shalaya Clump, the peculiar and beautifully stanky girl he claims to love, as they become Black, Southern time travelers. The pair leap between "the future," where they steal a laptop and cell phone from a Black girl rapper, also named Baize

---

18. A few of the texts that influence my thinking here are rooted in thinking explicitly in considering love, intimacy, and kinship (but that aren't explicitly dissected in this chapter) follow: Joy James's *Seeking the Beloved Community*, specifically the chapters "Politicizing the Spirit," "Black Suffering in Search of the 'Beloved Community,'" and "The Dead Zone"; Kristie Dotson's "Radical Love: Black Philosophy as Deliberate Acts of Inheritance"; Audre Lorde's *Sister Outsider* (New York: Crossing Press, 2007 Reprint Edition), especially the line, "We have to consciously study how to be tender with each other until it becomes a habit" (175); and also Audre Lorde and Pat Parker's *Sister Love: The Letters of Audre Lorde and Pat Parker 1974–1989*, edited by Julie R. Enszer. These texts help seed the questions about Laymon that we explore here. I am also animated by my experiences reading Angela Flournoy's *The Turner House*, Natashia Deón's *Grace*, and Jesmyn Ward's *Sing, Unburied, Sing* because how they compelled me to think about love as act, love as inheritance, love as mourning, and love as hurt cannot be untethered from my thoughts here; I cannot disentangle my critical approach to love as a concept and the conclusions and questions derived from that approach from my experiences reading these novels, despite not critically approaching them in this particular project.

Shepard, and "the past," 1964, where they learn of, witness, and attempt to intervene in the personal histories of anti-Black violence that directly shape their presents. Laymon's metafictional narrative structure, his focus on the importance of sentences and the work of their creation and arrangement, his play with the figure and function of ellipsis, and his honest, caring exploration of Black love and growth found an untimely world where and when a bit of the fullness of Black life, dying, and death, might be witnessed and felt.

The locus of all of this is Shalaya Crump: how she speaks and thinks establishes an interesting entanglement between ellipses, futurity, and love. Shalaya issues imperatives and pronounces her punctuation. City's failed attempts at spitting game, usually because his spitting is a performance of some jilted form of swagger, usually summon forth a combination of both forms of Shalaya's speech: "Look, City . . . I could love you the way you want me to, really. I could if you *found a way to help me change the future* in, I don't know *dot-dot-dot* a *special way*."[19] Shalaya is "worried about the future"[20] in a way that drives her character and seems to destabilize her temporal existence. Her repeated pronunciation of ellipses, "dot-dot-dot," is routinely bound up with this existential, metaphysical, and untimely worry. Further, how this worry and this elliptical enunciation relate to City turns on a conditional statement hiding an imperative declaration. The conditional: My love is available, but if and only if you dot-dot-dot help me mitigate this future oriented worry that troubles my being. The imperative: Helping me this way is love; love is helping me change the future in "a special way"; love me by helping me change the future. And both the conditional and imperative signal that what Shalaya considers to be a haptical gesture or an act of unreasonable love is this, or is only this, insistence upon changing the future.

Shalaya's worry is not unwarranted. After time traveling to the future and learning of the unimaginable devastation wrought by Hurricane Katrina, Shalaya discovers that she and City disappear during the storm, never to be found. She worries that this disappearance implies death, so her desire to "change the future" can be thought of as a form of preventative rescue or recovery, something like a preemptive form of what M. NourbeSe Philip calls "exaqua," the recovery of Black bodies from water. This becomes the impetus for the time-travel mission on which she and City (and eventually Jewish Evan Altshuler) embark throughout their narrative arc. They

---

19. Laymon, *Long Division*, 25.
20. Ibid., 54.

repeatedly leap into and out of the black hole in the Melahatchie, Mississippi, woods because they hope for a better future, an alternate timeline in which they are not disappeared by the cataclysmic storm.

Though unreasonably following Shalaya without question on her journey through time to preemptively un-disappear them both, City ultimately and belatedly uncovers a crucial problem with their mission. While in the future, he encounters, befriends, and begins to love a young Black girl named Baize Shepherd, who mysteriously shares her name with a missing girl in the world of the other City reading this time-travel story. A budding but talented writer and lyricist, Baize has been looking for her parents ever since their disappearance during Hurricane Katrina. Too late does City realize that Baize is the daughter that he will one day have with Shalaya, and later still does he recognize that Shalaya's desire to un-disappear their future selves has as its condition of possibility the disappearance of Baize from her own timeline. Like the fictitious alchemical principle of equivalent exchange, it seems that City and Shalaya must determine whether or not the complicated arithmetic of their yet-to-be-lived lives, their eventually realized love, and all of their current and future desires is mathematically greater than the life, creativity, and love of their future daughter. The outcome is a product of a comparative mathematics of multiple forms of love or care: the gestures of care that compose City's attempts to help Shalaya complete this mission, the shared and individual care they have for the well-being of present and future selves, the care they each develop for Baize, and the care Baize has for her parents in their current (teenage) or future (adult) forms.

The "dynamic sentences" of their lives are punctuated by what they decide to do about, with, or to Baize. Asked what kind of punctuation she would be, Baize replies, "I'd be an ellipsis ... the dot-dot-do you were talking about" because "an ellipsis always knows something more came before it and something more is coming after it."[21] Baize elliptically punctuates the comparative arithmetic of their future-oriented care. She refigures, or disfigures, all that comes before and after her. She embodies a temporal dereliction of the relationship between the established past, the unstable present, and the unwritten future. She lives this embodiment in a way that centers an indeterminacy reminiscent of the bird/language in the hands of the petulant youth; what language appears beyond her punctuation will determine her aliveness or deadness, and will also speak to the aliveness or deadness of particular forms of care. The unstable potentiality of her elliptical existence serves as a pivot for the problems of care, writing and creation, and

---

21. Ibid., 254.

futurity that knot into Kiese's interest here. Ellipses, under the constraints of the plot and the constraints of Baize's definition of them—particularly, that something must follow their appearance in the dynamic sentence—issue a demand for a "radically different kind of . . . continuation"[22] or resolution.

So when Baize fades from existence because Shalaya makes the decision to time travel with Evan Altshuler instead of living with City toward their inevitable disappearance/death, self-preservation as self-care seems to be positioned as the form of Black care that has the highest value for her. This does not add up for City. This is a devastating valuation with horrifying consequences: The untimely story of a dynamic sentence this produces can only be described as "the saddest story in the history of a state like Mississippi."[23] That Shalaya's future clears and opens a way to unknowable possibility provides no closure to City, whose opportunity at a future with the girl he loved and the daughter with whom he could only begin to fall in love evaporates, just as Baize does: suddenly, and without the possibility of real redress. As one form of care for Black life is written into existence—a care for a very particular futurity for Black lives very literally imperiled by disastrous conditions (here, Hurricane Katrina)—another falls away.

But not in totality. Alone and in the dark of the black hole on the outskirts of the woods of Melahatchie, City sits and reconsiders the blank pages left at the end of the novel, *Long Division*, that Baize suggests that he read just before she disappears. Animated by his own desire to recover the disappeared—his daughter, Shalaya, Evan, and every other character they encountered on their journey through time—he begins to write, read, revise, reread, revise, write, and write his version of what "comes after" the ellipses of the dynamic life/death sentence of his existence. While there is no recovering the dead, the disappeared, and the lost, City recognizes that "knowing all we needed to know about how to survive, how to live, and how to *love* in Mississippi"[24] was in his hands. Differently put, and differently than Shalaya, City embraces the "ethical responsibility" to create an at least textual or imaginative spacetime where time traveling, care, and life for Black folks might be possible. Adjudicating whether or not City's form of literary creation or Shalaya's form of self-preservation is the more appropriate form of care for Black folk under untimely conditions is unnecessary.

I am less than certain that this leaves or leads us anywhere I/we hoped to go, more than it reveals the nowhere I/we have been from the outset. The nowhere we are, and the destructive void we keep reestablishing as our

---

22. Spillers, "Mama's Baby, Papa's Maybe," 68.
23. Laymon, *Long Division*, 22.
24. Ibid., 273.

destination, at least appears to emphasize the spatiality of the questions at hand. Thinking about the spatial qualities of the kinds of imaginative invention that must be passed on, or that must pass on, or both—the spatial qualities of this perplexing, indeterminate, remembered and forgotten, dying and "living" word-wake-work—might illuminate what has been a present absence in our discussions thus far. How to conceive of untimely movement and creation through and with space undergirds the work already done, and defines the questions that vex us now. Specifically, thinking about how we might navigate the space of the ergosphere (just outside or before the event horizon) to cross the spatiotemporal boundary of the event horizon, and to arrive in the unknowable nowhere of the singularity that defies our capacity for knowledge, thought, and invention becomes imperative if we are to remark more wholly and precisely on where we're headed.

If our destination is an infinitely crushing nowhere, how to get there? Understanding the temporal mechanics and capacities of the stories we wrote, write, and seek to write—as well as the contradictions and questions emergent from thinking about these mechanics and capacities—how does this word-wake-work mark our present relation to the space outside, near, and inside the Black w/hole? Further, how does this word-wake-work move us through the empty nowhere we are, the fragment-filled accretion disk around the Black w/hole, and then to the singularity—the nowhere that spatially telegraphs what, if we return to Sharpe and Hartman, is unimaginable and impossible about what we do when we write? We boldly go to this crushing nowhere, imaginative invention as our vehicle, hoping to cross the event horizon, which is to move wholly over the threshold beyond which there is no possibility for return.

Without looking back, and with hope, dot dot dot.

THIRD ARRANGEMENT

Transmissions from Out of Nowhere

VII

Prelude

No Place, Not Any Place, Out of Place

> It comes as a great *shock* to discover the country which is your birthplace and to which you owe your life and your identity has not *in its whole system of reality* evolved *any place* for you.
>
> The world has prepared no place for you, and if the world had its way, no place would ever exist.
>
> —JAMES BALDWIN[1]

AFTER OUR EXPLORATIONS of Black untimeliness and Black work under untimely conditions, we time travelers arrive "here" at Baldwin's words and what they say about "place"—about "not any place," about "no place"—surprising no one. Inevitable, really. We know that to intervene into a conversation about the nature of a particularly peculiar relationship to and collective experience of time would necessarily be to leap into a conversation about space. We knew this, understood the stakes and consequences of bearing untimely fragments and of inevitably losing one's bearings. We know this not in the least because theories like general relativity and indigenous cosmological concepts like *pacha*[2] teach us about the inextricability of space

---

1. The first quote comes from a 1965 debate with William Buckley in the documentary *The Price of the Ticket*; emphasis mine. For more information on the documentary, visit: https://www.pbs.org/wnet/americanmasters/james-baldwin-film-synopsis/2647/. The second comes from Baldwin's "The Black Boy Looks at the White Boy Norman Mailer," published in *Esquire*, May 1961.

2. *Pacha* characterized how Incan culture understood the order of the cosmos. The three levels of pacha mapped the three planes of being that the Incas understood to name the structure of the universe and their position in it. Each level was not only spatial but also temporal, revealing a "premodern" understanding of the inextricability of time from space. Obviously, this also suggests what should be commonly understood: These conceptualizations—though most famously formulated through the "hard" (and

from time: that there is no unraveling the knot between space and time, and that to think about the violent dereliction of one (time) means that we must consider at least the possibility, if not the certitude, of the violent dereliction of the other (space).

Consider, for example, the nature of an "event." "Events," or more aptly "resonances,"[3] occur at a unique moment and position in the larger fabric[4] of spacetime, so each resonance must be spatial and temporal at once. Let us press on and flesh this out a bit more: Consider gravity and gravitational waves. Generally, gravity is considered to be a phenomenon or force resulting from the curvature in the fabric of spacetime; gravitational waves are changes produced by certain gravitational interactions (e.g., the collision of two supermassive Black holes) that ripple, or propagate, through this curvature. For our purposes, we time travelers liken the deathly force of anti-Blackness to the force of gravity, that crushing product of the curvature of the fabric of Black spacetime. So keeping in line with the theoretical influences of relativity and pacha, when gravity warps this fabric, this means that it must warp both time *and* space. If the gravitational interaction is forceful enough, this means that violent ripples will propagate through and radically alter the whole fabric of space and time in observable ways. Thus, as we discovered in the opening section, the way this force warps, bends, crushes the Black relation to time into untimeliness suggests that a similar warping, bending, or crushing alters the Black relation to space. Conceptually and analytically, this is the place we arrive; it is "here," with no place else to go, that we must continue our investigation into things Black and untimely.

---

supposedly more legitimate) sciences and Western, imperial practices of hypothesizing, experimentation, and theorization—are not unique to or wholly emergent from Western thought; in fact, they often long-predate the belated, Westernized "discovery" of the same understanding.

3. In a talk delivered at Omni Commons in June 2015, Frank Wilderson spoke, in part, on the temporality of Blackness. At one point, he made the following clarification: "Social death elaborates a sentient being whose temporal resonances can never be transposed to temporal events—they're resonances, but they're not events." This is because, as in the first chapter of this project, Wilderson also conceives that Black time is no time at all, and that the time of Blackness cannot so simply be thought of in the terms of a conventional temporality.

4. The use of fabric to visualize the otherwise more abstract idea of spacetime is both useful and pervasive. Not only does this gel well with current prevailing metaphors in the world of theoretical physics, but it seems to have found a comfortable home in popular culture. Across science fiction, ranging from parody, to reference, to serious work, we find versions of the idea: "the fabric of spacetime," "the fabric of space and time/time and space," "the cosmic quilt," and so on and so forth. Tellingly, it is almost universally mentioned if it is already imperiled, or in danger of being imperiled.

How Saidiya Hartman describes the archive in "Venus in Two Acts" affirms our recognition of the inextricability of space from time, especially as this inextricability pertains to our writing about Blackness, death, and creation, so let us briefly return to her writing in order to help us flesh out our burgeoning spatial concerns. As we reckon with above, what we discovered to be "untimely Blackness," the name we give to the Black problem with time, suggests a Black problem with space. As we revisit "Venus in Two Acts," we recall that Hartman characterizes the archive of slavery as a "tomb." In this light, the term "archive" signifies a specific space where we might locate time. The stuff of time, "history," or what the time travelers prefer to describe as "untime," can be accessed through or in the archive. That the archive is a tomb conjures the ensemble of sensory associations we make when we imagine death and the dead. As the archive, "tomb" signifies the untimeliness of "the dead, the dying, and [we] living lives consigned, in the aftermath of legal chattel slavery, to death that is always-imminent and immanent,"[5] compelling us envision what this place of the lost might look like. Overlaying archive and tomb forces us to consider the architecture of the archive/tomb's corridors and the caskets and ossuaries that line the walls. Ultimately, in this arrangement of meanings death, untime, and space become inextricable from one another.

Of creation and destruction, this developing inquiry into Black spatiality catalyzed by the imagery Hartman uses to describe the archive drives us to think anew about our particular and peculiar worries about the literary and the imaginary. New questions abound. What do we make of all the literary and otherwise imaginative spaces—communities, worlds, universes—we create in relation to our inescapable vulnerability to invasion, violation, removal, and other forms of violent displacement? Of what we've read in this project's Second Arrangement, what do we make of House 124's spitefulness[6]—the spitefulness and vengeful aliveness (which is really living deadness) of the space itself? Of what we will read next, what do we make of Dickens, California's omnipresent, unbearable *Stank* in Paul Beatty's *The Sellout*? What might we make of what all of these questions tell us about the capacity to create parallel, or intersecting, or interjecting Black literary universes, from words to the worlds? Of that capacity in relation to both the fact of our loss and lost-ness, and the desire and imperative to mourn, "tend to, care for, comfort and defend" those/we subject to that fact?

---

5. Sharpe, "Black Studies: In the Wake," 60.
6. This is taken from the first line of *Beloved*.

Claiming to know "where" to go from here is to ignore the real and powerful "vengeance of the vertigo" we experience. Lovingly, I want to make the untimely journey to where nowhere might be. This is an imaginative enterprise preceded by a necessary, if daunting, need to map the contradictory topographies of our untimely relationship to space. As description, cartography, the creative process spanning the desire and inclination to create the map of some/nowhere, the ethical necessity of the accuracy and truthfulness of the map, and the actual creative work of drawing, scaling, detailing, and providing a key for the map, both implicitly and explicitly describes spatial relationships—between cartographer, traveler, terrain, and the physicality of the map itself. Lovingly, then, what I desire to do is map the relationship between a Black theorist theorizing (myself); the terrain of the anti-Black cosmos; Black folk (my mother, my auntie, and all) who might make use of this map as we travel and navigate that anti-Black terrain; and the untimely, imaginative, and real Black spaces we might create.

Our doubled imaginative work—the work of recognizing the problem of time the tomb/archive signifies added to the simultaneous work of imagining the space that problem of time forms or occupies—suggests that what we discovered about untime laces this space's architecture. Stitches in time compose the complex lattice that gives the archive/tomb its structure. If a Black relation to the archive/tomb is untimely, the archive/tomb's very structure adopts the "wibbly-wobbly" characteristics of untime as well. The space of the tomb becomes wholly unwieldy if not completely unimaginable, and we will do well to examine the mechanics, stakes, and possibilities of this unwieldy spatiality.

We know this. And so we inevitably fail to integrate what we discovered about time into a clear "image" of the tomb, the dead zone,[7] Ursa's womb,[8] the ship and its hold and/in the wake,[9] the break,[10] the rupture,[11] the tear in the world, the room in which "history" waits,[12] the labyrinth,[13] venomous

---

7. This is Joy James's concept.

8. See the reading of *Corregidora* in the First Arrangement, chapter 2.

9. From Sharpe's brilliant, path-breaking, and caregiving text *In the Wake: On Blackness and Being*.

10. See Fred Moten's *In the Break* (Minneapolis: University of Minnesota Press, 2003).

11. See Hortense Spillers, "Mama's Baby, Papa's Maybe: An American Grammar Book."

12. Both the room and the tear are formations imagined by Dionne Brand in *A Map to the Door of No Return: Notes to Belonging*.

13. From Anthony Paul Farley's "Behind the Wall of Sleep"; we will discuss it further in the forthcoming chapters in this section.

124,[14] or whatever name or shape this impossible place of the dead takes to hide, lose, dismember, or otherwise render irretrievable the refractive fragments of Black life.

Our "arrival" at a series of new questions about space, which is really an arrival at a new mode of seeing and hearing the few fragments we can bear, which is really a *recognition* and reexamination of our bearings: where we are, how we are there, how we bear these fragments in relation to ourselves, and how the site of these arrangements appears. How might we describe the orientation of our Black and untimely position, there, just there, among and holding the fragments? We recall carelessly writing: "Here are the entangled arrangements of the ones I could collect, the ones I hold the closest. I sit with all the bits that I can bear, listening and looking with intent."[15] What even constitutes "closeness" in this context? What "arrangements" does the preposition "with" even locate? *Can't you see it?* What are the wheres of here or there, of then, of him? Are the wheres every which where—the zones, the tomb, the womb, the ship, the hold, the break, the rupture, the tear, the room, the haunted house—all at once, and more? Or by virtue of being "all at once," are they what Baldwin means by "no place," "not . . . any place," and so nowhere in particular? *Can you imagine?* Or is this parallax of a problem of Black spatiality so much more unwieldy than the neatness of even these two forms?

Eyes up in a sudden panic. Disoriented, we cry out that we do not know where (or when) we are. We exclaim, "We cannot find ourselves! We are lost!" but our words drown in the call and clamor of all those scattered bits and pieces of Black life, telling and retelling our fractured narratives.

Each and every black fragment matters. But with only nowhere to speak of, and with nowhere else to go or be, we time travelers can only reach out again, grasping, looking, and listening for the stories that speak the loudest, the ones with the greatest resonance, the ones that might offer some semblance of guidance for the lost.

~~Here~~, or

~~There~~, or

On these pages, we look closely at one fragment calling through the dark.

---

14. The opening lines of Toni Morrison's magnum opus, *Beloved,* grant us entry into the novel's world by way of a haunted house: "124 was spiteful. Full of a baby's venom."

15. From chapter 1, "Prelude: Untimely Fragments and the Beginnings of a Reflection."

Fragment 34
BEING OUT OF PLACE

His whole body buzzes, raw with the raging electricity of the movement, the moment, there. His feet vibrate in his shoes as he stands on asphalt that seems to quake beneath all the bodies speaking, touching, pacing, thinking quietly, and otherwise mourning atop it. The air churns and crackles, too, unsettled by the troubled kinetic energy emanating from the corner of 183rd Street and Pires Avenue. Unremarkably, and like that of the rest, his flesh becomes conduit and custodian for the rippling rhythm of dying that is the cadence of the scene, channeling it like a node in the shifting circuitry of loss he and they try their best to sustain there.

There, Zachary Wade, guided by an unspoken resonance, finds him. In the waning light of day on this May 17, 2015, Zachary's eyes gloss, spark, and flicker with what he announces and repeats is an eerily uncanny recognition, "You know, you look like him, my nephew."

Something in him crumbles beneath the weight of this resonance, raining down upon his flesh with profound gravity. The buzzing becomes audible between his ears. It might be the frequency emitted by the collapse of the lie of distance between himself, his self, and the one they all gathered in sorrow and rage to mourn, or the sound of the perilous closeness to death between and among the living nodes of trauma and defiance. And so there he stands, inches from Zachary, overlain with the lost, buzzing, stunned.

What holds him there, grips him so? What stills him there, sticks him in the static there—right there, just there, locked in the buzzing hum of looking-like and being-like the dead? What is it about being so very close to loss there, so very proximal to the lost there that shocks him into the paralysis that preempts and prevents any response?

Throughout the day and against suburban silence, Zachary had spoken and stepped with the *breath* and *boom* of thunder.

Boom! Over the smooth quietude of quietly policed Cerritos streets, be it over Bloomfield passing in front of the town center or through the occupied ventricular intersection at South and Gridley, he shouted the improvised calls to which the marching crowd of hundreds responded. He discovered himself to be a stormcaller, a warlock conjuring the jagged arcs of chained lightning between them; each chant rang out like a Westbrookian bellow, meant to stun, awe, and jolt all in earshot and line of sight of its repeating crash.

Breath. Sharp. The murder of his nephew, Nephi Arreguin, on May 7, 2015, ripped open a new rift in the spatial arrangements of Cerritos, California, slashed open yet another "tear in the world," another "fault line" and so a site of a routine cataclysmic "rupture," a break and quake that were ultimately part of the very terrain on which they stand, move, and otherwise mourn.[16] *Escúchela: La ciudad respirando.* The earth trembles at the opening of this new gash, agape and gasping at the tectonic shock of the loss and losers and the electric energy of their booming losing, thundering atop the spot where Nephi's flesh was emptied by an emptied clip of an unremarkable Space Enforcer. *Escúchela.*

See, Nephi was lost.

Driving with a companion in search of a friend's home. His companion knocked on a door, on the wrong door, on the door of one who would soon come to dole out death. Afraid, like all suburban Death Dealers are, the homeowner called the "Police." The Space Enforcers, as Black folk name them, travel faster than the fastest tachyon at the Death Dealer's call. The black-and-whites of their vehicles unmistakably signify in, through, across, and against space and spaces that which is being enforced: the strict, rigid boundaries between polar absolutes, between being and nothingness, between life and death, and between the pristine space of everywhere else and Black space.

Their mode of conveyance, the way they move through, interrupt, and warp the domain of their "patrol"—by their mere presence alone they establish the jurisdiction upon which their violence is inflicted.

Like they often say of us, they say that he attempted the impossible. It is reported that as they confronted him at his driver's side window, and after he refused to exit his vehicle, he flew into enough of a frenzy to try impossibly to run over the officers to his left. Fearing they might be crushed via a violation of basic physical principles, they fired, striking him (at least) in the heart.

Violently ejected from his flesh, his soul could only watch alongside the Space Enforcers with their guns drawn as his vacant body careened into a fire hydrant, the water of which burst and struck loose electrical wires overhead. According to the Space Enforcers, this is why his body was inaccessible to paramedics: The wires created a hazardous environment, and they would not endanger themselves to reach his lifeless form.

The accounts of Space Enforcers, death dealers, and their accomplices that emerge in the aftermath describe he and his companion "not belonging" in the area, as "being out of place," double emphasis on *being*.

There was no place, here, or anywhere, for him or for her to belong, and because he was Black in his refusal to be removed from where he was parked, from where he, in that moment, wanted and needed to be, because

---

16. Brand, *A Map*, 4–5.

he defied the imposition of their jurisdiction upon his existence, he was removed from life itself.

"You know, you look just like him, my nephew. Just like him—he used to wear his hair pushed back like that. You've seen him, right?" He had. Of course he had. The memorial pictures lined the walls just over there. Alex, Josh, Natali, and Tania ensured and would ensure that they remained and would remain on the walls despite repeated removals by Space Enforcers, death dealers, or their acolytes. Differently sized photographs of Nephi, some with his hair pushed back into the nimbus of dense curls crowning his head, occupy the center of posters perched above flowers and flickering candles. Words of mourning, statements of love, and vows of action surround the small space of each photograph. All of it, all of them, suspended there, held in and by the wake.

"Yeah, just like him. You remind me of him, the way you got your hair back like that . . ." his sigh punctuating his words. *Escúchela*. The boom and breath quieted then, just for a moment. There in the stillness swept clean by Zachary's sigh, he stands unable to conjure a response, just buzzing.

To look into his eyes is to see that his stasis there is also a departure *from* there. What suspends him there suspends him only to displace him: The space of his flesh opens out and Nephi's afterimage fills it; at once, Zachary's words fling him out and disperse him, jettisoning him into the bullet-riddled body, the coroner's office, the memorialized photographs on the wall, and the grave. He is there and gone, present and lost. In the worst way and like Nephi, he, too, is singled out, out of place, belonging neither here nor there nor anywhere—or, more precisely, nowhere.

The collective mourning this evening interrupts the space of Pires Ave. there. They all hold each other to behold the echoes of his presence there. They stand there, Black and out of place there in the name of his absence, framed by the glaring headlights, the gaze of Space Enforcers' surveillance there. They know of the Enforcers' gleeful overseeing, acknowledge it in their periphery. But their eyes focus only on and *try to really see* each other, which is to say they hold and behold each other, there, just there, lost in/to the electricity of the moment.

※

We might be lost. Or, at least, at a loss—for words, directions, and even the coordinates to relatively locate ourselves in the void—so how might we continue? After interrogating, unraveling, and reimagining how we imagine the entanglement between time, Blackness, and creation, we "find" ourselves in an encounter with the peril of space.

We are worried about the arrangements—of the fragments, the terms, the bodies, the landmarks, the feelings, and the beings. Not solely do we worry about the material and abstract spatial arrangements made possible within the framework founded upon this unethical relationship between Blackness and space, but we also worry about the kinds of spaces—gatherings, worlds, universes—we create from within and against this framework. Differently put, while we must worry about our spatial relationship with armed officers (e.g., Darren Wilson) and deputized citizens (e.g., George Zimmerman), stampeding military boots, lobbed teargas canisters, and flying bullets, we also discover that we worry about the mass of Black folk convening in Cleveland lovingly and critically moving for Black lives, and what the space they occupy, the space they indict with their collective presence, tells us. We worry about the destruction of the spaces we occupy, the spaces of our flesh, and the spaces of our imaginations, and we also inextricably worry about the spaces we create and maintain to channel, contend, and outdo—because undoing is impossible—that destruction.

Triggered, we might begin to encounter rememories of similar removals, of ourselves, of others we can name, of still more that we will never be able to imagine. More menacing and unbearable questions: What do we make of the space of Kendrick Johnson, whose body, following an "investigation" of his yet unsolved murder, was stuffed with old newspaper after his internal organs were "discarded"—what of that displacement/replacement, and the flesh encasing it? What do we make of Aiyana Stanley-Jones's space, the small and cozy space of the living-room sofa where she slept across from a television, and its vulnerable openness to stampeding boots, flash-bang grenades, and bullets? What do we make of the space of Elisha Walker's shallow grave, how it housed her trans flesh, or the voids between the many "wheres" in the incomplete narrative that left her there? What do we make of the many voids in the archive—all the failures to locate the lost—all those empty spaces, all those lost names and the Black folk that, should we ever rediscover them or their remains, might not ever be able to bear or claim?

Triggered again, we encounter more menacing and unbearable questions: What do we make of the space of the Mondawmin Mall, which was at once a space of deliberate provocation and aggression created by the Baltimore Police Department, *and* a space of active resistance and Black rage spontaneously carried out by stranded Black school students? Of the space of the riots, created by an explosion of Black pain, rage, and love? What do we make of the space of the convening of the Movement for Black Lives in Cleveland, Ohio, which was simultaneously a space of creation and critique and also a space for action and resistance? What do we make of the space of the MOVE compound, or of every gentrified (e.g., Compton, California), imperiled (e.g., the Black Student Union of the University of California, Irvine), or destroyed (e.g., Black Wall Street) Black community, organization and space? What do we make of what happens to the spaces we create?

How do we locate those/we who at the level of our being are, as Dionne Brand writes, "flung out and dispersed"? Or, how do we reckon with the impossibility of locating ourselves—the flung out, dispersed, removed, displaced and lost—as the defining characteristic of how we relate to space? And, if we can bear this total "loss of bearings," this vengeful vertigo, in our thinking, being, and creating, how can we orient ourselves, in the flesh and in the imagination, to the parallel universes we make out of the nowhere where we are? Perhaps it is dangerous to ask without recourse to the spatial and temporal affirmation of a definitive set of answers.

But this is about boldly going. This is about venturing into the dark. With love, we set out, are cast out, are jettisoned into the void. Adrift, without the right (read: correct; ethical) words or phrases to catch hold on, or of, just the imaginative journey, the sense that we must move, and the propulsion of our "menacing and unbearable" questions.

"Whatever we make of this, so long as we make it out of nowhere," we might think, tumbling, tumbling, in the dark.

VIII

Nowheresville

> The archive is, in this case, a death sentence, a *tomb*, a display of the violated body, an inventory of property, a medical treatise on gonorrhea, a few lines about a whore's life, an asterisk in the grand narrative of history.
> —SAIDIYA HARTMAN, "VENUS IN TWO ACTS"[1]

> "Westside, nigger! What?"
> —PAUL BEATTY, *THE SELLOUT*[2]

WE'VE BEEN here before.

The arrangement of narrative fragments, the scattered refuse of untimely stories, guided us here. Leaping, falling, tumbling; listening, looking—we have arrived at these questions, concerns, and conclusions, our eyes traveling from fragment to fragment. But we only begin to take note of the surrounding space. Our gaze sharpens, and our eyes linger at previously, haphazardly passed-over details. Focused in the dark, we take note of two structures: the vague outline of a door, and the labyrinthine walls that occlude the fullness of its shape. We take these into consideration and begin our examination, which is our imaginative exploration of what we're able to do next, which is our cartography of the possibility of return or exit.

Before us are the daunting labyrinth and its walls. Our job in the forthcoming analysis will be to explore this labyrinth, examine its structure, and attempt—sensing that failure might be inevitable—to locate ourselves in relation to this structure. Our aim is to begin this perilous process of mapping to whatever degree what it means to be Black and untimely in space. Traversing the labyrinth and observing its structure as closely as possible

---

1. Hartman, "Venus in Two Acts," 2; emphasis mine.
2. Paul Beatty, *The Sellout* (New York: Farrar, Straus, and Giroux, 2015), 41.

will help us build a theory and a sense of how space plays out on our beings and how we navigate the space(s) of the anti-Black cosmos under such violent and vexing conditions. Further, taking the labyrinth as the conceptual and symbolic backdrop behind our considerations of Black spatiality will help us work through Paul Beatty's *The Sellout*, which itself offers us significant guidance toward a real sense of the, at present, undefined "where" of Blackness.

Our problem with the labyrinth, and really the problem of Black spatiality, inheres in problems of orientation and recognition: our capacity to discern where we are and where we might go, as well as the characteristics of our surroundings (which will influence the care and vigor with which we will try to navigate the space). Anthony Paul Farley's "Behind the Wall of Sleep," his response to Maria Aristodemou's *Law & Literature: Journeys from Her to Eternity*, offers us some of the guidance we seek; rather, since Farley's stylistic choices and claims bewilder us as much as they propel us through the labyrinth—since Farley's response to Aristodemou is itself labyrinthine— "guidance" might best be sandwiched between quotation marks. Farley's dissection of Aristodemou provides us key insights into the complex architecture of the labyrinthine structure that frames Black spatiality. Specifically, his writing compels us to consider how Black spatiality might inhere in a failure of spatial orientation—a constitutive spatial dislocation—which will allow us to better direct our investigations into the fuller mechanics, stakes, and possibilities of Black spatiality that follow. Farley singularly investigates Aristodemou's opening chapter, "A Rebeginning," because, as it establishes the methodological and conceptual groundwork for the entirety of the text, "the rebeginning is the most important chapter of *Law & Literature*."[3] Aristodemou's "retelling of the story of Ariadne and Theseus and Asterion," one of the many "tales of retelling" she retells throughout her text, allows us to think about the complex relationship between reason, desire, repression, and law. Specifically, Farley's winding reading parses the key symbolic and conceptual elements Aristodemou draws from the story of Ariadne as she examines this relationship through the figure of the minotaur, the structures of the wall and the labyrinth, and the repressed performance of the dream in order to orient us to her argument. We worry about this orientation, as it governs how meaningful the relationship between the repressive "wall of sleep," the labyrinth of law, and the desirous, symptomatic dream will be to our capacity to imagine an escape or an exit.

---

3. Anthony Paul Farley, "Behind the Wall of Sleep," *Law & Literature* 15, no. 3 (2003): 423.

The wall is an obstacle. More precisely, it is "a *political* obstacle, an instrument of repression"; it is "the form taken by repressed desire."[4] The wall works as the materialization of repression's force, barring us access to the "forbidden" country of desire we imagine to be on its other side; the imaginative labor instigated by an encounter with the wall as an obstacle, as repression reveals and clarifies the nature of the desire. Perhaps it is the recognition of the wall's repression that transforms desire from the potential for movement into propulsion itself, driving us through the entrance and deeper into the labyrinth. The labyrinth and its peculiar characteristics are the spatial realization and arrangement of our desire meeting structural political repression. How it twists and turns, where it leads, and whether it has any exit at all seems to turn on our capacity to orient ourselves to the length, detail, and durability of its structure. If our desire helps propel us through the structure—our imaginative resistance to repression, mobilized into our attempt at navigating the labyrinth—and its full realization is the forbidden country that might be on the other side of the labyrinthine wall, then the power relation between the force of our desire and the force of repression that has materialized into the walls that impede us structurally determines how far we might travel, where we might go and how quickly, and whether we "make it out" or resign ourselves to the impossibility of escape.

This is simultaneously an imaginative and political problem, which means it is also a problem of position, capacity, and orientation: Where we are in relation to the walls impeding us, and our capacity, at the level of our very being, to imaginatively and politically locate that position, worry us here. The nature of the walls becomes more important. What they look like, or, at least, what their structural composition is will help us unravel our dilemma. Following Farley following Aristodemou, we look:

> To look at the wall is to wander into the endless complexity of the stonework. The wall, as we stare at it, becomes a labyrinth—a network of lines that enlace. Each line is a philosophy, an explanation of its own necessary connection to each of the other lines. . . . This side and the other are both made by the wall. The wall is made of writing. And this leads to reading.[5]

Or we begin our attempt at reading. Reading becomes the groundwork of our movement through the labyrinth, as it tests our ability to discern the

---

4. Ibid., 424.
5. Farley, "Behind the Wall of Sleep," 425.

characteristics written, etched, painted onto the wall(s) before us. For Aristodemou, the labyrinth's walls are inscribed with the literature and narrative of law. Looking intently, we find the constitutive features of what makes the wall a wall, and law, law. Reading the lines and in between them, we "enter" the labyrinth of the wall's structure, the labyrinth within the labyrinth we already struggle to begin to navigate, getting lost, or even losing ourselves, in the complexity. Reading is both necessary and perilous, then: We must read the writing on the wall to have a chance at moving along it toward what we hope or imagine will be the exit to the land of our desire, but we risk losing ourselves in, or to, the details of the structure and what they tell us about where we are. Our reading is a mandatory test of our desire against the stricture and structure of repressive reason, and it is also an encounter with the real, and likely fatal, possibility of being lost, of losing our bearings, or realizing we'd lost them some indeterminate, immemorial time ago. We recall Ursa and the originary "method for reading" screaming through the "materialized scene" of her fleshy blues.[6]

For Farley, depending on the paradigm, the name of the writing on the wall might change: "Gender is a wall. . . . Race is a wall. Class is a wall. The nation is, of course, a wall."[7] The labyrinth and the labyrinths composed by the lines of the stonework of its walls form a complex, intersectional structure. The writing on the wall(s) are the philosophies and explanations necessary to give the structural formations of gender, or race, or class, or sexuality, or disability, or nation, their meaning and form. Examining the structure of the wall(s), reading the writing, then, as a means of entering the labyrinthine logic that gives them their dimensions, frames this process of orientation as one of identification.

We locate ourselves in relation to the structure in our careful examination of the walls and stonework that give it form by way of a measured identification with what's written there—about whatever feature of our structural position, only a few of which are listed above. We who are behind the wall of sleep, performing this identification, this orientation, this reading, articulate ourselves only in "symptoms and dreams" and blueshifted screams produced as our interpretation of the structure. If, following Farley

---

6. Spillers, "Mama's Baby, Papa's Maybe," 68. For a sustained reading of the relevant passages of Spillers's "Mama's Baby, Papa's Maybe," revisit the First Arrangement. Also, recall that in the passage in which the phrase "method for reading" appears, Spillers specifies Black female flesh as the primary subject of her analysis. As we see throughout this project, her analysis is absolutely foundational to how we understand Blackness; here, how we locate Blackness in space.

7. Farley, "Behind the Wall of Sleep," 426.

into Du Bois, this symptomatic, dreamy language is the language of problems, "problem language," then what might we be able to say about when, where, who, and what we are in the labyrinth? How might this "problem talking" help us navigate, let alone escape, the walls of sleep?

The problem of spatial orientation becomes one of reading and communicating; the process of our interpretation and our capacity to translate that interpretation into meaningful communication become the conditions for locating ourselves in relation to the repressive structures framing our untimely existence. Reckoning with this, we recall having conversed with the words of Hortense Spillers, who sought out a "vocabulary" and a "method for reading" the "undecipherable hieroglyphics of" and on the brutalized flesh of Blacks. Farley confirms that we move in the right direction: "The wall, then, is made of skin. . . . Whiteness is a wall of skin; gender is skin; class is also a skin. . . . We are able to negotiate the labyrinth because we have, inside *our* skin, an orientation."[8] What is written on the skin of the wall can be "read," or deciphered by way of the key coded into our flesh; the wall's repressive literature interacts what we bear in the flesh, revealing our structural position, and allowing us a sense of place. Following Farley, knowing this would be enabling: "All these lines, all these fates, *enable* us to orient ourselves in the *dark* of the labyrinth, and, seemingly, find our way out."[9] Ariadne seems to leave us a thread, a "method for reading" space, or maybe a way out, by revealing to us the content and nature of our very beings in relation to the repressive structure barring us from the real and proverbial other side.[10]

But we've yet to attend to something. Farley seems to miss something; or rather, given the meticulousness and clarity of his analysis, to hide something from us—he might leave it unattended in a way that draws our attention to it. The room of the labyrinthine tomb is dark. All its possible walls surrounded by darkness; what is the nature of this darkness? Is it blank, like the darkness Morrison describes? What does it do to our capacity to read the writing on the walls, to know where we are? Certainly, there are many kinds of walls, so many kinds of repressions, and many kinds of identifications produced in relation to those varied repressions. The problem remains that the walls appear to be, for all the difference in their inscriptions, equally walls—hence the indefinite article of Farley's list. Gender is *a* wall, race is *a* wall, class is *a* wall, nation is *a* wall, sexuality is *a* wall, (dis)ability is *a* wall,

---

8. Ibid., 429.
9. Ibid.; emphasis mine.
10. I also use this phrase as an intentional reference to a song by The Roots entitled "The OtherSide" from their 2011 album, *undun*.

and so on. The indefinite article links these together, not quite appositively, so not quite synonymously; rather, since the walls are at least political, the continuous indefinite article creates a political equivalence. The walls of the labyrinth are equally walls, equally political. Struggling to grasp the flattening consequences of this logic, we worry about the singular impenetrability of the darkness we'd taken for granted in Farley's retelling of Aristodemou's retelling of the myth. We are reminded of the singularity of Blackness that brought us here, and find ourselves at a loss.

This thick Blackness obscuring the glyphs on the walls, the narratives in the flesh, illuminates a question we never thought to ask. Perhaps, in Farley's response to Aristodemou, it was not only unthought, but also unthinkable: Knowing how imperative it is we locate ourselves in relation to the labyrinthine structure of repression before we can begin to imagine a way out, what happens to the writing on the walls, the structures themselves, and our capacity to orient ourselves in the dark—in relation to the dense, atmospheric Blackness before us? We realize we have yet to proceed. Worse, we realize that there is a dark space surrounding us, that there is in fact a structure we wish to escape and the glimmer of what might be an exit, we find that we remain lost. The walls, in their obstructiveness, in the political identifications (race, gender, class, nation, sexuality) they produce, still offer us a chance, a way to find a way out; the walls, then, are flawed. But Blackened by the darkness, their texts become, as Spillers wrote, undecipherable. Reading between the lines of that undecipherability, we find that we cannot orient ourselves, that we do not know where we are, and that we are incapacitated: We have yet to move; we are going nowhere.

I believe that Farley recognizes this, and encodes it into what otherwise appears to be an analysis that makes the mistake of analogizing Blackness to (any) race, to gender, to class, to sexuality, and so on. The darkness of the room is constitutive to the scene from the myth he recreates, and it is only after the introduction of darkness to the space that he writes: "The moment of capture was the one in which the watcher began to stare at the wall: the wall became labyrinth and the watcher began blindly searching its many mansions, its many law rooms. Ariadne's thread never leads us out. Theseus never escaped." In Farley's retelling of Aristodemou's retelling, he appears to place Blackness on a different plane of physical space than forms of identification that compose the walls. How I envision this structure parallels his placement of Blackness here.

My understanding is that Blackness frames the structure of the labyrinth as darkness. Being unable to meet the demand of the space (to read, and so to escape), locating ourselves within the labyrinth, let alone navigating it, let alone escaping into the imagined space of our fulfilled forbidden desires, becomes impossible *because* of the Blackness/darkness. Perhaps this is why Farley leaves us with a final question, confirming our darkest fears: "What if we only *think* we escape the labyrinth?" What if the nature of the darkness of the labyrinth is to merely give the impression of possibility—of the chance we have at locating the method for reading the walls, of interpreting the writing on the walls, of finding ourselves in the flesh, politically, physically, and imaginatively? What if, instead, there was never a way out, never an Ariadne, and we are, as feared we were at the start, lost, left in the dark?

This is going nowhere, and Farley appears to anticipate the worry we experience after recognizing the fact of the Blackness/darkness that encroaches and positions us. Given where we are, Aristodemou only suggests that we "must dream harder . . . dream of a [new] beginning,"[11] a new entry into a new story without the darkness, the labyrinth, or, perhaps, the need for an exit; an alternate reality altogether, without the perils of being in, surrounded by, with, or subject to the force of Blackness. This is to do the symptomatic, problematic speaking or enunciating against what the structure tells us about itself and ourselves; this is the imaginative work of recreation performed in the flesh.

Outthinking the labyrinth . . . This is the "wake work" we aspire to perform for Black folk. Thinking outside the labyrinth is the "wake work" Sharpe calls on us to do and that we will bring to our explorations in this project's Second Arrangement. We must attempt to impossibly wield it against the dominating force of the "symbolic order" we, through and with Spillers, trace in the first section. Taking Aristodemou beyond the intended conceptual bounds of her work, the impossible labyrinth(ine) work manifest in the following pages might be the only way out. To perform it is to work under the recognition that our capacity to imagine at all is sutured to the obliterating force of the darkness that keeps us here in the first place. To attain force and meaning at all, our "wake work," our dream work, must reckon with the fact of the labyrinth and the darkness; to dream at all, we must reckon with the fact of our inability to locate ourselves, the fact that we are and were always lost.

All that there is for us to do from here, all that we might do, is speak through the dream of an exit. Farley seems to anticipate this, too, and enlists Ursula K. Le Guin to confirm what we begin to understand. "There is only 'the Telling,'" he tells us, a "practice," and a "form of attentiveness" that, we hope, affords us the capacity to at least attend to the fact that Blackness

---

11. Farley, "Behind the Wall of Sleep," 429.

structures our position and the possibility of our spatial orientation. In Le Guin's words:

> It appeared that in the old Akan way of thinking any place, any act, if properly perceived, was actually mysterious and powerful, potentially sacred. And perception seemed to involve *description*—telling about the place, or the act, or the event, or the person. Talking about it, *making it into a story.* But these stories weren't gospel. They were essays *at* the truth. Glances, glimpses of sacredness. One was not asked to believe, only to listen. . . . There were no rules. *There was always an alternative.*[12]

If cartography is not journey—our movement through and out the labyrinth—but "description"—the dream-wake-work of "Telling" about an "alternative," a way out, another reality altogether—then what we must take from Farley in his layered retelling of Aristodemou, Du Bois, and Le Guin becomes clear. We are to imagine the map to the way out, to elsewhere. And as she clarifies, "there is only 'the Telling,'" there is only the story, and so there is only the "making" of the narrative map, the "story," to the way out. We know as much: In our rememories we encounter our reading of *Beloved* and thinking about what it means to "pass on" a story—is this our way out? A story as a description of a way to the way out, an approximation of the "truth" of the exit; a story in orbit of the dark, real, "actual,"[13] deathly Blackness surrounding our very being, gripping our every gesture—*this is it.* Our access to the exit of an "alternative" that was "always" here, always with us in the dark. Armed with the fragments of Le Guin's language curated by Farley—"Telling," "making," "description," and "story" as different but similar approximations of the "alternative" that, as Le Guin writes, "always exists"—this, we think, blinded by the dark, looks like our way out.

A moment of informed, but blind optimism, then, and we're searching the backs of eyelids and the spaces of our imaginations for stories that tell toward, or about, the "truth" of the map, the way out, the elsewhere, the other side. We think hard, clamoring for stories of new beginnings and dreams, of spaces where we might "be." In boundless want, we encounter Paul Beatty's *The Sellout*, and find ourselves hoping to find ourselves in Dickens, California.

---

12. Ursula K. Le Guin, *The Telling*, 96–97, cited in Farley, "Behind the Wall of Sleep," 430–31; emphasis mine.

13. Meant to evoke Spillers's "Mama's Baby, Papa's Maybe," which we engage in the First Arrangement.

Our section opens with a line that stands alone as a chapter in Beatty's *The Sellout*, an exclamation at the intersection of imperative and declaration: "Westside, nigger!" Me, aka Bonbon, aka the titular Sellout (or at least one of them), who we only know by his last name, declares by name a black space, a black region, and commands that we recognize it as itself. As we read this at the highest volume, this is a dense, loud sentence that forcefully asserts the legitimacy of the framework and premise of the novel: the reclamation, or "reanimation," of Black space subject to denial and erasure. This is not to suggest that Beatty explicitly or even primarily concerns himself with establishing this as the central problem of the terrain he maps, but to reckon with the fact that for all the brilliance, scope, and incisiveness of the sometimes satirical, always if awkwardly loving, and relentlessly Black setups, scenes, jokes, characters—main and peripheral—the novel never loses hold of a fundamental concern for what constitutes Black space, being Black in space, and how Black untimeliness operates as the grammar suturing being to Blackness to in-ness to space.

But I am also, if not more, intrigued by the immediate shift from that exclamation to an interrogative: "What?" "What" is the matter, but what's "what"? If "Westside, nigger!" exclaims both the affirmative declaration of a connection between Blackness, belonging, space, and representation, and the imperative to "recognize" the invocation and reality of this connection, then this "What?" can express a critical vexation with that connection. Tonally, given the absence of exclamation juxtaposed with the exclamation right next to it—Beatty seems deliberately to call attention to the distinction between the sound of both the exclamation-declaration-imperative and the interrogative—the vague emotionality of the question mark expresses confusion, indignation, disgust, and/or explicit critique, in all a calling into question of the nature of the preceding exclamatory-declarative-imperative "Westside, nigger!" claim.

To what ends? The deliberate vagueness[14] of the relationship between "Westside, nigger!" and "What?," whatever the intended tones of the expressions, shares across the array of interpretations an attempt to trouble the terrain of the connections captured and invoked by the opening exclamation-declaration-imperative. A quaking of the world presumed, declared, to be underfoot of the claim, a shaking of the grammar that gives

---

14. I say *deliberate* because Beatty has implied across several of his interviews that the obfuscations he typically includes in his work—the way he masks or at least coats what he's "really" doing in humor, parody, and absurdity—is always deliberate, and that he has no intention of clarifying, let alone outright stating, what he "means" when he does X in this novel (or his others). There are always hints.

the exclamation its force and shapes or directs its meaning, what's what is the unthought "how" whispering behind the loudness of the claim: How does this relation work, look, operate, and/or exist, given what we know about where we "are" (or aren't)? If this "what" channels the force or our predicament in the labyrinthine tomb of this "nowhere" where we work to locate ourselves into the form of a question, then what's the matter, at least at the foundations of all that is written in the novel, is what it might mean to think, move, and create in terms of reanimating, reclaiming, or making space when we know what we know about the structure that positions us. If "lost" and "nowhere" characterize where we are/aren't and how we are there/here, then "what?" elucidates the stakes in naming, declaring, exclaiming, recognizing, and belonging or laying claim to space, and calls into question what it is we do when we try or aspire to "make ways out of no way," literary or otherwise.

Before we arrive in Dickens, there is yet another detour in the "making" here—this is, after all, a labyrinthine task. We ask: How might that making-a-way take place? What are the constitutive features and elements of that process transform "nowhere" into "a way out," or "elsewhere," or, at least, a space where we might do wake work?

An inappropriate—but generative in its inappropriateness—metaphor written by popular science writer and theoretical physicist Lisa Randall will help us think about structural formation in relation to Blackness (in ways very likely unintended by the author), which will frame how we think about both Black spatiality and Black creation. We take a detour to her recent writing about dark matter to lay a bit more groundwork before pressing on into Beatty's *The Sellout*. In October of 2015, Randall's fourth book, *Dark Matter and the Dinosaurs: The Astounding Interconnectedness of Everything*, emerged to a generally positive reception. Aimed at a lay audience, her text works as a thought experiment in which Randall hypothesizes about how the existence and behavior of dark matter might deepen our understanding about the nature of the extinction of the dinosaurs. She divides her text into three parts. The first, "The Development of the Universe," explains the science of cosmology, presenting the Big Bang theory, cosmological inflation, and the general composition of the universe, and defining what dark matter is, how it was ascertained, and what its role is, or might be, in influencing the structure of the universe. The second focuses exclusively on the solar system and the constituents that relate most closely to the thought experiment at the center of her work—meteoroids, asteroids, and comets—and how those constituents relate to life's formation and destruction on earth. The final section integrates the work of the first two, and works to map out and compare various models of dark matter, each of which presents what dark matter, or at least the effects attributed to its existence, might actually be, and how this dark matter's interactions with matter and with itself continue to pose theoretical problems.

We are concerned primarily with the first and final sections of the text, specifically Randall's explanations of dark matter, galaxy and structure formation, and her use of analogy to help explicate both—it is this last concern that will be our ultimate problem. We will walk through some of the key scientific information Randall provides about dark matter in order to set up our examination of the analogy between Black people and dark matter that Randall crafts in order to help explain dark matter's relation to structure formation to a lay audience. Dark matter remains elusive, invisible. It only feebly, imperceptibly, interacts with the matter that we currently know. Detectors have yet to achieve the necessary sensitivity to directly measure its effects; much of the belief in and theorization about its existence comes somewhat inferentially. Dark matter might be best thought of as existing, as Randall puts it, in and as "a society totally separate from the matter that we know," one of countless distinct, invisible "'universes'" that "passes right through our bodies,"[15] while eluding our capacities to sense it. At the particulate level (if it is composed of some new type of particle), those particles might have a mass comparable to known particles. If those particles behave as expected given current understandings of dynamics, however, dark matter would remain a problem for thought for those in search of it.

The most important evidence for what this "'dark universe'" and its composition might be appears to inhere in dark matter's importance to the formation of structures like galaxy clusters and galaxies via its gravitational influence.[16] Dark matter's abundance and apparent immunity to electromagnetic radiation, which in the early universe "initially prevented ordinary matter from developing structure on scales smaller than about a hundred times the size of a galaxy,"[17] heavily contributed to the attraction of ordinary

---

15. Lisa Randall, *Dark Matter and the Dinosaurs: The Astounding Interconnectedness of the Universe* (New York: Ecco, 2015), 2.

16. Scientists have been able to study this particular interaction between dark matter, gravity, and galaxy structure by way of measuring gravitational lensing. Lisa Randall explains it thusly: "The idea behind the gravitational lensing proposal," first put forth by Swiss astronomer Fritz Zwicky, "was that the gravitational influence of dark matter would also change the path of light emitted by a luminous object elsewhere. The gravitational influence of an intervening massive object such as a galaxy cluster bends the paths of the light rays that are emitted by the luminous object. When the cluster is sufficiently massive, the distortion in the paths is observable" (*Dark Matter*, 15).

17. Randall, *Dark Matter*, 59.

matter into increasingly dense regions of space. These density perturbations, "regions that are slightly denser or less dense than others, which are created when" the period of cosmic inflation ended,[18] precipitate in the collapse of matter that seeds the creation of structures like galaxy clusters,[19] galaxies, and stars. The "diffuse spherical halo"[20] of dark matter framing these regions heavily contributes to the gravitational attraction that maintains the structure of the formation; allows gaseous matter to cool, condense, and fragment into stars; and even attracts back into galaxies "some of the matter that is ejected by supernovae . . . [helping] to retain heavy elements that are essential to further star formation and ultimately to life itself."[21] Before we really arrive at how Randall actually analogizes Black people and dark matter, considering these theoretical interactions between dark matter, galactic structure formation, and star creation will influence how we begin to theorize Black spatiality, especially as we think about Black creation as a form of dark and cosmic structure formation. Considering this now primes us to see why, problematic as it will be, Randall's analogy can be generative for us.

Aside form the theoretical knowledge about dark matter and structure formation that Randall's work offers us, her approach to the writing is important to us because it influences *why* she resorts to the explanatory power of analogy in the first place. In *Dark Matter and the Dinosaurs*, Randall works to consolidate research from ongoing investigations into the problem of dark matter into one textual space, and to render that material accessible for lay readers. This is characteristic of work written by so-called science popularizers who write about this complex, fascinating research in ways that offer textual points of entry into what is otherwise treated as esoteric material. Crucial to Randall's venture into clarifying some of the research and theorization about dark matter (including her own) are analogy and metaphor. In the opening section of her text, she makes two central, framing comparisons: between the dark matter's involvement in structure formation to the planning and layout of a city, and between dark matter itself and the "rank-and-file of society." Of the first, she writes:

---

18. Ibid., 60.
19. Of particular import is an example Randall uses in her text, a galaxy cluster known as the Bullet Cluster. Formed by the merger of two galaxy clusters, the peculiar structure of the galaxy has been difficult to explain without accepting the influence of some noninteracting matter (possibly dark matter), and is thus an important source of evidence for dark matter's existence.
20. Ibid., 67.
21. Ibid., 61.

> Urbanization has been vital to many of the advances in modern life. Put enough people together and ideas bloom, economies flourish, and abundant benefits emerge. Cities develop organically as they expand ... but once a city becomes too dense, expensive housing, crime, or *other urban predicaments* frequently drive people out into more sparsely settled neighborhoods, or even farther away—outside the city altogether. ... And without stable urban centers, suburban communities won't flourish either, in which case mall developers will be disappointed too. ... It turns out the same general pattern might apply to the growth of structure in the Universe. ... As with predictions for large-scale urban growth, predictions of large-scale structure in the Universe agree with observations extremely well.[22]

I quote her at length to express the full shape of what is a facile at best, anti-Black at worst comparison between the nature of urban development and large-scale structure formation—of galaxies, galaxy clusters, stars, and so on. Randall flattens the process of modern urbanization in a way that necessarily, if haphazardly, displaces the anti-Black violence inherent in the organization and growth of cities to clarify the effects of dark matter on large-scale structure formation in the universe. She presents an idyllic, simplistic framing of urbanization without addressing the violence animating the planning, arrangement, rearrangement, and maintenance of "urban" spaces: gentrification and the ensuing displacement (New Orleans, in the still-burgeoning wake of Hurricane Katrina, provides a case study);[23] the creation of food deserts and the destructive responses to the ways Black communities attempt to develop self-sufficient sources of nourishment (Afrikatown in

---

22. Ibid., 303.
23. From an article written by Ben Casselman entitled "Katrina Washed Away New Orleans's Black Middle Class," *Five-Thirty-Eight*, August 24, 2015: "But they also worry about rising rents, gentrification and the erosion of the culture that made New Orleans special in the first place. All of those changes are closely entwined with issues of race. *More than 175,000 black residents left New Orleans in the year after the storm; more than 75,000 never came back.* Meanwhile, the non-Hispanic white population has nearly returned to its pre-storm total. ... Together, the trends have pushed the African-American share of the population down to 59 percent in 2013, from 66 percent in 2005. But it isn't just that there are fewer black New Orleanians; their place in the city's economic fabric has fundamentally changed. African-Americans have long accounted for most of the city's poor, but before the storm they also made up a majority of its middle class and were well represented among its doctors, lawyers and other professionals. After Katrina, the patterns changed: The poor are still overwhelmingly black, but the affluent and middle classes are increasingly white. ... The influx of young, educated—and *overwhelmingly white*—professionals ... [has] brought with [it] a wave of gentrification"; emphasis mine.

Oakland);[24] forms of environmental racism (e.g., the poisoning of the water in Flint, Michigan, and in likely several predominantly Black regions of the United States); and the overpolicing of Black communities (e.g., everywhere Black people are). To make this critical elision in the name of clarification is to knowingly or unknowingly ignore the realities of anti-Black violence at the level of spatial arrangement and relation. How she chooses to make this clarification for the lay audience obfuscates the violence that emerges in the arrangements, infiltrations, intrusions, displacements, and death that characterize the relation between Blackness and space.

This problem of obfuscation persists as she crafts the second metaphor, in which dark matter metaphorically stands in for the "rank-and-file of society." In an article about *Dark Matter and the Dinosaurs* that she wrote for the *Boston Globe* entitled "Seeing Dark Matter as the Key to the Universe—and Human Empathy," she clarifies and focuses what she might mean by "rank-and-file." Recounting a reading from the first chapter of her book for an audience at the artists' colony Yaddo, during which she ventured to help clarify the dark matter's "unseen but important influences" on the universe, Randall recalls being asked, "I know this might sound like a crazy question, but were you really talking about race?" In her telling, Randall beams at the thought: "The real issue I was addressing was the transparency—both metaphorical and literal—of people, phenomena, particles, and forces that we don't necessarily appreciate but that are important to our shared reality." She revels in this connection and extends the metaphor into seminars she teaches at Harvard. But her own inability to see the problem with both her analogy and her bafflingly, but predictably, uncritical use of it, as well as the language she wields here—namely "transparency"—might continue our exploration of dark matter's utility for our analysis.

Dark matter is the most abundant form of matter in the universe, but it goes unnoticed and remains undetectable to current research methods and instruments. Ordinary matter does not interact strongly with or resemble dark matter; dark matter merely passes through ordinary matter, and

---

24. The Afrikatown Community Garden's Facebook page provides the most current updates of its ongoing battle with the owner of the once-empty, dilapidated lot in which the garden thrives. The owner sought to sell the land to luxury condominium developers, and in April 2015, the standoffs with bulldozers began. On April 3, declared Liberation Day by protesters, organizers invited guest speakers for a day of music, food, lecture, and dance meant to prevent the destruction of the garden. In November, when Danae Martinez and Qilombo volunteers began to clean the lot—littered with discarded needles and human excrement—they sought to establish a space where the predominantly Black community members could work together toward collective physical, psychological, and spiritual nourishment.

ordinary matter phenomenologically exacts more influence on the known universe, its shape, contents, and so on. Some might consider dark matter dangerous because of its "ominous-sounding name." Dark matter's very existence confounds and fascinates scientific and lay intellects alike, prompting extensive research into what it is, how it behaves, and what the full extent of its influence on reality might be. All in all, thinking critically about or researching dark matter demands an attempt at understanding the invisible, the underthought, the unimaginable, the terrifying, the otherworldy . . . in other words, the Black. For Randall, research into dark matter, and the parallels between dark matter's function in the universe and the positions of Black folk and non-Black people in the world, prompt questions of empathy: What is it to think through and about, and to identify with, the constituents, sentient or particulate, of another world? Of another universe?

Randall's curious and problematic analogy between Black folk and dark matter is peculiar in its own right, particularly given the position of power Randall occupies. Occupying the political-ontological position of the human, as a white, blond woman of increasing acclaim in a field that continues to marginalize not only Black people (and on a different register, people of color), but Black *women* (cis- and transgender) in particular—providing fewer research opportunities; accepting fewer candidates to elite programs, research laboratories, and projects; and offering little or no access, reinforcement, or encouragement at early ages[25]—she presents this metaphor, like the first, in a way that works to obfuscate the anti-Blackness undergirding it.

Worse, in the second instance in particular, Randall wields Blackness, via the invocation of race and the focus on the "dark" of dark matter, as a tool to make a general claim about the need for empathy (the very concept of which Saidiya Hartman tears asunder in her work)[26] without a substantive recognition of the singularity of Blackness. In both instances, clarification and connection turn on Randall's blindness to the realities that character-

---

25. One of the most compelling writers and thinkers on this problem as it intersects with the sorts of metaphors Randall employs is theoretical physicist Chanda Prescod-Weinstein. Her research into the viability of axions as the strongest candidate for dark matter constituents, as well as her commitment to centering problems of inclusion and access for Black people and people of color in STEM fields, is the driving force behind the use and critique of Randall I'm presenting here. One conversation in particular, a chat we had online about the inappropriateness of Randall's analogy, brought this problem with Randall's framing to the fore.

26. I'm drawing attention to Saidiya Hartman's *Scenes of Subjection*, specifically to the chapter entitled "Innocent Amusements," in which Hartman dismantles the concept of and capacity for empathy between white/non-Black observers of Black suffering and the Black people who are political-ontologically, psychically, psychologically, and physically terrorized by the anti-Black world.

ize the Black position in the anti-Black world, in the field of physics (and in STEM fields in general), and with regard to the spatial formations created by the violent process of urbanization that she so casually and callously uses in her analogy. In all, while dark matter can at least draw and hold the fascination, care, adoration, research, and funding of physicists, researchers, and laypersons with scientific interests, dark matter—at least in Randall's metaphor—does not experience or capture the profound, debilitating, exclusionary, and fatal violence generally characteristic of Black life and death for Black folk around the globe.

Troubling as these elisions are, they intersect with what are useful metaphors for our consideration when thinking about the relation between Blackness and space. If for Randall Black folk and dark matter function similarly, as the structuring, transparent—or rather, unseen, unthought—feared condition of possibility for the formation of the structure of the universe, the very condensation of matter that eventually produces the earth, its inhabitants, and the structures those inhabitants create to house and arrange themselves or others, then this metaphor proves useful. That Black folk qua dark matter likely facilitates the condition that make what we call "space" possible, be that space physical, political-ontological, psychic, or imaginative, clarifies the darkness before us in the labyrinthine structure of the mausoleum before us. Not only does it affirm what we understand to be the violent mechanics that edify this structure to begin with, but it also directs our questions about how we might make or inhabit a space to do the wake work of mourning and moving with the dead. The "dark universe," this "zone of nonbeing,"[27] this nowhere, that gives the (non-dark) universe form, as a metaphor for the spatial arrangement we occupy primes us to read what Beatty and Me are doing with and in Dickens, California.

How Beatty and Me work with the dark matter of Blackness to shape the space of Dickens as a site of Black interaction, confrontation, and creation will help confirm and challenge both what we know about being and going nowhere, and also better frame our understanding of the possibilities afforded us by being lost.

---

27. This is a Fanonian concept, introduced by Fanon in *Black Skin*, 2. He writes, "There is a zone of nonbeing, an extraordinarily sterile and arid region, an utterly naked declivity where an authentic upheaval can be born."

IX

Stanky Shrines and Hollow Bastions

> "Shit, when Cuz and my brother picked me up from work and we drove back here, *soon as we crossed that white line you painted*, it was like, you know, when you enter a banging-ass house party and shit's bumping, and you get that thump in your chest and you be like, if I were to die right now, I wouldn't *give a fuck*. It was like that. *Crossing the threshold.*"
> —MARPESSA IN PAUL BEATTY, THE SELLOUT

1

Beatty's *The Sellout* follows Me as he tries to "reanimate the city of Dickens," California, an agrarian "ghetto community on the outskirts of Los Angeles."[1] Dickens recently suffered a silent erasure from the map as "part of a blatant conspiracy by the surrounding, increasingly affluent, two-car garage communities to keep their property values up and their blood pressures down."[2] Or because of the "widespread local political corruption,"[3] lack of open police and fire stations, poorly staffed city hall, and nonexistent school board—whatever the reasons, and without announcement, editorial piece, brief sound bite on the daily news, or anything resembling the promise of recognition or memorialization, Dickens was deliberately dissolved from cognitive and geographical maps into topographical nothingness. This casual, quiet, and violent alchemy transmutes "somewhere" to "Nowhere,"[4]

---

1. Beatty, *The Sellout*, 93.
2. Ibid., 58.
3. Ibid.
4. This dissolution parallels the first step in the alchemical process, tellingly and usefully called "nigredo," the "black process," which consists of the disintegration of material to its most fundamental, essential elements, at which point it is no longer recognizable as itself; it becomes the material, for our purposes the (dark or black) matter, with which our creative practice becomes possible.

a clear parallel to the singular quotidian violence to which Black folk around the globe remain subject—consider as evidence the ongoing slow poisoning and murder of the predominantly Black community of Flint, Michigan[5]—prompts Me into action.

His plan wins him the juridical lottery, a congratulatory summons to the Supreme Court of the United States of America, stamped with the word "IMPORTANT! in large, sweepstakes-red letters."[6] The novel begins here, almost all of its plot told in a series of layered flashbacks as Me reclines while smoking weed in the Supreme Court chambers, as an infuriated parody of Clarence Thomas is prompted by rage to speak for the first time in almost a decade.[7] Referred to as "the black Justice," his fury stems from precisely how Me tries to "reanimate" Dickens, California: by violating "the hallowed principles of the Thirteenth Amendment by owning a slave . . . willfully [ignoring] the Fourteenth Amendment and [arguing] that sometimes segregation brings people together."[8] Me's project entangles notions of life, (re)birth, and (re)creation with the political-ontological, psychological, temporal, and spatial implications and consequences emergent from slavery and segregation, and inadvertently calls into question the relationship between Blackness, creation, erasure, and space.

Beatty's framing narrative asks: What gives a space life? What about being Black in space must we understand differently when the "life" of a space is sutured to the way it contains or houses and advances anti-Black practices and policies? Differently, what is it to be Black in space when anti-Blackness affords space recognition as space in the first place? Worse, when a "Black space" becomes a "dead space" that must and can only be "reanimated" by anti-Blackness? If that "dead space" is a "nowhere," and an anti-Black space is a "living space," and so a "somewhere," then what even *is*

---

5. The city of Flint, Michigan, is *still* experiencing a crisis because of the lead-contaminated water it's been pumping into its residents' homes and throughout the water system. This problem has been protested by residents of Flint for years, and parallels several similar, deliberate poisonings in predominantly Black cities like Baltimore, Maryland, and New Orleans, Louisiana. This subjection to what has been called "environmental racism"—in which the access to environmental resources and the quality of those resources dramatically differs across racial positions—usefully and necessarily parallels our concern with the relationship between Blackness and space.

6. Beatty, *The Sellout*, 1.

7. A *New York Times* article by Adam Liptak published on February 1, 2016, entitled "It's Been 10 Years. Would Clarence Thomas Like to Add Anything?" addresses the fact that the real-life justice has maintained a "decade-long vow of silence" during oral arguments and his reasons for doing so. Which makes this parody especially absurd and funny, given what he ultimately and ironically says of Me at the end of the prologue (24).

8. Beatty, *The Sellout*, 23.

a Black space, given the labyrinthine enclosure, the door, and the darkness that form the architecture containing our structural position? To put this as Me and Beatty do: "So what exactly is *our [Black] thing?*"[9] Here, nowhere, can whatever it is ever be "ours"?

Beatty situates these questions in two distinct but overlapping frames: the external, meaning institutional and communal, and the internal, meaning subjective. The institutional frame deals with the juridical processes that seem to end up being the way to legitimize Dickens as a space. The communal element emerges from the need to compel LA's denizens to take Dickens's territory seriously, both of which depend on recognition from without. The internal frame is captured by Beatty in a recurring question first asked by Me's father, "Who am I? And how may I become myself?" Overlaying these frames, Beatty reveals the inextricable entanglement between spatial arrangements and coordinates, and the assertion and definition of Black selfhood via identification with, or an emplotment in, space. Examining the way Beatty stages and characterizes this set of internal and external spatial relations through Me, specifically the strategies Me devises to accomplish his goal, will afford us insight into the limitations of a framework that draws internal identification and external recognition as its boundaries without reaching into the realms of the political-ontological. And doing so will also throw into crisis the ways we conceptualize space itself: what we take to be the defining features of a space; what we take to be essential to locating oneself, one's community, and one's being in space.

Dickens was founded in 1868, perhaps some time between the founding of the Hampton Normal and Agricultural Institute (later, Hampton University) and the ratification of the Fourteenth Amendment. It was founded as an agrarian community that sought to remain free of "Chinamen, Spanish of all shades, dialects, and hats, Frenchmen, redheads, and unskilled Jews."[10] It is the "Last Bastion of Blackness," a hollow bastion, not just vacated of the recognition of its space, but denied the spatial relations of having so much as a sibling/sister city. Me is from the Farms, a "ten-square block section of Dickens" spanning "five-hundred acres" occupied by grown men and children riding dirt bikes through crowds of wandering livestock, and various series of failed and successful crops grown by Me and others. At different intervals and depending on the season and the movement of the Santa Ana winds, it stanks, or it reeks of cow manure, weed smoke, slices of square and pyramidal watermelon, and satsuma oranges. There is a dank sweet-

---

9. Ibid., 288.
10. Ibid., 27.

ness and a sweet dankness to the peculiar nourishment this land provides the mostly Black and brown folk that find themselves in the middle of this cultivated nowhere.

The Stank arbitrarily drifts into and looms over Dickens as a cosmic effluvia composed of chemical pollutants, blackness, death, and decay. As Me describes it, the Stank is

> an eye-burning, colorless miasma of sulfur and shit birthed in the Wilmington oil refineries and the Long Beach sewage treatment plant. Carried inland by the prevailing winds, the Stank gathers up a steamy pungency as the fumes combine with the stench of the lounge lizards returning home from partying in Newport Beach, drenched in sweat, tequila shooter runoff, and gallons of overapplied Drakkar Noir cologne. They say the Stank drops the crime rate by 90 percent, but when the smell slaps you awake at three in the morning, the first thing you want to do is kill Guy Laroche.[11]

The Stank is an unnatural sensory force with political-ontological scents and physical and psychological effects. It operates invisibly, lacing the life-giving air Dickens's constituents breathe with a mix of White power and privilege embodied by the drunken, sweaty Newport Beach "lounge lizard";[12] an aroma of sulfurous, gaseous byproducts of manufacturing refined black fuel—for transport, for commerce, or whatever other nefarious process, and perhaps produced by insidious and environmentally devastating California fracking projects with effects that disproportionately affect Black folk; a stench of shit from mismanaged and massive sewage treatment plant; and an unmistakable, musty, and as-advertised performative, faux-black hypermasculinity in the name and color of the bottle of Drakkar Noir cologne. Perhaps deadlier than even the massive methane leak in Aliso Canyon, California, in 2015,[13] it is a curious Stank, but no less violent for its peculiarity as it, at least for Me, awakens Black rage aimed at the cologne's creator, Guy

---

11. Beatty, *The Sellout*, 113.
12. Typically, "lounge lizard" pejoratively refers to a lounge musician, but it can also just refer to someone who idles at lounges and clubs in a general sense.
13. From the California Air Resources Board web page on the aftermath of the event: "CARB and SoCalGas have developed a proposed agreement that will fully mitigate in California at least 109,000 metric tons of methane emissions, the amount of methane released during the Aliso Canyon Natural Gas Facility leak from October 2015 through February 2016. Implementation of the Mitigation Agreement will achieve the mitigation principles and objectives outlined in the Governor's Proclamation of January 6, 2016, and CARB's Aliso Canyon Methane Leak Climate Impacts Mitigation Program."

Laroche, who is a proxy for every White or non-Black contributor to the wretched Stank that the wretched of the earth must breathe as if air.

We recall thinking about Black breath as disturbance through Sharpe. We found that Black creative work is aspirational, at its best catalyzing, facilitating, and continuing the putting and keeping of breath in Black bodies. And we will do well to think on another resonance between Sharpe's *In the Wake* and this project: between our ideas about the Stank and Sharpe's ideas about what she calls "the weather": "the *totality* of our environments; the weather is the total climate; and that climate is *antiblack*. . . . Antiblackness is pervasive *as* climate. . . . [I]t is the *atmospheric* condition of time and place."[14] Under the conditions of an increasingly perilous global climate due to changes that continue to accelerate toward environmental catastrophe, changes that were once totally preventable, were recently preventable to a degree, and are now realistically characterized by questions like, "How might we adapt to the gutting losses and radical changes to come?," thinking about anti-Blackness in terms of "total climate" has a particularly disturbing and urgent, if apropos, resonance to it. Sharpe's "weather" diffuses anti-Blackness into the atmosphere; anti-Blackness no longer has the tactility of something like a "structure" or an "institution," however massive or overwhelming that tactility might be, and is instead beyond tactility, beyond visibility, beyond destruction—it is everywhere, and it determines the conditions of everything and everyone everywhere.

In one sense, Stank appears to be adjectival in relation to the weather: One might describe the weather by how Black folk experience it as "stanky"; in this relation, "Stank" describes the atmospheric conditions as well as the phenomenological constraints under which Black folk variably experience those conditions. But in another sense, Stank adds a layer of particularity to the idea of the weather, being both synonymous—so, serving a similar conceptual and grammatical function for us—and more narrow, describing anti-Blackness as atmospheric in a general sense, but describing it as miasmatic in particular for Black life.[15] We may suppose that the distinction rests in this sense of specificity, and only builds on the foundational work Sharpe does when she introduces us to the anti-Black weather. To think of Blackness

---

14. Sharpe, *In the Wake*, 104–6; emphasis mine.

15. Sharpe uses the word "miasma" on page 112 of *In the Wake* to describe a moment in which slave masters would still continue to force slaves to work in unfavorable or even disastrous weather conditions, even when "the rain produced a miasma or 'bad air.'" So the idea is seeded here a bit, but Sharpe does not pursue it in developing her conceptual map of the weather, likely because she's approached the weather in a way that for her includes or precludes any assessment of bad air or miasma as their own concepts.

in the anti-Black cosmos as stanky is to presume that the conditions of the weather do not hold the promise of changing or being ameliorated in any capacity, especially under the realities of radical climate change accelerated by the capitalistic industrialized society that characterize the Anthropocene, and especially for Black folk who already have, do, and will certainly continue to experience the effects of the growing Stank in different ways than all others. Furthermore, aspiration under stanky conditions always means negotiating the problem that any air that we try to put and keep in Black bodies will be on some level poisonous or harmful because the air is always already a toxic miasma; Black breath as disturbance will itself come "disturbed" because it is polluted with the deathly spores of anti-Blackness and the particulate toxins produced by a horrifyingly destructive human world. In both cases, thinking about the atmospheric conditions of the weather and/or of the Stank is essential to understanding Black space.

The Stank might be a fundamental feature of being Black in space, the odorous marker borne by Black folk marked by Blackness in the labyrinthine mausoleum of the variously dead, deathly, and dying. Differently put, it might be the amalgamated smell of death, and all its attendant meanings for Black being. Following a two-day symposium entitled "Black Thought in the Age of Terror," held at the University of California, Irvine in 2006, Frank B. Wilderson III offered the closing comments to the brilliant work shared by the scholars in attendance.[16] Entitled "Do I Stank, or Was It Already Stanky in Here?; or, Notes from an Impossible Negro," the anecdotal sections of his comments provide insight into how we might name and decipher Me, Dickens, and Beatty's Stank. Wilderson recounts a ride to the airport in a shuttle with a South Asian driver, a White woman, and a White man, soon after the "ground at Ground Zero had stopped smoldering."[17] They converse about Wilderson's position at Cal and discuss the supposedly generalized injustice of the Patriot Act. All the while, Wilderson responds, either speaking in a parody of a minstrel's voice or describing it narratively. Never do we hear precisely what he speaks as he speaks it; rather, we read it relationally, as if his very capacity to speak on and for himself, his beliefs, and his works has been mutilated by the nature of this confined, communal space "in mixed company." As a proxy for empathy and suffering, the White passengers prompt the South Asian driver to disparage the Patriot Act's immorality by

---

16. These included David Marriott, Fred Moten, Lindon Barrett (rest in power), Cheryl Harris, Zakiyyah Iman Jackson, Jared Sexton, Akinyele Umoja, and Frank Wilderson.

17. Frank Wilderson, "Do I Stank, or Was It Already Stanky in Here?; or, Notes from an Impossible Negro," 3.

recounting the kind of suffering he and his family endured prior to entering this country, only to suffer continuously, if differently, because of legislation like the Patriot Act. After sharing and lamenting, the South Asian driver wonders aloud to everyone and no one in particular, "I don't know why I ever brought my family here." Unthinkingly, half-jokingly, and sorrowfully, Wilderson responds, "Me neither," and the space of the van shifts. The air reeks of Frank's Stank.

Too comfortably, Wilderson responds operating on what he recognizes is a misreading of the space of the shuttle and the structural relation between the passengers. For a moment, in their discussion of the Patriot Act and a shared disdain for the supposed un-American nature of it, he allows himself to believe in a "common sense," a connective thread of shared thought between beings of otherwise different structural positions, and a "common purpose," a shared purpose. In both, he allows himself the dream of a common people-ness, a shared humanness, a collective "we"—"we are all people"—and a flattening "just"—"just people"—a "multicultural consensus" indicative of some form of organic "community," an "intrepid coalition of affect."[18] The intoxicating, sweet scent of the fantasy of this kind of political-ontological flatness radiates from a momentary desire for and belief in not only the possibility of assimilation but also in the capacity of Black folk (here, Frank) to directly facilitate the realization of that possibility, in spite of the distinctions in structural position between Black folk and the non-Black "people" occupying the space. This fantasy becomes an unspoken, imagined truth wafting through the air of this enclosure, the transformative, invisible force transmuting the anti-Human deathliness of Wilderson's Black position into human life, comparable to the differential human status (modified by gender, race, class, and citizenship) of who he believed to be his compatriots. But once it is uttered aloud—"me neither"—once the fantasy is spoken into the air *as if*, the air clears, the fantasy's aroma dissipates, and the way for the very pungent odor of the fact of his Blackness reaches the nostrils and lungs of the passengers and driver, an untimely truth prompting a rude awakening, and introducing an "uncommon" silence.[19]

This shift embodies the paradigmatic question of the title; does Frank stank, or was it already stanky in the airport shuttle—in the world beyond it? This is, in part, a version of a Fanonian question, indicative of a temporal problem and a set of spatial relations: Was I a "dirty nigger" before the boy invoked it, was I Black and stanky before I spoke, or was that fact (re)

---

18. Wilderson, "Do I Stank," 4.
19. Ibid., 6.

introduced into the air anew in a way that is distinct from any prior version of it? Here? Everywhere?

We pursued the temporal implications of Fanon's narrative while dissecting Dana's character development in Butler's *Kindred*, and now Wilderson adds, or excavates, a different layer to the problem of the (timing of the) stench. Temporally, Wilderson is always already untimely, and as such, the answer appears to be both: The Stank operates as a confirmation of what is already true; it is a removal of the perfumed, fantastic mask that had been carefully crafted by both Wilderson's Sambo dialogue and the favorable responses of the White and South Asian passengers. Once he speaks, once the fact of his Blackness becomes undeniable in this space, his Blackness becomes the muting, suffocating force that sutures together the real, unmasked, coalition of silence formed by what Wilderson would call the master/settlers (Whites) and their junior partner (the South Asian). The anti-Blackness lurking behind the varied structural positions occupied by each putrefies behind the lie of the common erected in the shuttle, and its revelation manifests in the "uncommon" silence, the shared holding, or withholding, of breath by the three non-Black people.

Spatially, if Frank stank Blackly before he entered the space—if it is an untimely fact of his deathly existence—and this Stank is only made the odorous equivalent of "legible" to everyone he encounters in the space of the shuttle, then the answer to his titular question affirms not only the fact of his Stank as it pollutes the civility of the shuttle's space, but also the fact of his Stank in all spaces he enters and exits before and after his ride to the airport. Yes, it was already stanky in here, but only because it, and I, and Blackness is stanky already everywhere. Blackness operates as a kind of pollutant that, perhaps in the performative self-deprecation and degradation of appeasement with aspirations for assimilation (e.g., Frank's Sambo), might be masked or rendered odorless (like methane) in the name and fantasy of civility, here captured by the sonic space of a particular kind of utterance. But should it suffer some form of Fanonian exposure, whether on the part of Black folk or from an antagonistic encounter, the way its stench had already expanded to fill the volume of the space it occupies becomes undeniable. So much so that, in the end, given the opportunity to symbolically recant, to deny the emission of the stench, Frank straightens his posture and affirms the stankiness of his Stank. This time, the Stank smells distinctly of burning, "a cornfield up in flames," a conglomeration of, perhaps, singed hair, the smoldering feces of livestock, and disintegrating possibilities for nourishment; everything—the fantasy of coalition, the desire for and belief in assimilation—ablaze.

Me and Beatty's Dickens, California, Stank, for all the specificity of the components sutured to its geographical location, stanks of a Blackness that is always already present. It waxes and wanes in odor; it stanks differently on different days, is at one moment in the text infuriating and interruptive, then at another wholly unbearable.[20] The Stank operates as an omnipresent, "omnipotent"—in a quite different sense of potency—isolating force, singular to the nonexistent city of Dickens, a site at which its amalgamated smell and all its components might conglomerate, linger, become one with and inseparable from the air Dickens's denizens must breathe. On one particular morning, the Stank becomes overwhelming. At the height of his efforts to wield segregation as a tool to "reanimate" Dickens by segregating Dickens's Chaff Middle School, which is to say earn its recognition as a legitimate space within the larger space of the anti-Black world, the Stank rolls in with a particularly devastating force. Children in the Farms stumble and stagger to Me's plot of land in flight from its stench, some retching and vomiting on the elm tree, and some devouring peanut butter to keep their mouths and minds occupied.[21] All try to flee the World-War-I-mustard-gas-esque[22] miasma as if seeking sanctuary from the omnipresent violence, both symbolic and intestinal, of this iteration of the Stank.

I am interested in what draws the children to Me's farm. Me's plot of farmland is at the nexus of nourishment and subjugation, satiated life and social death, Stank and citrus, for Dickens's constituency. In this instance, "it was the smell [of satsuma oranges] that brung 'em."[23] The "refreshing pungency of citrus"[24] interrupts the violence of the Stank's omnipresence in a way that entices the children of the Farms to seek refuge near Me's satsuma tree. Satsuma citrus perfume holds a set of promises: a reprieve from, or at least a masking of, the overwhelming and unbearable Stank, and several entangled forms of nourishment, physical, psychic (relational), and political-ontological. Bound up with the satsuma's "perfectly balanced bittersweet flavor"[25] is its restorative, protective magic. Satsuma, like Me's other cultivated fruit, promise health benefits akin to shiny hair, clear skin, ultra-white

---

20. Jared Sexton's essay and presentation, both entitled "Unbearable Blackness," are worth investigating here for their dissection of the many meanings of "unbearable."
21. Beatty, *The Sellout*, 185–86.
22. Ibid. As he writes it, "I stood in the middle of Bernard Avenue, the kids beckoning me over, waving frantically like World War I soldiers urging a wounded comrade out of the mustard gas and back in to the relative safety of the trenches."
23. Ibid., 186.
24. Ibid., 187.
25. Ibid., 172.

eyes, and a general state of relaxation.[26] Furthermore, this fruit promises wrinkle-free skin, a stronger immune system, decreased likelihood of cardiovascular disease, and relief from hypertension. Satsumas, not tangelos, clementines, or tangerines, remedy strained and broken kinship ties, romantic and otherwise: After Marpessa, a Black woman bus driver who enters and exits an on-and-off relationship with Me, "face . . . slathered with Satsuma juice,"[27] suddenly dons an "irrepressible smile" and speaks joyously and affirmatively on the renewed status of their romantic partnership. On another occasion, the satsumas' scent on a photograph prevents Marpessa's younger brother, Stevie, from pulling the trigger. Their sweet (16.8 percent sucrose)[28] juice "[removes] the nasty taste . . . of cooning," which sometimes tastes like "nasty . . . comic-relief watermelon,"[29] and acts as a way of masking the wound and pain of performatively "selling out" on television and movie screens (and, by extension, in songs, dance, in government institutions, and so on). Satsuma juice, pulp, and rinds work as an elixir for physical ailments and hunger, romantic relationships, life-and-death situations, and affirmations of one's property status; they attract children, appease ex-lovers and their antagonistic (perhaps murderous) younger siblings, and shield children and adults from the overwhelming and unpredictable Stank of Blackness. They are, in every register, "what freedom smells like."[30]

The congregation of children that gathers on Me's farm daily continues to devour the newly ripened satsuma oranges in order to escape the warlike terrorizing violence of the Stank, masking the bitterness and stankiness of Blackness with the sweet scent, food, and juice of a fantastic kind of freedom. The farm becomes a pocket universe, housing a reality in which Black children might taste and ingest a kind of life-giving and life-sustaining freedom from the symbolic, sensory, psychological, physical, and political-ontological violence composing the Stank of the life-denying, poisonous air they otherwise breathe. Perhaps satsumas smell like the pristine containment of Wilderson's airport shuttle, the kind of fantastic space, the kind of sanctuary, from the omnipresence and omnipotence of Black Stank that seems to make real a dream of the alchemy that turns fugitivity into free-

---

26. Ibid., 184. Specifically, Me's papayas, kiwis, apples, and blueberries seem to provide these effects.

27. Ibid., 194.

28. Ibid., 187. Beatty takes great care to detail the characteristics, cultivation, and quality measures of satsuma oranges.

29. Ibid., 173.

30. Ibid., 185.

dom, freedom into life-giving nourishment and satisfaction, and life into joy and pleasure.

Satsuma oranges, like the "coalition of affect" of Wilderson's airport shuttle, are the fruit borne by that dream behind the wall of sleep, and they too wake to the nightmarish question Farley poses: "What if we only *think* we escape the labyrinth?" To reframe the question, what if the Stank and the sweet scent of satsumas are so inextricably entangled that the latter is not only not an escape, but also not the marker of the creation of a space, an elsewhere to the nowhere we occupy, a somewhere where we might be and, so, be free—what if that entanglement reveals that the sweetness of the satsumas, and all the relational, physical, psychological, and political-ontological dreams they fulfill, to be similarly violent, similarly bound up with Blackness and its attendant, deathly features?

Me offers an answer in his peculiar choice to bury his father in his backyard. Specifically, *why* Me buries his father in his farmland as well as the circumstances of Me's father's death will lead us toward an unnerving answer to that question. Me's father, a "liberation psychologist"[31] so invested in dissecting what it meant to be Black that his son became his primary and most important experiment-cum-patient, worked, often with the police, as Dickens's "Nigger Whisperer," a Black community crisis manager who was called "whenever some nigger who'd 'done lost they motherfucking mind' needed to be talked down from a tree or freeway overpass precipice."[32] Not unlike many Black folks who work within anti-Black institutions like the system of policing,[33] he inevitably faced and succumbed to the overwhelming and gratuitous anti-Black force of that same institution. Having impa-

---

31. Me introduces his father as "the founder and, to my knowledge, sole practitioner of Liberation Psychology" (27) at the outset of the novel.

32. Ibid., 36.

33. The following list is not exhaustive by any stretch of the imagination. And while I have written repeatedly on the foundational unethicality of the police as an institution, and that because of its unethicality I am of the mind that reforming it is impossible, let alone from within, this list is indicative of the way Black officers/people who work or worked with the police are imperiled by their Blackness in ways they may deny, but that remain real and unavoidable. Both barring and including actual wrongdoing these officers have done: Christopher Dorner, for example, and the notorious "burn that motherfucker alive" uttered by police who had cornered the former officer who'd allegedly murdered two people; Christopher Owens, a Black police officer of the Providence Police Department in Rhode Island who was beaten on his day off; Cariol Horne, who, after witnessing another officer choking a suspect and intervening on his behalf, was punched in the face—she had to have her bridge replaced—fired, and denied her pension; and Howard Morgan, who, while off-duty in 2005, was stopped for driving the wrong direction down a one-way street, shot twenty-eight times—twenty-three in the back—tried twice for the crime of attempted murder (found guilty the second time), and thrown in

tiently driven around a pair of officers mindlessly blocking an intersection while talking to a homeless woman and "yelled something," Me's father was stopped, lectured, and about to be issued a ticket when, quoting Bill Russell, he replied, "Either give me the ticket or the lecture, but you can't give me both." The officers "took exception, pulled their guns, [Me's] dad ran like any sensible person would, they fired four shots into his back and left him for dead in the intersection."[34] I recount this at length because it resonates with accounts like Nephi Arreguin's and other stories about what happens to Black folk of any age, class, gender identification, sexual orientation, or disability, for driving while Black or fleeing, unarmed, from the promise of dishonorable death, like Sandra Bland, Walter Scott, or Terrance Kellom. This real, quotidian, spectacular anti-Black violence that contextualizes and gives meaning to the moment of the murder in Beatty's novel also gives meaning to the corpse of Me's father left in this moment's wake.

When Me claims and protects this corpse and all its spectrally attendant meanings by burying it in the farmland he inherits from his father, that spectral and spectacular violence, *that untimely deathliness*, dissolves—decomposes—into and becomes one with the very earth on which Me produces his crops. Black death, even in some infinitesimal way, fertilizes the fruit and cotton Me grows. Standing in the mud atop his father's grave, Me recalls attempting to plant an apple tree—his father loved apples—how that tree died almost immediately, and how the fruit tasted fertilized by, or at least in close proximity to, Black death: "Two days later it was dead. And the apples tasted like mentholated cigarettes, liver and onions, and cheap fucking rum."[35] From atop the grave while encountering the rememory of the Stank-and-death-infused apples, he observes the farm in its entirety: "Rows of fruit trees. . . . Lemons. Apricots. Pomegranates. Plums. Satsumas. Figs. Pineapples. Avocados. The fields, which rotate from corn to wheat, then to Japanese rice . . . [and] the greenhouse sits in the middle . . . backed by leafy processions of cabbage, lettuce, legumes, and cucumbers . . . grapes . . . tomatoes . . . cotton."[36] The panoramic view projects outward from a vexed position, one that is untimely for its concurrence with the foundational and fertile memories of death, violence, bitterness, and decay, and deathly for its position atop a corpse produced and haunted by quotidian, but spectacular, forms of anti-Black police violence. "In the mud" mixed with decomposed

---

prison for, as his attorney puts it, "driving while Black." Morgan was released in 2015 and is trying to have his conviction reversed.

34. Beatty, *The Sellout*, 50.
35. Ibid., 213.
36. Ibid.

Black matter directly from his father's corpse; the mud dark and fertile, perhaps the color of the flesh of the one dead below, and the one imperiled by death above; the mud melding the untimeliness of the rememory, the Me remembering, and the corpse violently vacated of life—from here, Me spies it all. It is *only* from this position in the mud that melds the space of death and decay with the space of life and growth, that the whole expanse of the farm becomes visible, legible in its totality. Black death fertilizes this totality, how Beatty envisions it, and how Me witnesses it; it is only at this nexus that the full promise and complexity of the flourishing farm becomes clear.

Black death fertilizes the satsumas, too. The fruit the children devour cannot be disentangled from the Black death feeding the tree at its root; there is no way to discern how much of the refuse produced by Me's father's corpse is directly responsible for the growth and development of the oranges (or any other fruit or crop). Initially, at first whiff and bite, against the waking nightmare of a Blackness that cannot and does not stop stanking, this succulent fruit-shaped dream plays on a desire for affirmation, protection, assimilation, and inclusion that momentarily masks the stanky and untimely fact of Blackness. This many-tiered, sweet, and juicy trap of the farm's pocket universe entices. But in actuality, and perhaps more devastatingly, the "pungency" of "freedom" and all its attendant sentiment, satiation, and affirmation, is nonetheless fleeting and illusory. It stanks just as much as, and of, untimely, deathly Blackness. If they are different, that difference is not at the level of fundament, the level of the soil and the root. The pocket universe carved out of this violent miasmatic Blackness looming over all of Dickens, California, becomes nothing more than a fantastic reiteration of that miasma made more palatable, more digestible, to those forced to bear its overwhelming force. Like Blackness, bad dreams, and waking nightmares, satsumas stank of death, and the space of their creation and cultivation is made both possible and fertile only by the decay of Black flesh. Flight from the suffocating violence of a labyrinthine nowhere, in the name of ascertaining fugitive nourishment or cultivating some semblance of freedom, is a lie.

If the answer to "So what exactly is *our thing?*," which is also, "What even is a Black space?," is something like, "A nowhere produced, at least in part, by a violent and arbitrary erasure, shrouded in variously sweet, pungent, and foul iterations of a Stanky Blackness that is an inescapable labyrinth, where even life, growth and nourishment are made possible, at least in part, by Black death(liness)"—grimy—then the possibility of making a way out of no way or nowhere collapses. Instead, what becomes clear is that all ways always stank—that is, there is not only no escape from the stanky Blackness of our position in the labyrinth, but even the large and small spaces we make and cultivate out of nowhere cannot be disentangled from that Stank.

While we understand that dark matter condenses and congregates, providing a framework for and giving a form to the masses of ordinary matter, the large and small structures that dominate our conceptualizations of the universe, and what it is to be in it as we understand it now, dark matter only imperceptibly and undetectably interacts with ordinary matter. Its effective invisibility and implicit effectuality is bound up with the way ordinary matter dominates the visible, interactive plane of the universe. While under erasure, while rendered spectral, this condensation of dark matter, of Blackness, named Dickens, California, remains structurally entangled with the anti-Black world that transformed it into a stanky, ghostly space.

What Beatty suggests through Me and his farm's entanglement with the Black death that variably fertilizes its crops is that spaces for or of Blackness, spaces where Black folk might congregate, be nourished, and dream of freedom, must also be sites that stage confrontations with this stanky death that never really leaves. Both because they are structurally bound to do so and because the possibility for an "authentic upheaval"[37] inheres in doing so, Black spaces must wallow in the muddy contradictions and act as sites where we confront the series of knots binding life with death, cultivation with decay, nourishment with nausea and hunger. This appears to be the logic animating Me's plan to reanimate Dickens, to get it back on the map: painting white boundaries around the territory,[38] creating Whites-only seats on local buses,[39] segregating Chaff Middle School, and unofficially reinstituting chattel slavery by honoring the wishes of Hominy Jenkins. While on the surface this is a totally absurdist plan, superficially purely interested in appealing to desires for inclusion and assimilation via juridical recognition and implicitly legitimizing the same juridical process that both erased Dickens in the first place and casually snatched life from his father's flesh, these strategies appear to hyperbolize the inextricability of this Black bastion from the labyrinth. In their own, Beatty-ful, absurd way, these strategies might be aimed at their own version of amplifying the impossible. Me's machinations for recognition attempt to elucidate and make unavoidable a confrontation between this looming question of Black space and what it might look like, or what might be its constitutive element or problem, and the way Black spaces, like condensations of dark matter, remain structurally bound up with the anti-Black world and all its constitutive matter.

37. This is another reference to Fanon's "zone of nonbeing."
38. Beatty, *The Sellout*, 99–100.
39. Ibid., 127–28.

In sum, *The Sellout* theorizes that Black folks occupy a space, a nowhere, constituted of unresolved and unresolvable contradictions—antagonisms—in which we must wallow. That Dickens quietly returns to recognized status in a weather report on the news one day and that Me accomplishes his self-appointed mission do not obscure the nature of Dickens as a hollow, stanky bastion of Blackness in the anti-Black world. Rather, given that Me only comes to the understanding that he will never understand himself or precisely what animated his mission, and that its accomplishment occurs so unceremoniously, this achievement of the novel's superficial goal might only affirm the importance of the theorization that undergirds—fertilizes—it.[40] Beatty leaves us lost, irresolute. To enter into the novel and to travel to Dickens is, paraphrasing Marpessa, to cross the threshold into nowhere, its irresolvable contradictions and hyperbolically impossible entanglements. It is to enter into a forced, forceful, stanky reckoning with the knots binding Blackness, being, space, death, and life into something at once flourishing and dying.

The Last Bastion of Blackness is inextricable from the anti-Black labyrinthine mausoleum in which we are structurally positioned. It is a land of the living dead, littered with crops that thrive in toxic air and promise nourishment with the sweet poison of dreams, dreams of elsewhere and escapes that only mean to jettison us deeper into the muck and the mire of a confrontation for which we must "make way" in this "no way."

2
LOST PASSAGES

Here we are, in Dickens, California, the middle of Nowhere, lost, dreaming of impossible sanctuaries, doors, and exits, enrapt in the miasma of the dark. We worry about the nature of this space across the threshold, this site of contradictions; our concern is for the mechanics of our passage, for the structure framing our crossing, for where we've ended up now that we seek a reckoning with the door and the stanky Black deathliness looming over this space beyond the threshold. In our collective rememory, Dionne Brand's *A Map to the Door of No Return* comes to mind. In it, we travel with her with and toward the figure of the eponymous "door of no return." The "door,"

---

40. The final chapter of the novel is entitled "Closure," and the lack thereof appears deliberate for the sake of the need to leave unanswered this lingering question about Blackness and space.

which "is really the door of *dreams*,"⁴¹ as a figure and concept, allows us entry to the labyrinthine dream for an exit. Through its conceptualization we might find our way to imagining and telling the stories that will take us to the nowhere we want to go. Hoping to imaginatively make a way out of no way, and knowing that though we fear what monsters might lurk in the dark this has been about boldly going into the black (w)hole's abyss, we do what we set out to do from the beginning.

We leap, we fall.

The door calls for as much. After all, it is "the place of the fall"—into hysterectomies and blueshifted blues, into deathliness, into untimeliness, into nonbeing, into Blackness. What it is and what it is not will frame what we might be able to do and where we might be able to go in our imaginations. We must map the door's characteristics. Contrary to Aristodemou in Farley's reading, it is not the marker of or access to a "beginning," new or otherwise—not precisely, anyway. In discovering our untimeliness, we reckoned with what Brand calls "a tear in the world . . . a rupture in the quality of being . . . the end of traceable beginnings,"⁴² so it is where the connection between Blackness and meaningful "beginnings" dissolves. In the First Arrangement, we briefly thought with Brand about how slavery inaugurates a kind of time and temporal relation, untime, that violently severs the connection between us and being, and between us and the possibility and sense of origins. Following Brand's thinking, "too much has been *made* of origins."⁴³ The door, the tear, seems to locate the inaugural moment at which Blackness becomes antithetical to being, at which we might emplot ourselves at the beginning of the grand, anti-Black narrative of modernity. In actuality, the door only marks the site at which we lost our temporal and spatial bearings; it is the place of the event of a metaphysical, physical, and imaginative "dislocation,"⁴⁴ in which our being, our flesh, and our imagination was "flung out and dispersed"⁴⁵ from any sense of time and space. The door is not neatly framed, or pristinely crafted; it is not the beauty of an old or new point of entry. It is the jagged and distorted site memorializing our dislocation from the capacity to know where we are in time and in space, an indictment against the very possibility of "beginning" for Blacks. *A* beginning, *new* beginnings, the "rebeginning"—these possible destinations recede into the dark; they cease to mean what they might have.

---

41. Brand, *A Map*, 28; emphasis mine. But also "dream harder," Aristodemou urges.
42. Ibid., 5.
43. Ibid., 64; emphasis mine.
44. Ibid., 73.
45. Brand, *A Map*, 26.

If not exactly a point of beginning, but one of a fatal and untimely injury and entry, how might we orient ourselves in our imaginations to the door? Further, if "too much has been *made* of origins," what's been made of their dereliction? What can we make of the door, then? As always and like us, these questions are untimely, "too early, or too late." We need(ed) more information.

Brand's text offers numerous descriptions of the door that might guide us toward the orientation we seek. The door exists triply: physically, psychically, or imaginatively, and metaphysically or political-ontologically. The door of no return "is not mere physicality. . . . [I]t is a spiritual location . . . [and] also perhaps a psychic destination,"[46] which is to say that "the door is a place, real, imaginary, and imagine . . . which exists or existed . . . the door of a million exits multiplied . . . a door which makes the *door* impossible and dangerous, cunning and disagreeable."[47] The door's existence bleeds across the planes of spatiality in which we find ourselves lost, but it is not even precisely a door. It is a site, a "location" plotted on the map of the anti-Black world, a mark demarcating "the place of the fall" that happened and keeps on happening; it is also a "destination," a psychic spatial place to which we might like to return, through which we might exit, or, at least, where we might end up. It is both singular, *the* door of no return, and potentially infinite, the chimeric structure of "a million exits multiplied." It is a door with its very door-ness thrown into disarray; perhaps it is not even really best thought of as a door at all.

The door and its threshold appear to open us into an unfamiliar and contradictory space. On the one hand, its opening "exists as an absence . . . a thing in fact which we do not know about,"[48] the dereliction of our capacities to imagine and think ourselves toward its presence both because we cannot grasp its precise location and because it is both present and absent and if present it is paradoxically singular *and* infinite—or, absent in the way that it exceeds thought. It is "really *the* door of dreams,"[49] and yet it is also "*a* 'vastness,' indeed 'beyond imagination,'"[50] the kind of spatial excess that exceeds the bounds of the dream and strains and stresses the dreamer. Finding our way to the door, and so also being able to orient ourselves to its place, might require nothing more than the mind. The door might best be thought of as Black consciousness itself, and reaching it, or finding oneself

---

46. Ibid., 1.
47. Ibid., 19.
48. Ibid., 15.
49. Ibid., 28.
50. Ibid., 61; emphasis mine.

in its multiplicitous space, the door is what it is to think or imagine while Black at all: the door of Black dreams, the door as Black imagination. And yet, from the outset, Brand reminds us that "there is as it says no way in; no return."[51] But maybe this is less a set of contradictions than it is a reflection of our imaginative capacity. Passage to and through the door requires nothing more than the imagination, but the violence marked by the door (it is the site of the fall) creates an imaginative set of barriers and limits that both ensure that we are unable to conceive the door's totality and also bar our imaginations access/entry should we ever impossibly find our way to it. So imagine or "dream harder," Aristodemou might suggest.

In the end, if, for all the qualities of its imaginative, spiritual, political-ontological structure, and its many permutations in the material world, the door both sets and exceeds our capacities to imagine what and where it is. Our work might only be able to aim "at the truth" of what it is, and what it does and means to us. We might do well to track its presence in what it has touched, in its resonant effects on we who "fell" through it. Perhaps we hold the clues and the keys in the flesh, in the imagination, and in our very beings. The question might be, "How did we end up here?" Which, relative to the door and our initial passage over its threshold, is to ask, "How did that passage happen? What was the nature of our crossing?" and also, "What hieroglyphics or marks do we bear because of it?" These are questions aimed at characterizing our movement through the violent space of the door, the tear,[52] and also at the traces of that movement we bear in our flesh, imagination, and being.

In terms of movement, we worry how what we understand to be the deathly and untimely force of enslavement propelled us through the door. To know the way this force moved and moves us would be to better understand our capacity to move and orient ourselves in relation to it. From the door, we are "flung out and dispersed,"[53] catapulted through the portal of terror and domination (of enslavement), and into the darkness devoid of being, the void or "zone of nonbeing,"[54] the Black space of the labyrinth. Being jettisoned, we suffer a violent "dislocation"[55] from the world, from time and space, from each other, and from ourselves; the labyrinth's walls

---

51. Ibid., 1.
52. I am evoking Brand's language here. In the opening anecdote of *A Map to the Door of No Return*, she describes slavery as having ripped the entire world asunder; it produces "a tear in the world" (5).
53. Ibid., 26.
54. Fanon, *Black Skin*, 2. Here, he maps what he calls the "zone of nonbeing."
55. Brand, *A Map*, 73.

are the structural manifestation of this dislocation. Brand's language is the language of violent breaking; the scatter and shatter of relations, orientations, and the capacity to create or maintain either in "dispersed"; the disturbance of the connections, or joints, between us and the constitutive features and forces of the world—namely time and space—in "dislocation."

Passage through the door appears to be a quick and haphazard spaghettification: We are "atomized" in our being, being forced through the violence of the door, as are the connections that might allow us to locate ourselves in relation to the door's threshold, to each other, and to ourselves. The broken refuse of our flesh, our imagination, and our being is "dispersed" across the "vastness" of the void; our "dislocation" inhibits if not prohibits our ability to locate ourselves "here" or anywhere beyond the door's threshold. In our rememories, we encounter Dana in the moment her arm is amputated by the wall, and hear her screams; we also remember Hartman's analysis of the amputated flesh; we reconsider Fanon's sense of being dismembered.[56] We find our many fragments scattered at the labyrinth's entrance.

This is what lost us. This is why we *are* lost. Our lostness is the product of our subjection to a force that flung us out, shattered us, and scattered the pieces at the "entrance" to the dark and labyrinthine structure of terror and domination. What we have named "lostness" is not merely a condition characterized by our inability to orient ourselves to the structure as well as we might like, which is a problem created, in part, by the darkness encroaching our bodies and the walls around us, but also a state of being-in-space characterized by being broken at the level of our flesh, our imagination, and our being, the innumerable fragments dispersed. "Lost," unable to find our way; "lost," unable to recollect ourselves into the wholeness of singular beings or positions; "lost," multiplied by the countless bits dislocated from one another; "lost," it seems, irretrievably. This is to be "captive" to being lost: bound to our lostness by both the labyrinth's structure and by the state of being broken. Our broken flesh is of "captive bodies," our bodies are the "(places) of captivity." Our being and imaginations are bound up with and bound to the shattered space of Black flesh.

This entanglement is inextricable: To be "captured in one's own body" is to be captured "in one's own thoughts," is to be captured in the untimely shatter of the flesh, is to be possessed by, is to be "out of possession of one's own mind" as well.[57] As Brand writes, "our cognitive schema is captivity":

---

56. For the corresponding readings: chapter 2, "Black Holes and Generations" (discussion of Dana's arm); also chapter 5—"Of Shadows and Diamonds" (reading of Hartman).

57. Brand, *A Map*, 29.

The framework for the production of thought, and for the stimulation of the many gestures that would and do compose our movement within the dark of the labyrinth is our captivity to the force and effects of the door of no return. Our capacity to think and move, to imagine and orient ourselves, in the dark is captive to being broken, captive to breaking, broken, itself. We, our means, and our way, are lost.

The horror.

Brand tells us that this is the stuff of waking nightmares: Stank. These are the stanky, "bad dreams," to which "the dreamer is captive," and in which we are "overwhelmed by the spectre"—the living dead, or undead, or Beloved, presence—"of captivity."[58] We face the nightmarish reality of immeasurable and "perpetual retreats and recoveries,"[59] the maneuvers necessitated by the perils of the structure with which we hope to contend. When we do move, when we do think, we do so like Fanon, piecing together fragments as other selves—broken selves, the spaces of which break again and again in untimely encounters with old and new trauma; we move and think in the breaking wake of enslavement, against the overwhelming force of the door. Our body/flesh, imagination, and being, being broken open to all forms of gratuitous anti-Black violence, are "constructed and occupied by other embodiments";[60] in our dispossession, we are possessed by captivity's specter. As Wilderson writes in "Grammar and Ghosts," "violence and captivity are the grammar and ghosts of our every gesture,"[61] which for our purposes is to say that our movement and thought are at least framed, if not wholly possessed, by this specter; our capacity to move and think in space emanates from and gestures back to the door, its force, and all it signifies.

There is no way out. None we can imagine or locate, but we knew this before we arrived at this conclusion; we've been in Dickens, and we have yet to leave. What Brand reveals is that in addition to being unable to locate some form of escape, engage in some form of meaningfully fugitive flight from the labyrinth, or cultivate a space for life and nourishment, we also remain unable to imagine or locate even the possibility of the wholeness of our own flesh, imaginations and beings. It is stanky where we are, and at least a portion of the particulate refuse composing that Stank's miasma is itself composed of the particulate dark matter into which we shattered, scattered indiscriminately throughout nowhere. Even following Farley's method of retelling—reTelling, to conjure Le Guin—the broken narratives

---

58. Ibid.
59. Ibid.
60. Ibid., 38.
61. Wilderson, "Grammar and Ghosts," 119.

of our beings, or the narratives that broke, break, and will break our beings, will not redress the wounds, nor repair the breaking.

Brand discovers as much while she reads J. M. Coetzee's *Disgrace,* on the verge of falling asleep and drifting into dream. Stunned by Coetzee's reductive characterization of Blacks as "acquisitive, predatory, rapine, and brutal," specifically by his deployment of the anti-Black "trope of the Black rapist," Brand worries about the creative possibilities of myth, allegory, and reality in relation to Blackness. She worries that they "fail as imaginative devices," that their structures crumble when they must describe, or map, the position of Black flesh, imagination, and being. She worries, as she falls asleep, that Farley's kind of revisionary myth- or allegory-making, or dreaming (harder), or "reTelling," will not take us to where we imagine we would fundamentally like to go: elsewhere; away; out. But doing so might take us deeper, might allow us to wallow, might afford us the place where we might confront Black deathliness's Stank without retreat.

Having the sense that we have yet to meaningfully move from where we began, from where we were flung—Dickens, Flint, Chicago, Los Angeles, Detroit, Irvine, whatever the name borne by our coordinates in the labyrinth—what have we made and what do and can we make out of the nowhere where we are? Better, how do we inhabit this place, and what's at stake in embracing that inhabitation—in allowing ourselves to meld with mud and Stank?

We encounter one more guide here, in our rememory. Recall the framework for what we understand as "work," specifically Black creative work in the shadow of the door, in the dark of the labyrinth, "in the wake" of enslavement. Sharpe reminds us that the guiding question animating our work concerns the deathly nature of our *being* being broken and scattered into the void, of various being stricken by the incapacitating and mutilating force of death: "How do we who are doing work in black studies *tend to, care for, comfort,* and *defend* the dead, the dying, and those living lives consigned, in the aftermath of legal chattel slavery, to death that is always-imminent and immanent?"[62] Thought differently, given where we (fail to) find ourselves, this is in part a question of how we create spaces of mourning for the loss that characterizes and plagues our position, and for the variously lost in the dark. We think with Brand about the simultaneously meticulous and automatic (re)cognition that allows us to think the world and its structures into "solidity":

---

62. Sharpe, "Black Studies: In the Wake," 59–60. For a more extensive discussion of Sharpe's essay, return to the Second Arrangement, chapter 4's introductory section.

> There are ways of constructing the world—that is, of putting it together each morning, what it should look like piece by piece—and I don't feel that I share this with the people in my small town. Each morning I think we wake up and open our eyes and set the particles of forms together—we make solidity with our eyes and with the matter in our brains. . . . We collect each molecule summing them up into flesh or leaf or water or air. Before that everything is liquid, ubiquitous and mute. We accumulate information over our lives which brings various things into solidity, into view.[63]

We accumulate information as particulate dark matter in our imaginations; that information is framed by, rearranged, and stored in relation to the cognitive schema grammatically structuring our thought; and we deploy that inflected information in order to construct the world(s) around us. Inextricably bound up with the captivity and breaking that characterize at least our structural spatial relationships, the world(s) we produce out of the silent liquidity are the product of an attempt to account for death spatially—to make a space for death, the dead, and the dying.

Broken and broken open, we must and do make space for the fact of our lostness in the dark terror of the world's labyrinthine structure. The careful summation of all that we know means to do the work with which Sharpe tasks us. Our creations are not imaginative exits, escapes, or returns, but *deeper descents into the dark, into nowhere.* To make space "out of nowhere" is to sculpt what indomitably stands before us into an examination of this lostness and into a space where we might actively honor and mourn the dead. In the labyrinthine tomb of the archive, we sit, think, and imagine in the space of death, with the dead spread out like dust all around us.

Out of the particulate refuse of our flesh, imagination, and beings, out of that illegible dark matter, and out of nowhere, we only work to make the necessary arrangements.

---

63. Brand, *A Map*, 140.

OUTRO

Out of Time in the Middle of Nowhere

There
is nowhere
like this place, and
no time
like the present.

WE WORK with the shards of Black life and death that called out to us because we knew and know that the critical, caring, and perilous work we need to do is bound up with destruction. These fragments of Black life and death surrounding us affirmed our sense of our own untimeliness against the neatness of time, and of our stankiness in the middle of nowhere. The untimeliness that signals our destructive relationship to human models and experiences of time and the stankiness that signals our destructive relationship to human spaces and spatiality act as the Black *prima materia*, the Black and essential material, with which we must work to create these impossible stories we imagine, witness, bear, conjure, and live in and against the anti-Black cosmos where and when we cannot be. What we knew, and now know with excruciating intimacy, to be the violent, distorted fabric of spacetime shaping the field of fragments around us *is* the material we must bend to create Black pocket universes from streets to pages (and everywhere and when between). We knew and know that in order to conjure Black spacetimes that might upend the anti-Black cosmos, we would have to become avatars of destruction, able to bend the forces of untimeliness and stankiness and love toward the kinds of authentic upheaval that must be born if we are to save the earth and conjure the impossible story of a wholly unimaginable world.

Wherever and whenever we've ended up, nowhere is better or more apropos, and we've got no time to celebrate. We wordly wanderers wandered wondering about the possibility of other worlds, word worlds that would warp and rend and otherwise radically reimagine the fabric of spacetime, especially since we understand the ways that our pain, terror, and subjection stitch that fabric together. We traversed the perilous folds in space and wrinkles in time in search of the fragments of a theory of Black spacetime because we recognized that understanding not only how time and space tear Black life, death, and creation absolutely asunder, but also how Black life, death, and creation unsettle and upend time and space,[1] would be essential if we aimed to take time and make space for Black folk, in theory, in word, and in deed.

Our many lingering questions about the actual possibilities of Black creation are the connective force arranging the field of these fragmented, impossible stories we sought out and that sought us out, that we write and we tell, around us. For Jasmine, Shakara, Dajerria, Sandra, Kalief, Nephi, for my students across time and space, for my wife and my family, and for all the Black folk living and dying untimely lives and deaths in the middle of nowhere, these questions illuminate the path forward, propel and direct the vector of our imaginative journey, and shape our vision of a destination. Asking how we have, do, and might better marshal the violent energy of our spatiotemporal dereliction and transmute it into the creative, caring energy required to conjure moments and sites for Black folk to disturb the air with our breath opens us into a serious consideration of the stakes and potentiality of Black creation. Our visitations with Black words and worlds created and lived by Black folk allow us to advance this consideration and to move ourselves toward taking the leap into the wholly Black black hole of it all.

Ultimately, our leap leads us to recognize that to make the arrangements, conjure ways out of no way, and take and make time when there is none to spare is to engage in dangerous work—and not in the least because the work tends to draw the fire, bullets, terror, and domination of the anti-Black

---

1. There are a few good visual analogs/metaphors that I think of as I write this line. One would be how the universe of *Fullmetal Alchemist* characterizes alchemy as transmutation derived from an equivalent exchange: Whatever the material being manipulated, the energy required for the manipulation depends on an equivalent exchange made by the alchemist. There are dangers to this process, and there are forbidden forms of transmutation for which the offering is either impossible to produce, or the exchange cannot possibly be made equivalent (e.g., transmuting a human life/soul). This is akin to the way Blackness manipulates the force of the anti-Black cosmos.

world, its institutions, and its agents;[2] we work with volatile material, this stuff of untimely death and destruction, and this stank of nowhere, so we must negotiate how we imperil ourselves and the variously dead and living Black folk for whom we care. How we handle the forces that destroy us, that remove us from a subject position—that is, from a stable location relative to space and time—has significant import for us because our handling of these forces will impact those who encounter the creations we destructively produce.

How we alchemically transmute destruction determines the shape the product takes and the effects it might have on those for whom we endeavored to create it. How we treat this material across each step of the process of alchemical creation affects what form that material is able to take. Nigredo, alchemy's first step, signifies blackness and requires the dissolution of our source material, compelling us to think about how we break our material down to its volatile essential components. Albedo, alchemy's second step, signifies whiteness and requires the distillation of the usable from what nigredo produces, compelling us to consider how we scrub clean or purify what we can or want to use of that material. And rubedo, alchemy's final step,[3] signifies redness and results in the synthesis of the fabled philosopher stone itself, compels us to consider how we alter and synthesize that destructive force into a radically different product. When we think of Black creation, especially when that creation is inherently a "working-with-fragments," we must think (and have thought) about the ways we handle these fragments throughout the complex process of transmutation under untimely, spatially dislocated conditions.

This is a good way of thinking about what has been the subject and the work of *Impossible Stories*: On the one hand, we spent pages trying to think about how this process works (its mechanics) and to what ends (its stakes and possibilities); on the other, we spent pages performing this work by unraveling the entanglement of Blackness, spacetime, care, and creation,

---

2. I really want us to think of the ongoing disappearances and deaths of several activists from the Ferguson protests in 2014 and beyond, as well as the deaths of their friends and family members as I mention this—most recently, the supposed suicide of Danye Jones reminds us of the ways the anti-Black world seeks out those who would dare to confront it.

3. In alchemy, the Great Work, or the Magnum Opus, names the process of working with the prima materia, the first matter or essential matter, to create the fabled philosopher's stone, which in *Fullmetal Alchemist* promises the ability to transmute anything without adhering to the principle of equivalent exchange, there are three steps (condensed from an original four steps): nigredo, albedo, and rubedo (which was previously preceded by citrinitas, but this step was consolidated with rubedo).

extracting what is essential to this entanglement, and producing a theory of Black untimely creation out of nowhere. This has been a written account of a difficult and dangerous transmutation. Working with and through our destructive relationship with the fabric of the cosmos produces what we understand to be an essential contradiction of Black creative work: In this cosmos, our untimeliness and our displacement are constitutive to our capacities to make time or take a minute, and to make space or find our way; that which destroys our relationship to time, space, and each other remains inextricably bound up with our creative aspiration and imaginative aim. We knew this, and we know this, and we have created, and do and will continue to create under these conditions.

Fragment 117
DESTRUCTIVE WRITING AND FRAGMENTED WORK

How
    to tell
        a
shattered
    story?[4]
What is required to . . . tell an impossible story?[5]
I do not know
    when or how else
    to begin,
but I do know that
    each and
e   ver   y *Black* frag   ment
matters
Here are the fragments put together by another me[6]

The cord of cowrie shells drags across the polished dark wood of the floor beneath her feet, tracing a constellation through the small nodes of

---

[4]. This question comes from Arundhati Roy's novel *The Ministry of Utmost Happiness*. It is a poem engraved onto a tombstone, and it characterizes the framing and plot of the novel beautifully. I was moved by the question, as well as the full poem, especially since it resonates so powerfully with what we've done in this project.

[5]. Hartman, "Venus in Two Acts," 10.

[6]. Fanon, *Black Skin*, 89. The Markmann translation reads a bit differently: "Now the fragments have been put together by another self" (82). I prefer the one I play with here.

water she arranged before us. M. NourbeSe Philip conjures a liquid narrative arc from the watery remnants of the lost words and names, bodies and souls, and untimely timelines of Black lives lost at sea as she performs selections from *Zong!* for we who sought to bear water and witness.

Clamoring cowrie shells clatter a rhythm for our guided collective recollection. Like the beautiful fragments of shells to which she was condemned to beaches to search,[7] they are their own w/holes, and their arrangement along the snaking cord traces the coordinate field of the event horizon that she asks us to cross. The wet drag of heavy, shelled rope through water scratch-splash-crashes above a low rumble, the drumroll of tidal forces altering the fabric of the small, dark cosmos of the theater. Overwhelming, oceanic, Black, chant, song, dance, breath, wake, word, and work warp, wrinkle, and collapse into one another. We get lost in the riff, rift, and riptide of the performance, rhythmically called by shell fragments to where and when the lost might be. In the cosmic Black magic being conjured, uncertainty is our familiar.[8]

Zong! is M. NourbeSe Philip playing with fragments, a poiesis of destructive means and ends. There are orders of fragments at play here, and play is only possible under the parameters set by Philip in an agreement with the limitations of the archive brokered by the 150 Black folk thrown overboard. The first order is composed of the narrative bits of Black life and death that make up, but will always fail to fully add up to, the 150 souls lost beneath the waves. The second order is established by the fragmentary (and figmentary) nature of the available historical account—the insurance claim and the court case. To become both magician and censor, the poet locks herself inside the limits of the available archive of the legal case *Gregson v. Gilbert*, attempting to inhabit the same conditions endured by the slaves aboard the *Zong/Zorgue*. Sequestering herself to the language of the available record means situating herself in the "dysgraphia" characteristic of every untimely narrative fragment—of the Black lives thrown overboard from the deck of the *Zong*, of those left to die on a dinghy in the Mediterranean,[9] of all of us. The "dysgraphia: the inability of language to cohere around the bodies and the suffering of [we] Black people who live and die in the wake and whose everyday acts insist Black life into the wake"[10] is the condition of possibility

---

7. Philip, "Fugues, Fragments, and Fissures," 2–3.
8. See Philip, *Zong!*, 190.
9. Vivienne Walt, "Migrants Left to Die on the High Seas Continue to Haunt NATO," *TIME*, April 17, 2012, http://content.time.com/time/world/article/0,8599,2112173,00.html.
10. Sharpe, *In the Wake*, 96.

for Philips's magic. Incoherence makes her form of spellcasting—or spelling—possible. We read, we watch, and we are caught in the derangement of the spell.

The story of the *Zong*, the story that the dead demand to be told, can only be "un-told," or told in a deranged way by "re-presenting the sequence"[11] of signs and symbols that index the available information. The writing becomes its own process of disfigurement and the process produces the second order of fragments: the language. The falling, failing, ripped-apartness of language, as an echo of the "seared, divided, ripped-apartness" of the "primary narrative" of Black flesh,[12] becomes the manifestation of this destructive "praxis" and "theory," "text for living and for dying, and . . . method for [writing] them both."[13] Spacing the words out and exploding their letters into the unintelligible disarray littering the pages of *Zong!* produces imaginative and physical strain. Eyes arrhythmically fail to track the lexical debris across, up, and down pages of the text, and the lack of an orthographic anchor subjects the imagination to a form of interpretive disorientation. The difference in legibility produced by a creative process that depends on the disfigurement of language and the refusal to impose meaning jettisons writer, reader, and witness into a state of imaginative vertigo.

M. NourbeSe Philip as Black poet, censor, and magician becomes something like a poetic Galactus: a Black cosmic entity and destroyer of words and worlds; a sentient, vigilant black hole in search of something in excess of meaning and sense; an "underlying current" subtending all that is written and all that the written account could ever mean. Against grammar, the "mechanism of force" structurally imposed onto the available language as symbolic order—the order of ideas, knowledge, and imaginations that ceaselessly and repeatedly murders Black beings[14]—and the Black dysgraphia such grammar allows, Philip mutilates and disorders language, "literally [cutting] it into pieces, castrating verbs, suffocating adjectives, murdering nouns, throwing articles, prepositions, conjunctions overboard, jettisoning adverbs . . . [separating] subject from verb, verb from object—[creating] semantic *mayhem*" in the name of "reaching into the stinking, eviscerated innards . . . and [reading] the untold story that tells itself by not telling."[15]

---

11. Hartman, "Venus in Two Acts," 11.
12. This is from Spillers's "Mama's Baby, Papa's Maybe," 67. We visited this thought and some of its attendant meanings in the First Arrangement. But I make this parallel after reading a line from Sharpe's *In the Wake* that introduces *Zong!* thusly: "It is in and with such falling, such ripping-apart, of language that *Zong!* begins."
13. Spillers, "Mama's Baby, Papa's Maybe," 68.
14. Ibid., 67.
15. Philip, *Zong!*, 193.

This "not-telling" is both vengeful and protective. It is vengeful because it is aimed at mutilating, jettisoning, murdering, suffocating, castrating, cutting, and exploding the archive in the same way the archive mutilates, jettisons, murders, suffocates, castrates, cuts, and explodes Black being. And it is protective because Philip recognizes the need to avoid subjecting the dead "to new dangers and to a second order of violence," one that not only affirms the violence of the grammar that imposes meaning and structure, but reproduces that violence (by "maintaining order")—and this is a need recognized by Hartman, Spillers, Sharpe, myself, and countless others who know the perils of bearing fragmented witness and water.

Alchemically transmuting fragments is, in one sense, a form of violent play, a form of derangement and disorder that playfully transforms the violence that made them fragments into a form of violence that can challenge, or outright disintegrate, the symbolic order. Thinking in these terms frames Philip's creative praxis as a form of offense. In this light, Philip poetically plays with language in order to conjure an assault on the normative constraints of language, grammar, and knowledge. Philip works with the lexical, political, and metaphysical refuse of the lost and dead Black folk thrown overboard by first recognizing them as such—as refuse, as effluvium, as whatever one might call the end product of spaghettification—and then by subjecting them to a form of destructively creative and creatively destructive alchemy that transmutes the violence that produced this refuse into something that attempts to dispose of the symbolic order and all its attendant limits. The organizing principle or grammar by which the anti-Black fictions of the archive comes to be faces annihilation in the form of a poiesis that turns its refuse against itself.[16] Reanimated[17] or ghostly[18] or deathly, the variously dead resurge in the breaks of word and meaning, and usher in an imaginative form of warfare waged at and against the limits of creative possibility imposed by the symbolic order that made Black folk deathly in the first place.

Alchemically transmuting fragments is also a means toward manifesting a ward, a protection. This frames Philip's writing as a form of defense. Philip flings out and disperses[19] the lexical and semantic remnants, and scatters the broken words into a shifting, protective arrangement. Each poem, each section of the poems, and the Black w/hole collection of poetry compose an amalgamated force field of fragments. Warped by the tidal forces of grav-

---

16. Recall the "hardness that 'hurts' as it is heard" of Ursa's new, blueshifted blues.
17. As I wrote in chapter 3, untime is a zombified force and feature of Black being.
18. See the reading of *Beloved*, chapter 5.
19. See the reading of Brand's *A Map to the Door of No Return*, chapter 9.

ity beyond their composite barrier, the untimely, stanky force suturing the shards to one another undulates, shifting the spaces between the letters, words, names, and utterances that compose *Zong!* All meaning and order violently imposed from without faces inevitable obliteration should it venture beyond this waving event horizon of the Black w/hole of the text. The promise of annihilating incoherence and the embrace and weaponization of fragmentation, dysgraphia, and illegibility provide a destructive defense. To "defend the dead," Philips-qua-poet-qua-magician-qua-alchemist-qua-tactician marshals an absolute power cosmic that inheres in destruction.

In its adherence to working with fragments, to accepting the absoluteness of fragmentation and the centrality of it to Black creative work, *Zong!*'s destructive approach to creation offers us a name for what it is we might best do with our untimeliness in the middle of nowhere: destructive writing. M. NourbeSe Philip's poiesis is destruction. To leap into the Black w/hole of the text, the praxis, the theory, and the interpretive method necessary to operate on the same frequency of this work is to take very seriously the untimely, stanky, political-ontological relationship between Blackness, creation, and destruction. To "make generations" in the name of defending the dead, or to do the wake work, or to conjure the Black and cosmic magic, is to reckon with the paradoxical generativeness of destruction. It is to wholly embrace violence as violence, fragments as fragments, and incoherence as incoherence, in order to actively refuse, combat, and vie to destroy the very logic, or grammar, or order that murdered, continues to murder, and threatens to wholly obliterate Black being, or whatever deranged fragments of that being remain.

What have we done? What have we been doing? What should—*must*—we do? As we reflect upon the shards of thought, language, literary scene, physical property, lived experience, and unbearable inquiry that form the field of fragments called *Impossible Stories*, we consider how these arrangements we have made have all been an attempt at working with destruction. Arranging and deranging, ordering, reordering, and disordering, and always looking, listening, and attending to them carefully has always been the product of a continuous negotiation of the destructive forces that turned Black life and death into fragments. We spent our textual spacetime theorizing the nature of these forces in order to both understand how they destroy us (how they work—think of the First and Third Arrangements) and to begin to consider what ways we might refract/reflect them (how we can create with and from them—think of the Second Arrangement). Our arguments throughout have turned on establishing the significance or rethinking these spatiotemporal forces and how they shatter our existences, indeed because rethinking time and space and how they play out upon us as a project on its own will help us better grasp the nature of our subjection to the various orders and structures of the anti-Black world, but also because a deeper understanding of their mechanics and their essence radically transforms how we imagine, theorize, and perform Black creation.

We have performed out impossible alchemy thusly: (nigredo) the disintegration of our core materials—time, space, and work—shedding the ashen detritus inessential to our work and leaving only what we need; (albedo) the distillation of what remains—untime, nowhere, and refraction—into the material we can synthesize into a greater conceptualization; and (rubedo) the synthesization of a new, vexing, abstract material that might reshape our understanding of Black existence and imaginative creation—destructive writing. While we knew and know our work aims to produce an alternative theory of Black creation that embraces and works with the destructive forces that make us untimely and displace us into nowhere, we perhaps (re)discover that our work *is* its own negotiation of destruction, our own staging of these principles of destructive writing. That invisible force suturing the fragments surrounding us into a field, that unseen thing that amplified the call of the fragments we sought out and were able to hold and behold, that animating element of untimeliness, refraction, and being nowhere: That undergirds the whole of this work, argumentatively and creatively, is destruction, and in our endeavor to make time and space for our considerations, we contemplate and imagine and write toward an answer to our most difficult set of questions.

How to tell a shattered story, one not meant to be passed on or *passed* on? How to "un-tell"[20] a story that must be told? How to tell an impossible story?[21]

Perhaps it is not exactly as Sharpe says. Perhaps the goal is not to "imagine the unimaginable" but, as part of the same refusal NourbeSe writes and performs, to radically un-imagine the imaginable.

> How to defend the dead, the dying, and *we* who live untimely lives in the middle of nowhere?
> By

---

20. M. NourbeSe Philip's *Zong!* culminates in a "Notanda" I have cited throughout this conclusion, and one of the most intriguing, if not completely vexing, conceptualizations comes in the form of "un-telling" the story of the Zong massacre, and how this "un-telling" became the way Philip framed her archival, poetic work. I evoke her meditation on that word here.

21. See the reading of *Beloved*, chapter 5.

becoming
everybody?
No.
By destroying everything.

Cowrie shells drag across the hard, wet wood. A constellation has been traced in water. A spell has been cast. A conjuring has taken place. We bear the water and the witness. We are a clamor of fragments in the oceanic dark.

Telling and writing impossible stories is destructive work. Telling, writing, and living impossible stories is destructive, dangerous work when deathliness, untimeliness, and stankiness are the conditions of whenever and wherever we try to be. To really listen to Ursa's blues and take the leap into the Black hole toward total destruction is to leap toward the singular possibility of radical, unimaginable, and impossible creation. Only in the dark and clamoring shatter, only from the nowhere of there and the untimeliness of then, might we really make time and space for one another.

Nothing less, nowhere else, and with no time to spare, we leap.

BIBLIOGRAPHY

Austin-Williams, Jaye. "Black Achievement in the Face of Diversity." Black Graduation commencement speech, University of California, Irvine, June 2015.

———, dir. *The Liquid Plain*. Written by Naomi Wallace. Robert Cohen Theatre, University of California, Irvine, January 30, 2015.

———, dir. *The Trial of Dedan Kimathi*. Written by Ngugi wa Thiong'o. Xmpl Theatre, University of California, Irvine, March 2014.

Baucom, Ian. *Specters of the Atlantic: Finance Capital, Slavery, and the Philosophy of History*. Durham: Duke University Press, 2005.

Beatty, Paul. *The Sellout*. New York: Farrar, Straus, and Giroux, 2015.

———. *White Boy Shuffle*. New York: Picador, 1996.

Brady, Nicholas. "Louder Than the Dark: Toward an Acoustics of Suffering." *The Feminist Wire*, October 11, 2012.

———. "Monstrous Abundance—A Small Note of Gratitude." *Out of Nowhere*, January 18, 2015.

Brand, Dionne. *A Map to the Door of No Return: Notes to Belonging*. Toronto: Random House, 2001.

Butler, Octavia. *Kindred*, 25th Anniversary ed. Boston: Beacon Press, 2003.

Casselman, Ben. "Katrina Washed Away New Orleans's Black Middle Class." *Five-Thirty-Eight*, August 24, 2015.

Darling, Marsha J. Tyson. "In the Realm of Responsibility: A Conversation With Toni Morrison" (1988). *Ruth S. Ammon School of Education Faculty Publications*. 711.

Davis, Thadious. *Southscapes: Geographies of Race, Region, and Literature*. Chapel Hill: University of North Carolina Press, 2011.

Douglass, Patrice, and Frank Wilderson. "The Violence of Presence: Metaphysics in a Blackened World." *The Black Scholar* 43, no. 4 (2013): 117–23.

Dunbar, Eve. *Black Regions of the Imagination: African American Writers between the Nation and the World*. Philadelphia: Temple University Press, 2013.

Eady, Cornelius. *Brutal Imagination*. New York: G. P. Putnam's Sons, 2001.

Fanon, Frantz. *Black Skin, White Masks*. Translated by Charles Lam Markmann. London: Pluto Press, 1967.

———. *The Wretched of the Earth*. Translated by Richard Philcox. New York: Grove Press, 2004.

Farley, Anthony Paul. "Behind the Wall of Sleep." *Law & Literature* 15, no. 3 (2003): 421–34.

Ferguson, Rebecca. "History, Memory, and Language in Toni Morrison's *Beloved*." 1991. In *Contemporary American Women Writers: Gender, Class, Ethnicity*, edited by Lois Parkinson Zamora, 154–69. New York: Longman, 1998.

Finney, Brian. "Temporal Defamiliarization in Toni Morrison's *Beloved*." 1990. In *Critical Essays on Toni Morrison's* Beloved, edited by Barbara H. Solomon, 104–16. New York: G. K. Hall, 1998.

Furst, Jenner, dir. *Time: The Kalief Browder Story*. 2017, New York City, NY: Roc Nation. Netflix.

Gordon, Lewis. "Theory in Black: Teleological Suspensions in Philosophy of Culture." *Qui Parle* 18, no. 2 (2010): 193–214. Qui Parle. https://doi.org/10.5250/quiparle.18.2.193.

Gyasi, Yaa. *Homegoing*. New York: Knopf, 2016.

Harney, Stefano, and Fred Moten. *The Undercommons: Fugitive Planning & Black Study*. Wivenhoe: Minor Compositions, 2013.

Hartman, Saidiya. *Lose Your Mother: A Journey along the Atlantic Slave Route*. New York: Farrar, Straus, and Giroux, 2007.

———. *Scenes of Subjection: Terror, Slavery, and Self-Making in Nineteenth-Century America*. New York: Oxford University Press, 1997.

———. "Venus in Two Acts." *Small Axe* 12, no. 2 (2008): 1–14.

———. "Wayward Lives, Beautiful Experiments." Reading at the University of California, Los Angeles, November 19, 2015.

———. *Wayward Lives, Beautiful Experiments: Intimate Histories of Social Upheaval*. New York: W. W. Norton & Company, 2019.

Hartman, Saidiya, and Frank B. Wilderson III. "The Position of the Unthought." *Qui Parle* 13, no. 2 (2003): 183–201.

Hawking, Stephen. "Information Preservation and Weather Forecasting for Black Holes," arXiv:1401.5761 (Winter: 2014), 3.

Henderson, Mae G. *Speaking in Tongues and Dancing Diaspora: Black Women Writing and Performing*. New York: Oxford, 2014.

Hossenfelder, Sabine. *Back Re(Action)* (blog). http://backreaction.blogspot.com/.

Hostetler, Ann. "Resurrecting the Dead Girl: Modernism and the Problem of History in *Beloved*, *Jazz*, and *Paradise*." In *Toni Morrison: Memory and Meaning*, 33–42. Jackson: University of Mississippi, 2014.

James, Joy. "Afrarealism and the Black Matrix: Maroon Philosophy at Democracy's Border." *The Black Scholar* 44, no. 2 (2014): 124–31.

———. "Black Suffering in Search of the 'Beloved Community': Political Imprisonment and Self-Defense." *Trans-Scripts* 1 (2011): 212–20.

———. "'Concerning Violence': Frantz Fanon's Rebel Intellectual in Search of a Black Cyborg." *South Atlantic Quarterly* 112, no. 1 (2013): 57–70.

Jones, Gayl. *Corregidora*. Boston: Beacon Press, 1975.

Judy, Ronald A. T. *(Dis)forming the American Canon: African-Arabic Slave Narratives and the Vernacular*. Minneapolis: University of Minnesota Press, 1993.

Kaku, Michio. *Parallel Worlds: A Journey through Creation, Higher Dimensions, and the Future of the Cosmos*. New York: Anchor, 2006.

Koupelis, Theo. *In Quest of the Universe*, 7th ed. Burlington: Jones & Bartlett Learning, 2013.

Krauss, Laurence M. "Finding Beauty in the Darkness." *The New York Times*, February 14, 2016.

Lacy, Mackala. "Wake Work—Self Care for the Black Community." *Out of Nowhere*, February 18, 2015.

LaValle, Victor. *The Changeling*. New York: Spiegel and Grau, 2017.

Laymon, Kiese. *Heavy: An American Memoir*. New York: Scribner, 2018.

———. *How to Slowly Kill Yourself and Others in America*. Evanston: Agate Bolden, 2013.

———. "Kiese Laymon on Trayvon, Black Manhood and Love." Colorlines, December 30, 2013. https://www.colorlines.com/articles/kiese-laymon-trayvon-black-manhood-and-love.

———. *Long Division*. Evanston: Agate Bolden, 2013.

Liptak, Adam. "It's Been 10 Years. Would Clarence Thomas Like to Add Anything?" *The New York Times*, February 1, 2016.

Lorde, Audre. *Sister Outsider: Essays and Speeches*, Feminist Series Reprint ed. New York: Crossing Press, 2007.

Krumholz, Linda. "The Ghosts of Slavery: Historical Recovery in Toni Morrison's *Beloved*." 1992. In *Modern Critical Interpretations: Beloved*, edited by Harold Bloom, 79–97. Philadelphia: Chelsea House, 1999.

Macharia, Keguro. "Love." *Critical Ethnic Studies* 1, no. 1 (Spring 2015): 69.

Marks, Kathleen. *Toni Morrison's* Beloved *and the Apotropaic Imagination*. Columbia: University of Missouri, 2002.

Marriott, David. *Haunted Life: Visual Culture and Modernity*. New Brunswick: Rutgers University Press, 2007.

———. *On Black Men*. New York: Columbia University Press, 2000.

———. *Whither Fanon: Studies in the Blackness of Being*. Palo Alto: Stanford University Press, 2018.

Mobley, Marilyn Sanders. "A Different Remembering: Memory, History, and Meaning in Toni Morrison's *Beloved*." 1988. In *Modern Critical Interpretations: Beloved*, edited by Harold Bloom, 17–26. Philadelphia: Chelsea House, 1999.

Monáe, Janelle. *The Archandroid*. Big Beat Records, May 2010.

———. *The Electric Lady*. Wondaland Arts Society and Bad Boy Records, September 2013.

———. *Metropolis: Suite I (The Chase)*. Bad Boy Records, August 2007.

Morrison, Toni. *Beloved*. New York: Vintage International, 2004.

———. *Playing in the Dark*. New York: Vintage, 1993.

———. *Song of Solomon*. New York: Random House, 1977.

———. "The Nobel Prize in Literature 1993." NobelPrize.org. Accessed September 3, 2011. https://www.nobelprize.org/prizes/literature/1993/morrison/facts/.

Mos Def. *Black on Both Sides*. Rawkus Records, 1999.

Mos Def and Talib Kweli. *Mos Def & Talib Kweli are Black Star*. Rawkus, 1998.

Moten, Fred. *In the Break: The Aesthetics of the Black Radical Tradition*. Minneapolis: University of Minnesota Press, 2003.

Mughal, Muhammad Aurang Zeb. "Time, Absolute." In *The Encyclopedia of Time*, edited by H. James Birx, 1255. Thousand Oaks: Sage, 2009.

Murakami, Haruki. *1Q84*. New York: Vintage Books, 2011.

Murillo, John III. "Black (in) Time." *Indiana Review*, January 2016.

———. "Smile Undun, *Django Unchained*." *Out of Nowhere*, February 23, 2013.

Nemiroff, R.J. "Visual Distortions Near a Neutron Star and Black Hole." *American Journal of Physics* 61 (1993). 613–42. arXiv:astro-ph/9312003.

Pearce, Lynne. "Gendering the Chronotope: *Beloved*." 1994. In *A Practical Reader in Contemporary Literary Theory*, edited by Peter Brooker and Peter Widdowson, 430–40. Hertfordshire: Prentice Hall, 1996.

Philip, M. NourbeSe. "Fugues, Fragments, and Fissures—A Work in Progress." *Anthurium: A Caribbean Studies Journal* 3, no. 2 (2005): article 7.

———. *Zong!* Middletown: Wesleyan University Press, 2008.

Pössel, Markus. "Gravitational Wave Detectors: How They Work." *Universe Today*, February 10, 2016.

———. "Gravity: From Weightlessness to Curvature." *Einstein Online*, March 4, 2016.

Ramadanovic, Petar. *Forgetting Futures: On Memory, Trauma, and Identity*. Lanham: Lexington Books, 2001.

Randall, Lisa. *Dark Matter and the Dinosaurs: The Astounding Interconnectedness of the Universe*. New York: Ecco, 2015.

———. "Seeing Dark Matter as the Key to the Universe—and Human Empathy." *The Boston Globe*, October 26, 2016. https://www.bostonglobe.com/opinion/2015/10/25/seeing-dark-matter-key-universe-and-human-empathy/NXNMBXAa7WEWejN63fFCNL/story.html.

Raynaud, Claudine. "*Beloved* or the Shifting Shapes of Memory." In *The Cambridge Companion to Toni Morrison*, edited by Justine Tally, 43–58. Cambridge: Cambridge University Press, 2007.

Rody, Caroline. "History, 'Rememory,' and a 'Clamor for a Kiss.'" 1995. In *Modern Critical Interpretations:* Beloved, edited by Harold Bloom, 155–75. Philadelphia: Chelsea House, 1999.

Rushdy, Ashraf H. A. "Daughters Signifyin(g) History: The Example of Toni Morrison's *Beloved*." 1992. In *Modern Critical Interpretations:* Beloved, edited by Harold Bloom, 115–39. Philadelphia: Chelsea House, 1999.

Sexton, Jared. *Amalgamation Schemes: Antiblackness and the Critique of Multiracialism*. Minneapolis: Minnesota University Press, 2008.

———. "Ante-Anti-Blackness." *Lateral* 1 (2012). https://csalateral.org/issue/1/ante-anti-blackness-afterthoughts-sexton/.

———. "The Social Life of Social Death: On Afro-Pessimism and Black Optimism." *InTensions* 5.0 (2011). http://www.yorku.ca/intent/issue5/articles/jaredsexton.php.

———. "Unbearable Blackness." Keynote lecture at the Terror and the Inhuman Conference, Brown University, October 2012.

Selasi, Taiye. *Ghana Must Go*. New York: Penguin, 2013.

Sharpe, Christina. "Black Studies: In the Wake." *The Black Scholar* 44, no. 2 (2014): 59–69.

———. *In the Wake: On Blackness and Being*. Durham: Duke University Press, 2016.

———. *Monstrous Intimacies: Making Post-Slavery Subjects*. Durham: Duke University Press, 2010.

Shreiber, Evelyn Jaffe. *Race, Trauma, and Home in the Novels of Toni Morrison*. Baton Rouge: LSU Press, 2010.

Simpson, Ritashona. *Black Looks and Black Acts: The Language of Toni Morrison in* The Bluest Eye *and* Beloved. New York: Peter Lang, 2007.

Smith, Valerie. "'Circling the Subject': History and Narrative in *Beloved*." In *Toni Morrison: Critical Perspectives Past and Present*, edited by Henry Louis Gates Jr. and K. A. Appiah, 342–55. New York: Amistad, 1993.

Spillers, Hortense. *Black, White, and In Color: Essays on American Literature and Culture*. Chicago: University of Chicago Press, 2003.

———. "Mama's Baby, Papa's Maybe: An American Grammar Book." *Diacritics* 17, no. 2 (1987): 64–81.

Spillers, Hortense, Saidiya Hartman, Farah Jasmine Griffin, Shelly Eversley, and Jennifer L. Morgan. "'Whatcha Gonna Do?'—Revisiting 'Mama's Baby, Papa's Maybe: An American Grammar Book.'" *Women's Studies Quarterly* 35, no. 1/2 (2007): 299–309.

Tally, Justine. *Toni Morrison's* Beloved: *Origins*. New York: Routledge, 2009.

Terrefe, Selamawit. "Phantasmagoria; or, The World Is a Haunted Plantation." *The Feminist Wire*, October 10, 2012.

Thorne, Kip S. *Black Holes and Time Warps: Einstein's Outrageous Legacy*. New York: W. W. Norton & Company, 1994.

Tyson, Neil deGrasse. *Death by Black Hole: And Other Cosmic Quandaries*. New York: W. W. Norton & Company, 2007.

Wilderson, Frank. "Do I Stank, or Was It Already Stanky in Here?; or, Notes from an Impossible Negro." Closing comments at the Black Thought in the Age of Terror Symposium, University of California, Irvine, May 2006.

———. "An Evening with Frank Wilderson III." Lecture at Omni Commons, Oakland, California, May 2015.

———. "Grammar and Ghosts: The Performative Limits of African Freedom." *Theatre Survey* 50, no. 1 (2009): 119–25.

———. *Red, White, and Black: Cinema and the Structure of U. S. Antagonisms*. Durham: Duke University Press, 2010.

———. "The Vengeance of Vertigo: Aphasia and Abjection in the Political Trials of Black Insurgents." *InTensions* 5.0 (2011). http://www.yorku.ca/intent/issue5/articles/frankbwildersoniii.php.

Williams, John A. *The Man Who Cried I Am*. 1967. New York: Overlook TP, 2004.

Wright, Michelle M. *Physics of Blackness: Beyond the Middle Passage Epistemology*. Minneapolis: University of Minnesota Press, 2015.

INDEX

"Afrarealism and the Black Matrix: Maroon Philosophy at Democracy's Border" (James), 70n49
Afrikatown (Oakland), 159–60, 160n24
Afrofuturism, 18
Afropessimism, 4n10, 17–18, 38n15, 77, 95n1, 125n11
alchemy, 163–64, 163n4, 186n1, 187n3, 191–93
"Ante-Anti-Blackness: Afterthoughts" (Sexton), 54n3
anti-Blackness: aspiration and, 82–83; in Beatty, 164–65; as climate, 83n9, 167; in Fanon, 66; in Hartman, 97; in Randall, 161; theory and, 54n3; time and, 37–38, 67; untime and, 69, 87, 109, 117; violence and, 68, 123
Aristodemou, Maria, 149, 152, 154
Arreguin, Nephi, 57
articulation, 83–84
aspiration, 82–83, 87, 93, 100, 104, 107, 124, 167–68, 170, 188
axions, 161n25

Baldwin, James, 137

Beatty, Paul. See *Sellout, The* (Beatty)
"Behind the Wall of Sleep" (Farley), 140n13, 148, 150–51, 153–54
Beloved (Morrison), 7–8, 8n18–n21, 16–17, 17n29, 55n5, 92n23, 95n1, 96–97, 96n2, 102–14, 104n28, 106n35, 118–19, 139, 141n14
Bhabha, Homi K., 8n21
Black Arts Movement, 17
Black Atlantic, The (Gilroy), 36n10
black hole, 62–63, 63n25, 72–73, 101
Black Lives Matter, 88n15
Blackness: alchemy and, 187; in Beatty, 148, 171, 176–77; in Brand, 178, 183; in Butler, 60–61, 63–67, 69; death and, 54–56, 58n11; in Fanon, 66–67; in Farley, 152–54; in Hartman, 98, 139; humanity and, 40; in Jones, 44–45, 50–51; language and, 128; in Laymon, 123–24; love and, 123; in Marriott, 54–55; Middle Passage and, 34n6; in Morrison, 102, 107; narrative and, 91; police and, 173n33; in Randall, 161–62; slavery and, 98; spatiality and, 145, 150n6, 152–55, 160, 164n5, 177n40; in Spillers,

40–41; as stanky, 167–68, 172, 175; structural formation and, 156–57; theory and, 54n3; time and, 23–25, 37, 56–57, 98–99; trauma and, 95; as unthinkable, 92; untimeliness of, 123; untimely, 139; as violence, 88; violence and, 72, 88; in Wilderson, 138n3, 169–70, 173; work and, 79
Black on Both Sides (Mos Def), 1n1
Black optimism, 125n11
Black Skin (Fanon), 162n27, 188, 188n6
Black Skin, White Masks (Fanon), 2n3, 3n6, 33
Black studies, 79–80
"Black (in) Time" (Murillo), 50n52
Bland, Sandra, 27–28, 57
blueshift, 46–48, 47n39
Body in Pain, The: The Making and Unmaking of the World (Scarry), 89–90
Boyd, Rekia, 57
Brady, Nicholas, 47n41
Brand, Dionne, 3, 9. See also *Map to the Door of No Return, A* (Brand)
breath, 83–88, 99
Browder, Kalief, 29–31
Brown, Anna, 57
Brown, Michael, 57
Buckley, William, 137n1
Burke, Kenneth, 124
Butler, Octavia. See *Kindred* (Butler)

capitalism, 125–26, 168
care, 121–22, 187
Clark, Stephon, 57
Colbert, Stephen, 96n2
Corregidora (Jones), 5–6, 24–25, 42–51, 44n31–44n32, 48n43, 106n35

dark matter, 11, 15–16, 156–62, 176, 182, 184
Dark Matter and the Dinosaurs: The Astounding Interconnectedness of the Universe (Randall), 11, 156, 157n16, 158n19
deathliness, 53–58, 58n11
Dent, Jerome, 77
Deón, Natashia, 129n18

"Different Remembering, A: Memory, History, and Meaning in Toni Morrison's *Beloved*" (Mobley), 100n17
Doctor Who (television program), 10n26, 50n52
"Do I Stank, or Was it Already Stanky in Here?" (Wilderson), 168–70
Dorner, Christopher, 173n33
Douglass, Patrice, 87–89, 91–92
Du Bois, W. E. B., 36, 36n10, 154

Encyclopedia of Time, The, 33–34
environmental racism, 160, 164n5
events, 138–39
Eversley, Shelley, 38n15, 39n21

"Fact of Blackness, The" (Fanon), 66–67, 109
Fanon, Frantz, 2n3, 3n6, 4n11, 33, 54, 66–68, 71–72, 90–91, 109, 162n27, 188, 188n6
Farley, Anthony Paul, 140n13, 148, 150–54
Ferguson protests, 187n2
Ferguson, Rebecca, 111n53
Flint, Michigan, 164n5
Flournoy, Angela, 129n18
Fullmetal Alchemist (manga), 186n1, 187n3

Garner, Eric, 57, 88n15
Garner, Margaret, 96–97. See also *Beloved* (Morrison)
Gates, Henry Louis, Jr., 34n6, 36, 36n10
Gilroy, Paul, 36, 36n10
Gordon, Lewis, 54n3
Grace (Déon), 129n18
Grant, Oscar, 57
gravitational lensing, 157n16
gravity, 138–39
Green, Dionte, 57
Griffin, Farah Jasmine, 38n15, 39n21

hapticality, 125–28
hardness, 109, 109n44
Harlem Renaissance, 17
Harney, Stefano, 125

Hartman, Saidiya, 3n6, 17, 27n5, 37n13, 38n15, 39n21, 55n4, 88–89, 97–101, 101n20, 112, 139, 147, 161n26
Haunted Life (Marriott), 25, 53–59
Hawking, Stephen, 62–63
Henderson, Mae G., 101n20, 104n28
Hill, Marc Lamont, 64n27
"History, Memory, and Language in Toni Morrison's *Beloved*" (Ferguson), 111n53
Horne, Cariol, 173n33
Hossenfelder, Sabine, 62–63, 63n23
How to Slowly Kill Yourself and Others in America (Laymon), 66n35
Hurricane Katrina, 159, 159n23

In the Wake (Sharpe), 55n4, 82–83, 83n5
"It's Been 10 Years. Would Clarence Thomas Like to Add Anything?" (Liptak), 164n7

James, Joy, 70n49, 129n18
Johnston, Kathryn, 57n10
Jones, Danye, 187n2
Jones, Gayl, 42. See also *Corregidora* (Jones)

Kindred (Butler), 6–7, 25–26, 59–73, 60n15, 62n22, 71n50, 79, 91, 170

Lacy, Mackala, 82
Lateral 1 (Sexton), 5n12
Laymon, Kiese, 9, 66n35, 122. See also *Long Division* (Laymon)
Le Guin, Ursula, 154
Liptak, Adam, 164n7
logistics, 125
Long Division (Laymon), 9, 66n35, 122–33
Lorde, Audre, 129n18
Lose Your Mother: A Journey along the Atlantic Slave Route (Hartman), 3n6, 55n4
"Love" (Macharia), 124–25
"Love" (Mos Def), 1n1

M4BL. *See* Movement for Black Lives (M4BL)
Macharia, Keguro, 121, 124–25

"Mama's Baby, Papa's Maybe" (Spillers), 2n4, 26, 26n4, 37–42, 38n14–38n15, 39n19, 39n21, 44n30, 61n19, 67n37, 150n6, 190n12
Map to the Door of No Return, A (Brand), 3, 12, 177–84, 180n52
Marks, Kathleen, 104n28
Marriott, David. *See Haunted Life* (Marriott)
Martin, Trayvon, 57, 122
McBride, Renisha, 57, 57n10
McCoy, Willie, 57
memory, 104–6, 108–12, 111n53
metaphysics of violence, 87–89
"Middle Passage Epistemology," 34–35, 34n6, 36n10
Ministry of Utmost Happiness, The (Roy), 188n4
Mobley, Marilyn Sanders, 100n17
Morgan, Howard, 173n33
Morgan, Jennifer L., 38n15, 39n21
Morrison, Toni, 96n2, 101n20, 114–16. See also *Beloved* (Morrison); *Playing in the Dark* (Morrison)
Mos Def, 1n1
Moten, Fred, 17, 125, 125n11
Movement for Black Lives (M4BL), 35–36
Mughal, Muhammad Aurang Zeb, 33–34

narrative elements, 13–14
négritude, 68
New Orleans, 159, 159n23
Newton, Isaac, 33–34
"NuBluez," 47n41

Oda, Eiichiro, 1, 1n2
One Piece (Oda), 1, 1n2
"OtherSide, The" (The Roots), 151n10
Owens, Christopher, 173n33

pacha, 137–38, 137n2
Pantaleo, Daniel, 88n15
Parker, Pat, 129n18
Patriot Act, 168–69
Payne, Yazmin Vash, 57
Philip, M. NourbeSe, 80, 109–12, 189–92, 193n20

Physics of Blackness (Wright), 5, 24, 33–36
Playing in the Dark (Morrison), 100
police, 40, 50n52, 57, 142, 145, 173, 173n33, 174
Prescod-Weinstein, Chanda, 161n25
Prestia, Paul, 31n8
Price of the Ticket, The (film), 137n1
Proud, Penny, 57

racism: environmental, 160, 164n5
Ramadanovic, Petar, 8n18
Randall, Lisa, 11, 156–58, 158n19, 159–62
Rankine, Claudia, 20
Red, White, and Black: Cinema and the Structure of U. S. Antagonisms (Wilderson), 42n26
rememory, 104–6, 108–12, 111n53
reparation, 2, 93
Rice, Tamir, 57, 57n10
Ricoeur, Paul, 9n21
Roots, The, 151n10
Roy, Arundhati, 188n4

Sartre, Jean-Paul, 68
Scarry, Elaine, 89–90
Scenes of Subjection (Hartman), 27n5, 88–89, 161n26
Scherer, Stefan, 63n23
Schrödinger, Ervin, 114n55
Seeking the Beloved Community (James), 129n18
Sellout, The (Beatty), 11, 17, 17n29, 139, 147, 154–56, 155n14, 163–77
Sexton, Jared, 5n12, 54n3, 88, 171n20
Sharpe, Christina, 55n4, 80, 82–84, 87, 124, 167, 167n15
Signifying Monkey, The (Gates), 36n10
Sing, Unburied, Sing (Ward), 129n18
Sister Love: The Letters of Audre Lorde and Par Parker 1974—1989 (Lorde and Parker), 129n18
slavery, 3–4, 3n6; Blackness and, 98; in Brand, 177–84, 180n52; in Butler, 59–61, 62n22, 64–65, 69–72; in Hartman, 139; in Jones, 43–45; in Morrison, 102, 108–10, 114–15; in Wilderson, 42n26

"Smile Undun, *Django Unchained*" (Murillo), 90–91
Souls of Black Folk, The (Du Bois), 36n10
spacetime, 60–61, 64, 73, 78, 93, 98, 114, 128, 132, 138–39, 138n4, 185–87, 192
spaghettification, 47, 47n40, 181
spatiality, 139–40, 147–48, 150–51, 150n6, 153–54, 164–65, 168–69
Speaking in Tongues and Dancing Diaspora (Henderson), 101n20
Spillers, Hortense. See "Mama's Baby, Papa's Maybe" (Spillers)
Stanley-Jones, Aiyana, 57, 57n10
Szalay, Michael, 14

Tayeb, Roger, 54
Telling, The (Le Guin), 154
"Theory in Black" (Gordon), 54n3
Thomas, Clarence, 164n7
time: absolute, 5n13, 33–34; anti-Blackness and, 37–38, 67; Black, 41, 77; Blackness and, 23–25, 37, 56–57, 98–99; in Butler, 59–62, 64–65, 69–70, 71n50; death and, 54–55, 57–58; epiphenomenal, 36, 41; in Jones, 43, 45–46, 49–50; loop, 41–42; in Marriott, 53–58; memory and, 104–6; Middle Passage and, 34n6; over, 39–40, 43; in Spillers, 37–42; in Wright, 33–36, 41. *See also* untime
Toni Morrison's Beloved *and the Apotropaic Imagination* (Marks), 104n28
"Toni Morrison's *Beloved*: Re-Membering the Body as Historical Text" (Henderson), 104n28
torture, 89–90
Turner House, The (Flournoy), 129n18

"Unbearable Blackness" (Sexton), 171n20
Undercommons: Fugitive Planning and Black Study (Harney and Moten), 125
unreason, 123–25
untime: anti-Blackness and, 69, 87, 109, 117; Blackness and, 139; Black time as, 77; in Butler, 59–60; defined, 24; in Marriott, 58; in Morrison, 108–9

"Venus in Two Acts" (Hartman), 37n13, 97–98, 112, 139, 147

"Violence of Presence, The: Metaphysics in a Blackened World" (Douglass and Wilderson), 87–89, 91–92

"wake work," 92–93, 104, 153
walls, 151–52
Ward, Jesmyn, 129n18
Wilderson, Frank B., III, 17, 42n26, 87–89, 91–92, 125n11, 138n3, 168–70

work, 78–80, 92–93, 122. *See also* "wake work"

Wright, Michelle, 33n2, 34n6. See also *Physics of Blackness* (Wright)

Zong! (Philip), 12, 109–12, 189–92, 193n20

Zwicky, Fritz, 157n16

NEW SUNS: RACE, GENDER, AND SEXUALITY IN THE SPECULATIVE
Susana M. Morris and Kinitra D. Brooks, Series Editors

Scholarly examinations of speculative fiction have been a burgeoning academic field for more than twenty-five years, but there has been a distinct lack of attention to how attending to nonhegemonic positionalities transforms our understanding of the speculative. New Suns: Race, Gender, and Sexuality in the Speculative addresses this oversight and promotes scholarship at the intersections of race, gender, sexuality, and the speculative, engaging interdisciplinary fields of research across literary, film, and cultural studies that examine multiple pasts, presents, and futures. Of particular interest are studies that offer new avenues into thinking about popular genre fictions and fan communities, including but not limited to the study of Afrofuturism, comics, ethnogothicism, ethnosurrealism, fantasy, film, futurity studies, gaming, horror, literature, science fiction, and visual studies. New Suns particularly encourages submissions that are written in a clear, accessible style that will be read both by scholars in the field as well as by nonspecialists.

Impossible Stories: On the Space and Time of Black Destructive Creation
JOHN MURILLO III

Literary Afrofuturism in the Twenty-First Century
EDITED BY ISIAH LAVENDER III AND LISA YASZEK

Jordan Peele's Get Out: *Political Horror*
EDITED BY DAWN KEETLEY

Unstable Masks: Whiteness and American Superhero Comics
EDITED BY SEAN GUYNES AND MARTIN LUND

Afrofuturism Rising: The Literary Prehistory of a Movement
ISIAH LAVENDER III

The Paradox of Blackness in African American Vampire Fiction
JERRY RAFIKI JENKINS

www.ingramcontent.com/pod-product-compliance
Lightning Source LLC
Chambersburg PA
CBHW030137240426
43672CB00005B/168